Improve Your Writing:
An Interactive Desktop Resource

Dianne Myers Haneke, Ph.D.

Owner's Name:_____

TATE PUBLISHING *& Enterprises*

Dedication

To my husband, John, and to our grown children – Mark, Debbie and, Julie – each a competent writer in his or her own right.

To aspiring writers who passionately desire to improve the grammar and mechanics of their writing skills.

To classroom teachers, college professors, and other mentors who intentionally assist others to become competent writers for every occasion.

Acknowledgements

This publishing project would not have materialized without each of you . . .

My Dean and educational colleague at Concordia University in Austin, Dr. Sandra Doering – thank you for encouraging me to write this text for a course to enable teachers in training to become more proficient in their writing for various purposes.

My friend and CEO of Pro-Printers, David Scott – thank you for believing in me and for providing opportunities for my writing projects to get into print.

My friend and accomplished fellow writer, Beverly Caruso – thank you for believing in me, seeing the value of this work for writing workshops, and providing professional feedback.

My long-time friend and seasoned Wycliffe Bible Translator who wrote and edited many linguistic publications in the Philippines, Carl Dubois, thank you for your final editing expertise.

My publisher, Tate Publishing, Janey Hays, Jesika Lay, Rachel Sliger, Sommer Buss, Melanie Hughes, Lindsay Behrens, and others — thank you for your tireless support and helpful suggestions to make this project such a success.

My husband, John – thank you for urging me to simplify the format and make the text more readable for a wider audience — as only an engineer/technical writer can do. Thanks, too, for all your loving support as together we plodded through the various drafts of this work of art.

Our three adult children – Mark, Debbie, and Julie — thanks for all your loving support and feedback throughout the lengthy process of writing, rewriting, and searching for a publisher.

Our grandchildren – Tony, Erik, Angelina, Alyssa, Aaliyah, Ty, and Nico — thanks for loving "Dr. Grandma" and encouraging me throughout the long writing, publishing process.

My many students from over the years — thanks for all your writings – many who alerted me to the need, and prompted me to write such a text.

My professional education colleagues — thanks for your feedback, suggestions, and encouragement on a project that turned out to be much bigger than I ever dreamed of creating.

My reviewers – thank you for taking time and energy to review the early manuscripts of the text. You opened my eyes to see that this project is intended for a much wider audience than I originally envisioned. A special thanks to educators Shirley Trethewey and Sharon Ledbetter for urging me not to abandon my basic premise – the integration of basic grammar with basic writing enables everyone to improve their writing.

Table of Contents

Grammar Improves Writing

Foreword

The English language is the second most-spoken language in the world, second only to Mandarin Chinese. English is considered the most influential of all languages. Toddlers learn to speak it in their homes; school children are taught basic grammar and writing in their classrooms; and people coming from every national origin learn to communicate to some extent in English. Yet few learn the use of the language as a skill. We usually learn just enough to get our message across, whether in speaking or writing.

Many books are available that teach grammar. Others instruct the reader to write a letter, a term paper, or even a novel. Dianne Myers Haneke, Ph.D. has put the entire writing process under one cover.

Dr. Haneke gained experience first as an elementary teacher, then for twenty-two years as a reading and remedial English specialist from junior high through the college level. She has trained teachers and helped design a graduate Master of Education program.

Increasingly, Dianne's concern about the writing abilities of students heightened her interest, stirred her passion, and honed her expertise in the field of writing. Her educational perspective — "All students can learn when given appropriate instruction." — blends research-based theory with practical applications from real classroom experiences to enable all students to become successful readers and writers.

Drawing from her forty years of experience in classrooms from elementary to teachers-in-training, Dianne combines the study of how people learn grammar and literacy together with the nuts and bolts of English usage, and presents her findings in a comprehensive and logically presented form.

Dianne uses creative methods to help the reader understand English and to improve the use of the language in various writing forms. By using a line-upon-line technique, she leads the reader to add new knowledge to what he or she already knows. Dianne offers useful exercises that help to reinforce the concepts.

However, there is much anyone can learn from this book -

even if they are an accomplished English speaker or writer. Dianne's presentation is so well organized, and so clearly presented, that one can use the text as a quick reference guide, or to strengthen areas of weakness in their understanding of the language.

Beverly Caruso

Preface

Though all students participate in writing instruction from kindergarten through high school English composition, most still have gaps in their knowledge of the English language, word selection, parts of speech, parts of sentences, appropriate sentence structures, effective paragraph structures as well as writing for a variety of assignments. This text enables us to "plug the gaps" in our knowledge base as well as to learn how to write more efficiently for a variety of assignments across the curriculum. Our writing affects the way others approach, engage in, sustain engagement in, and complete writing tasks, and our knowledge of the basics, our confidence in our own writing skills, and our enjoyment of writing are contagious!

Audience and Uses. Improve Your Writing: An Interactive Desktop Resource is appropriate for a wide variety of audiences and uses including elementary through university students as well as for writing workshops, and it is a basic personal desk resource for writers of all ages. The content of this book enables both beginning and advanced writers to easily improve their writing skills, to quickly embrace writing tasks, and to thoroughly enjoy opportunities to express their ideas in writing. Most find this a handy desk-top resource.

Contributions to the Field. Most writing texts and instruction reflect English teachers' emphasis on literature and narrative text writing — creative writing, essays, prose, and poetry – but most writing assignments call for expository text. Few, if any, writing texts provide opportunities to learn how to write expository text – packaging facts in a variety of ways for mathematics, science, social sciences, etc. Improve Your Writing: An Interactive Desk-top Resource 1) reviews the basics of words, grammar, punctuation; 2) incorporates various sentence structures; 3) clarifies paragraph text structures; and 4) scaffolds step-by-step processes for writing a variety of practical writing tasks, especially expository genres.

Goals and Objectives. Improve Your Writing: An Interactive Desktop Resource enables the participant to: 1) learn more about the English language, 2) eliminate deficiencies in writing skills, 3) improve writing effectively for a variety of audiences and purposes, 4) read and study more efficiently in a variety of texts, and 5) influence others to read, write, and study more efficiently for a variety of purposes. Persons using this resource will be able to master: 1) basic word elements; 2) basic sentence structures, grammar, and usage; 3) basic paragraph and text structures; and 4) basic writing genres, styles, and processes required for various audiences and purposes.

Scope and Overview. Four sections comprise <u>Improve Your Writing: An Interactive Desktop Resource.</u> Part I reviews the Basic Word Elements of the English Language including aspects of language, learning styles, confusing words, plurals, possessives, antonyms, synonyms, and analogies. Part II reviews Basic Sentence Structures, grammar, and usage including various aspects of agreement. Part III explains the Writing Process as well as Basic Paragraph and Text Structures. Part IV clarifies Basic Genres of Writing and provides step-by-step processes for successfully writing a variety of papers, especially preparing expository academic writing assignments. Appendices include several reference helps, an Answer Key, and an Index.

Read a person's writings

And you take a tour of her heart and soul . . .

" . . . for out of the abundance of the

heart the mouth speaks . . ."

[Matthew 12:34 KJV]

And out of the abundance of the soul the pen writes.

Dianne Myers Haneke © 2005

Part I

Basic Word Elements:
English Writing and Reading

Table I-1-References for Review -- Part I

Topic In Workbook	Step by Step	Grammar Smart	Help Yourself	Writing Smart	Other Resources
I-C: nouns &	pp. 25-35	pp. 3-7;	pp. 2-6; 22; 339	pp. 4-5	
Pronouns		pp. 24-33	pp. 10; 341	pp. 5	
PN-antecedent			pp. 95-112	p. 7	
Pronoun referent			pp. 113-126	p. 7	
Pronoun case			pp. 127-164	p. 7	
I-C: verbs	pp. 35-44	pp. 11-16	pp. 7-9; 17-18; 20; 51-76; 343	pp. 4, 19	
I-C: adjectives	pp. 63-68	pp. 8-10	pp. 10, 22	pp. 5	
I-C: adverbs	pp. 69-77	pp. 17-18	pp. 11-12, 23	pp. 5	
I-C: conjunctions	pp. 95-99	pp. 21-23	pp. 14-15, 19		
I-C: prepositions	pp. 83-87	pp. 19-20	pp. 13		
I-C: interjections	pp. 96-99	pp. 34	pp. 16		
I-D: confusing words		pp. 98-103; 145-148	pp. 349-360		
I-D: plurals			pp. 78, 100		
I-D: possessives			pp. 189-191		

Grammar Improves Writing

Reference List

Lerner, M. (1994). <u>The Princeton Review: Writing smart: Your guide to great writing</u>. NY: Random House.

Mattson, M., Leshing, S., Levi, E. (1993). <u>Help yourself: A guide to writing and rewriting (3rd ed.)</u>. New York: Macmillan. [out of print]

O'Conner, P.T. (1996). <u>Woe is I: The grammarphoebe's guide to better English in plain English.</u> NY: Putnam.

Pulaski, M.A.S. (1982). <u>Step-by-step guide to correct English</u>. NY: Macmillan.

Staff of the Princeton Review. (1996). <u>The Princeton Review: Grammar smart: A guide to perfect usage.</u> NY: Random House.

Part I

Basic Word Elements:
English Writing and Reading

A. Introduction

Because humans learn language before they even talk much, adults tend to take language acquisition and structure for granted. Most adults do not remember how, when, or where they learned to listen, speak, read, or write. It just happened, somehow. The oral/aural acquisition of sixty to seventy per cent of the most-frequently used words of the English language transpired during pre-school years, and by the end of first grade, most students can read and write these high-frequency words (See Fry's <u>Reading Teacher's Book of Lists</u>.) Words – basic elements of any language – are most readily accumulated and assimilated through real-life experiences. Reading, travel, movies, videos, etc. as well as conversations expand vocabulary. Words, then, are the basic elements of writing and reading not only in English but also in other languages.

B. Overview

Part I presents foundational constructs for building and expanding vocabulary. Among these basic "building blocks" are 1) four aspects of language, 2) two learning style paradigms, 3) ten parts of speech, 4) homonyms, 5) plurals and possessives, and 6) antonyms, synonyms, and analogies. Reviewing and mastering these basic word elements provides students the opportunity to effectively select more appropriate words to construct more powerful and engaging sentences, paragraphs, and papers.

C. Procedure Suggestions

Since students' knowledge gaps and learning needs vary throughout the concepts and constructs covered in Part I, the onus for mastery of these principles is placed on the individual students. The format of Part I chapters generally provides a Check-Up, some tutorial review or teaching, and a post-test or post-assessment of the skill.

When used in class with upper elementary and middle school students, more time may be required to master the concepts and contents of Part I and Part II. One suggested procedure that probably works best for upper elementary, middle and high school students is to use this text as a supplementary text, concentrate on Parts I and II for the first half of the semester and generally focus on one chapter per week. Then, during the second half of the semester, especially for writing paragraphs and papers in Part III and Part IV, focus on one chapter or assignment per week.

When used with accelerated high school, college or university students, Part I and Part II are designed to be quick reviews of content that should have been mastered earlier. One procedure that probably works best for college or university students is to review the word, sentence structure, and paragraph structure concepts (Parts I-II-III) – targeting 90% mastery by midterm. Then, spend the remainder of the semester writing some high-quality paragraphs and some high-quality two to three-page papers.

When used in home schooling, the above-mentioned procedures may be helpful. Ultimately, students need to spend time writing age-appropriate expository and narrative texts for a variety of situations.

In addition to all the above appropriations, Improve Your Writing: An Interactive Desktop Resource is a valuable desktop resource to refer to when one has a question about some aspect of word selection, sentence construction, paragraph structure, or paper organization.

D. Assessment Record

A Student's Score Sheet follows.

Notes & Questions

Table I-Intro Part I-1. Student's Scrore Sheet

#	Activity Name	Check-Up	Post-Test	90% goal?
I-3-P1	Parts of Speech Quiz Check-Up 1			
I-3-P2	Parts of Speech Check-Up 2			
I-3-1	Nouns practice A & B			
I-3-2	Pronouns practice			
I-3-3	Adjective & Articles practice			
I-3-4	Nouns practice			
I-3-5	Adverbs practice			
I-3-6	Prepositions practice			
I-3-7	Conjunctions practice			
I-3-8	Interjections practice			
I-3-Ch	Parts of Speech Check-up/Mastery			
I-4	Commonly Confused Words Check-Up			
I-4-1	Commonly Confused Words posttest 1			
I-4-2	Commonly Confused Words posttest 2			
I-4-3	Commonly Confused Words posttest 3			
I-5-1	Plurals Check-Up			
I-5-2	Possessives Check-Up			
I-5-5	Plurals Posttest Mastery			

Dianne M. Haneke, Ph.D.

Student's Scrore Sheet (continue)

I-5-6	Possessives Posttest Mastery			
I-6-1	Antonyms Check-Up			
I-6-2	Synonyms Check-Up			
I-6-3	Analogies Check-Up			
I-6-4	Vocabulary: Antonyms Checkup			
I-6-5	Vocabulary: Synonyms Checkup			
I-6-6	Vocabulary: Analogies Checkup			

Chapter 1

Four Aspects of Language and Vocabulary

A. Introduction

1. There are four aspects of language: reading, writing, listening, and speaking.

    a. **Receptive language aspect**: listening and reading.

    b. **Expressive language aspects**: speaking and writing.

2. The other way to categorize language is by **oral** (aloud) or **silent**.

    a. Oral language is received (receptive) through auditory/hearing/listening.

    b. Silent language is received (receptive) through visual/seeing/reading.

    c. Oral language is expressed (expressive) through speaking.

    d. Silent language is expressed (expressive) through writing.

B. Order of Language Development

1. First, infants receive language by **listening**.

2. Second, infants express language by **speaking**, responding to what they hear by listening.

3. Third, children receive language by **reading** – observing and reading environmental print, then books and magazines.

4. Fourth, children express language by **writing**, responding to what they hear and read.

C. Size of Vocabularies

1. The largest vocabulary for children and adults is their **listening** aspect of language.

2. The second largest vocabulary is their **reading** vocabulary.

3. The third largest vocabulary is their **speaking** vocabulary.

4. The fourth (or smallest) vocabulary is their **writing** vocabulary.

D. I-1.1. Four Aspects of Language

	Oral	Silent
Receptive	_____	_____
Expressive	_____	_____

{Check with Answer Key at back of book.}

E. I-1.2. Four Aspects of Language

Order of Language Aspects Development:	Order of Vocabulary Aspects Size:
1._____	1._____
2._____	2._____
3._____	3._____
4._____	4._____

So, why do you think we experience "writer's block"?

_____

_____

_____

_____

_____

F. Relevance to Writing

Basic to improving your writing is awareness of how writing is closely related to the other three aspects of language (reading listening and speaking), because all four aspects of language function interdependently — not independently. So, use your language strengths to strengthen your weaknesses, and use your abilities in reading, listening, and speaking to improve your writing skills.

Chapter 1 Notes

Chapter 2

Two Models of Learning Styles

No two people are alike. Each person learns best by a prioritized combination of several means. All people possess the components of all learning modalities, styles, or paradigms, but each person learns on a continuum of strengths to weaknesses or preferences to non-preferences. Theorists posit several paradigms of learning styles. Carbo, Dunn, and Dunn's School-Based Approach (1986) highlights four dimensions: environment, emotional support, sociological support, and personal/physical support. Gregorc's (1985) Style Delineator offers four clusters based on left and right brain hemispheric functions: concrete sequential, abstract sequential, abstract random, and concrete random. McCarthy's 4-MAT System (1987) integrates the learning styles into instructional strategies involving both left and right brain activities (Orton, et. al., 1990). To help you understand the ways individuals learn, we review two paradigms; learning styles may affect one's preferences, writing skill improvement, strengths and weaknesses, and the analysis of why some individuals have more difficulty than others in developing proficiency.

A. Learning Modalities

Learning Modalities are sensory-based: auditory, visual, kinesthetic, and tactile. This multi-sensory approach has three classic applications: a) VAKT - visual, auditory, tactile and kinesthetic; b) the Fernald Method (1988); and c) the Orton-Gillingham Method (Gillingham Stillman, 1970) [Richek, Caldwell, Jennings, Lerner, 1996]. All people utilize all four senses, but each person tends to learn best by one or by a combination of the senses.

B. Multiple Intelligences

Gardner's **Multiple Intelligences** (Gardner, 1983, 1993) theorizes at least eight "ways of knowing": verbal/linguistic, math/logical, spatial/artistic, musical/rhythmic, bodily/kinesthetic, interpersonal, intra-personal, and naturalistic. Each person utilizes all eight intelligences, but each person uses a preferred way of learning — a prioritized listing of ways of learning and knowing. These factors affect how people approach the task of writing, how they engage and sustain engagement in writing (including how they organize ideas and express themselves in writing), how they complete the writing task, and the quality of the final writing product.

C. I-2.1. Two Models of Learning Styles

Directions: Fill in the blanks in the following charts:

1. V-A-K-T = 4 Learning Modalities:

   a. Visual:
      learn best through activities they _____

   b. Auditory:
      learn best through activities they _____

   c. Kinesthetic:
      learn best through activities they _____

   d. Tactile:
      learn best through activities they _____

2. Gardner's 8 Multiple Intelligences:

   a. Verbal/Linguistic:
      learn best through _____ activities

   b. Math/Logical:
      learn best through _____ activities

   c. Spatial/Artistic:
      learn best through _____ activities

   d. Musical:
      learn best through _____ activities

   e. Bodily/Kinesthetic:
      learn best through _____ activities

   f. Interpersonal:
      learn best through _____ activities

   g. Intra-personal:
      learn best through _____ activities

   h. Naturalistic:
      learn best through _____ activities

{Check answers with Answer Key in back of book.}

D. I-2.2. References for Learning Styles

Carbo, M., Dunn, R., Dunn, K. (1986). Teaching students to read through their individual learning styles. Reston, VA: Reston Publishing.

Fernald, G. (1943/1988). Remedial techniques in basic school subjects. Austin, TX: Pro Ed.

Gardner, H. (1983). Frames of mind: The theory of multiple intelligences. New York: HarperCollins.

Gardner, H. (1993). Multiple Intelligences: The theory in practice. New York: HarperCollins.

Gillingham, A., Stillman, B. (1997). Remedial training for children with specific disability in reading, spelling, and penmanship (8th ed.). Cambridge, MA: Educators Publishing.

Gregorc, A. (1985). Gregorc style delineator. Maynard, MA: Gabriel Systems.

McCarthy, B. (2000). About Learning (The 4MAT System). Barrington, IL: Excel.

Orton, D.C., (Ed.) (2000). Teaching strategies: A guide to better instruction (6th ed.). Boston, MA: Houghton Mifflin College.

Richek, M.A., Caldwell, J.S., Jennings, J.H., Lerner, J.W. (1996). Reading problems: Assessment and teaching strategies (3rd ed.). Boston: Allyn Bacon.

E. Relevance to Writing

Being aware of the various ways in which people relate to and interpret their world — ways individuals learn — enables you to identify your learning styles and your stronger learning modalities. This awareness enables you to use your learning strengths to improve your writing skills.

Chapter 3

Ten Parts of Speech

A. Rationale:

Persons of all grades and in all subjects need to be able to recognize and utilize the parts of speech. For example, when identifying the main idea of a paragraph, a person looks for a subject that is usually a noun or noun phrase. Answers to the following questions are almost always a noun: Who? What? When? and Where? Answers to How? and Why? questions may be a verb, an adverb or adverbial phrase, a preposition, or a prepositional phrase. Understanding and utilizing the following ten parts of speech enables a person to read and write with greater efficiency.

B. Brief Review:

All words can be classified within the ten parts of speech categories as follows:

1. **Nouns** name a person, place, or thing and usually answer "Who?," "What?," and "Where?" questions.

2. **Pronouns** substitute for nouns—for (pro) nouns—and usually answer "Who?" or "What?" questions.

3. **Adjectives** describe or add to nouns and usually respond to "Please describe __" (noun).

4. **Articles** (a, an, and the) describe or add to nouns; they are classified as adjectives.

5. **Verbs** indicate action or state of being and usually answer "What is happening?" questions.

6. **Helping/Linking verbs** enable verbs to express past, present, and future tenses such as was, is, and will. They indicate time of action or state of being.

7. **Adverbs** describe or add to the verb, to an adjective, or to another adverb and usually answer "How?," "How much?," "How many?," and "Why?" questions.

8. **Conjunctions** connect or join two or more nouns, pronouns, verbs, adverbs, prepositional phrases, or independent clauses in a sentence.

9. **Prepositions** indicate positional relationship between two nouns and they usually answer "Where?" questions.

10. **Interjections** exclaim excitement and are followed by an exclamation point (!).

C. Format for this Chapter

Chapter Three offers the following overall as well as for each part of speech:

1. Parts of Speech Diagnostic Check-Up: Check understanding of definitions and uses.

2. Review: Review parts of speech with definitions, examples and tutorial, and practice.

3. Post-Test: Score at least 90% to demonstrate proficiency. (Answer Key is at back of book.)

D. Goals and Objectives for This Chapter

Understanding and correctly using the parts of speech strengthens and enhances one's writing; therefore, set the following goals:

1. Master each part of speech with at least 90% proficiency.

2. Master how parts of speech interrelate to convey meaning.

3. Master effective use of all parts of speech to communicate effectively in writing.

4. Master the parts of speech overall to achieve at least 90% proficiency on post-test.

Notes & Questions

E. I-3-Pre-1. Parts of Speech Check-Up — 1

Name_____ ____/10 = ____/100%
[Need 90% for proficiency]

Directions: Match the following parts of speech with their simplified meaning . . .

____1. noun
A. shows action or state of being; e.g., run, is, studied, walks

____2. verb
B. adds to verb, adjective, or another adverb; e.g., very, fully, rarely

____3. adjective
C. shows positional relationship of one noun or pronoun to another; e.g., to, from, in, out, over, under

____4. adverb
D. names person, place, thing, or idea; e.g. John, New York, home

____5. preposition
E. describes a noun; *tall, dark, pretty*

____6. pronoun
F. takes the place of a noun; subjective: I, you, we, they. objective: me, you, us, them; possessive: my, your, our, their.

____7. conjunction
G. expresses excitement or emotion; usually one word; interrupts; Wow! Super! Incredible!

____8. interjection
H. a, an, the; classified as adjectives

____9. article
I. is/are, was/were, has/have, will, be; enable verb to express past, present, and future tenses

____10. helping
J. connects series of nouns, pronouns, adjectives, adverbs; assisting verb adverbs; e.g., and, but, however, therefore

{Check answers in Answer Key in back of book.}

F. I-3-Pre-2. Parts of Speech – Check-Up - 2

Name_____ ____/33 = ____%
[Need 90% for proficiency.]

Directions: In the following sentences, write each word's part of speech in the blanks to the right hand side. Be sure to match the word # with the answer blank # at the right.

Use . . . N=noun, PN=pronoun, V=verb, HV=helping/assisting verb, ADJ=adjective, ADV=adverb, PREP=preposition, CONJ=conjunction, INT=interjection.

1 2 3 4 5 6 7 8
Jim and his wife drove to the store

1____ 2____ 3____ 4____
5___ 6___ 7___ 8___

9 10 11 12   13
to get some last-minute snacks

9___ 10___ 11___ 12___ 13___

14 15 16   17
for their evening guests.

14___ 15___ 16___ 17___

18   19 20 21
They shopped quickly, but

18___ 19___ 20___ 21___

22   23   24   25
some guests arrived early.

22___ 23___ 24___ 25___

26   27 28
"Wow!" said Jim.

26___ 27___ 28___

{Check answers with Answer Key in back of book.}

I-3-1. Nouns

A. Definitions:

All nouns function as subjects, direct objects, or as objects of prepositions.

1. **Common nouns** name general persons, places or things. Examples include president, nation, city, state, fish, birds, and house.

2. **Proper nouns** name specific persons, places, and things and as such are capitalized. Examples include President George Washington, United States of America, New York City, Texas, American Bald Eagle, and the White House.

B. Practice - Assignment-A:

*Directions: Circle all the **10 common nouns**; __/10*

We the people of the United States, in order to form a more perfect union, establish justice, insure domestic tranquility, provide for the common defense, promote the general welfare, and secure the blessings of liberty to ourselves and our posterity, so ordain and establish this Constitution for the United States of America. [Preamble to the Constitution, 1787.]

C. Practice - Assignment-B:

*Directions: Box all the **10 proper nouns**; ___/10.*

When in the course of human events, it becomes necessary for one people to dissolve the political bands which have connected them with another, and to assume among the powers of the Earth, the separate and equal station to which the laws of Nature and of Nature's God entitle them, a decent respect to the opinions of mankind requires that they should declare

the causes which impel them to the separation.   [Declaration of Indepen-
dence, July 4, 1776.]

We hold these truths to be self-evident, that all men are created equal, that they are endowed by their Creator with certain unalienable rights, that among these are life, liberty, and the pursuit of happiness. [Declaration of Independence, July 4, 1776.]

We the people of the United States, in order to form a more perfect union, establish justice, insure domestic tranquility, provide for the common defense, promote the general welfare, and secure the blessings of liberty to ourselves and our posterity, do ordain and establish this Constitution for the United States of America. [Preamble to the Constitution, 1787.]

{Check answers in Answer Key in back of book.}

Notes & Questions

I-3-2. Pronouns

A. Definitions:

Pronouns substitute for or take the place of nouns; they are for **(pro)** nouns. Examples follow in the subsequent sections.

B. Cases:

Pronouns fall into four categories, forms, or cases — depending upon how the pronouns are used in the sentence:

1. Subjective-Nominative.

2. Objective.

3. Possessive.

4. Reflexive.

The following charts present pronouns in the various cases:

C. Table I-3-2. Pronoun Cases

1. Subjective-Nominative case pronouns are used as subjects, i.e., usually doing the action.

Table I-3-2-1 Subjective/Nominative Case Pronouns

Persons	Singular	Plural
1st person	*I*	*We*
2nd person	*You*	*You*
3rd person	*it, he, she*	*They*
who	*Who*	*who*
whoever	*Whoever*	*whoever*

Pronoun Cases (continued)

2. Objective case pronouns are used as direct objects of the verb or objects of prepositions, usually receiving an action or an object . . .

Table I-3-2-2 Objective Case Pronouns

Table I-3-2-2 Objective Case Pronouns

Persons	Singular	Plural
1st person	Me	us
2nd person	You	you
3rd person – it	it, her, him	them
whom	Whom	whom
whomever	Whomever	Whomever

Grammar Improves Writing

Examples of Objective Case Pronouns:

a. Object of verb . . . Dad hugged me. Mom hugged us. The coach chose him and her to play. The coach chose them to play.

Whom are you choosing? You choose whomever you want to play.

b. Object of preposition . . . Bob threw the ball to you. The snow falls on you.

To whom did you give the gift? You give the gift to whomever you want.

3. Possessive case pronouns show possession or ownership either as a modifier or used alone . . .

Table I-3-2-3 Possesive Case Pronouns

Table I-3-2-3 Possessive Case Pronouns

Persons	Singular Modifier	Alone	Plural Modifier	Alone
1st person	*My*	*Mine*	*Our*	*ours*
2nd person	*Your*	*Yours*	*Your*	*yours*
3rd person – it	*Its*	*Its*	*their*	*theirs*
3rd person – he	*His*	*His*	*their*	*theirs*
3rd person – she	*Hers*	*Hers*	*their*	*theirs*
Whose	*Whose*	*Whose*	*whose*	*whose*
whosever (rare)	*whosever (rare)*	*whosever*	*whosever (rare)*	*whosever*

Note: The second option ("Alone") usually follows a state of being verb such as *is, are, was, were, etc.* For example,

a. Those are *my* (modifier) shoes; they are *mine* (alone).

b. That is *our* (modifier) home; it is *ours* (alone).

c. Those are *your* (modifier) clothes; they are *yours* (alone).

Also, possessive case pronouns (and possessives with nouns) must be used with gerunds. For example, "I enjoy him singing" is not correct; "I enjoy his singing" is the correct form. "I love to watch them playing basketball" is incorrect; "I love to watch their playing basketball" and "I love to watch their team's playing basketball' are both correct.

4. Reflexive case pronouns reflect or refer back to the noun subject . . .

Table I-3-2-4 Reflexive Case Pronouns

Persons	Singular	Plural
1st person	*Myself*	*ourselves*
2nd person	*Yourself*	*yourselves*
3rd person	*Himself, herself, itself*	*themselves*

For example,

a. The toddler said, "I can dress myself!" "We can feed ourselves!" said the preschoolers.

b. "Be careful, Ty, or you will hurt yourself." Take good care of yourselves.

c. The horse cut itself on the wire fence. The students helped themselves to library books.

D. I-3-2-D. Pronouns – Check-up

Name_____/25 = ____%
[90% = proficient.]

Directions: Circle the correct response(s).

1. The plaques were presented to (they, them) and to (she, her). [1–2]

2. In the beginning, both of (we, us) wanted to attend the concert. [3]

3. (They, Them) left the wedding after John and (she, her) had left. [4–5]

4. (She, Her) painted the picture for (whoever, whomever) she can find to buy it. [6–7]

5. Take (whoever, whomever) you want to the dinner dance. [8]

6. (He, Him) built the boat all by (his self, himself). [9–10] 7. (Who's, Whose) pizza should (we, us) sample today? [11–12]

8. (They, Them) are better athletes than (we, us). [13–14]

9. The Dean named (they, them) and (I, me) to be on the committee. [15–16]

10. From (who, whom, whoever, whomever) did you catch the flu? [17]

11. For everyone except (they, them) it was a trying ordeal. [18]

12. (I, Me) am (she, her), and (He, Him) is (who, whom) he says he is. [19–22]

13. (Whose, Who's) new red car is that? [23]

14. When we arrived, (he, him) and (she, her) greeted us. [24–25]

{Check answers with in the Answer Key in the back of the book.}

I-3-3. Adjectives and Articles

A. Definitions

1. **Adjectives** describe or modify a noun; e.g., *tall, dark, handsome, beautiful, red, white, blue.*

   a. Compound adjectives are comprised of more than one word and are hyphenated; e.g., *state-of-the-art, 12-year-old, etc.*

   b. Comparative adjectives add *-er* to express comparison when comparing two items such as *taller in Joe is taller than Jim.*

   c. Superlative adjectives add *–est* to express the extreme of a range when comparing three or more items such as *tallest in Joe is taller than Jim but John is the tallest of the three.*

2. **Articles** — a, an, and the — function as adjectives.

   a. *The* is a **definite article** referring to a specific noun.

   b. *A* and an are **indefinite articles** referring to a general noun.

B. I-3-3-B. Practice Adjectives Articles

Name_____/31 = ____%
[90% = proficient.]

Directions: Circle the adjectives and articles in the patriotic texts below.

*Oh, beautiful for spacious skies, for amber fields of grain [1-2-3
For purple mountain majesties above the fruited plain. America,
America, [4-5-6-7]*
God shed His grace on thee and crown thy good with brother-
hood from sea to shining sea. [8] [© Katharine Lee Bates,
1893; Samuel A. Ward.]
                              * * * * * * * *

*I pledge allegiance to the flag of the United States of America and to
the Republic [9-10-11]*
for which it stands, one Nation, under God, indivisible, with
liberty and justice for all. [12-13]
[© Francis Bellamy, 1892.]
                              * * * * * * * *

*You're a grand ole flag. You're a high-flying flag and forever and
peace may you wave. [14-18]*
*You're the emblem of the land I love – the home of the free and the
brave. [19-20-21-22-23]*
Every heart beats true 'neath the red-white-and-blue, where
there's never a boast or brag. [24-26] Should old acquaintance be forgot, keep your eye on the grand ole flag. [27-31]
[© George M. Cohan]

{Check answers with in the Answer Key in the back of the book.}

Notes & Questions

I-3-4. Verbs

A. Definitions

1. Verbs express action or state of being, and they may be one word or a group of words. As the key ingredient to the predicate half of the sentence, verbs tell what the subject does, what the subject is, or what action the subject receives. The Infinitive is the verb's base form such as *to sing*. Verbs are conjugated by singular and plural of the three persons just like the pronoun cases (see I-C-2): *I sing, you sing, we sing, they sing*, and the 3rd person singular usually adds an *s* such as *he, she,* or *it sings.*

Mnemonic: when the noun or subject ends in *s* (most plurals, e.g., *boys*), the verb does not end in *s*; but when the noun or subject does not end in *s* (most singulars, e.g., *boy*), the verb does end in *s*; therefore, *three boys sing* but *a boy sings.*

2. Helping, assisting, or auxiliary verbs -- such as *can, may, could, should, would, might,* and *must* -- are usually followed by the base or infinitive form of the verb; e.g., *The girls might sing their trio for the school program.*

3. Verb Parts and Classifications.
Verbs are classified by the way they form the past tense and past participle. The principal parts of a verb are its base/infinitive form, its past tense form, and its past participle.

a. Regular Verbs. Most English verbs are **regular**, so the past tense and past participle forms are created by adding *–ed* to the base form as in *walk, walked, walked.*

b. Irregular verbs change in other ways to create the past tense and past participle forms. One kind keeps the same form for past tense and past participle such as *play, played, played.* Another kind of irregular verb adds an *–n or –en* to the past tense to form the past participle such as *speak, spoke, spoken.* Another kind changes the spelling for each form such as *eat, ate, eaten* or *fly, flew, flown.* Still another kind of irregular verb uses the same spelling for all three forms such as *put, put, put* and *cut, cut, cut.* A large group of the irregular verbs change a vowel in both the past tense and in the past participle such as *begin, began, begun* or *sing, sang, sung.*

c. **Transitive verbs** have an object such as *singing* in *She is singing the song.*

d. **Intransitive verbs** have no object such as *singing* in *She is singing.*

e. **Linking verbs** occur in two structures. In one, the verb is followed by an adjective describing the subject such as *is* in *It is beautiful.* In the other , the noun following the verb links back to the subject such as *He is my husband. She is my girlfriend.*

f. A **finite verb** with a subject forms a complete sentence: *She writes. He is writing.*

g. A **nonfinite – verbal –** is a verb acting as another part of speech (noun, adjective) usually a gerund: (noun example: skiing) ***Skiing*** *is his favorite winter sport. (Adjective example: skiing) In the summer, many hike the* ***skiing*** *trails.*

h. **Infinitives** are verbs used as nouns, adjectives or adverbs. Here, *to write* serves as a noun: *To write a summary is difficult.* In *I have a summary to write, to write* serves as an adjective modifying *summary.* In *Julie wrote to become a better writer, to become* serves as an adverb modifying the verb *wrote.*

i. **Gerunds** are verbs used as nouns such as *writing* in *Writing is fun.*

j. **Participles** are verbs used as adjectives such as *winning* in *Tony hit the winning run.*

B. I-3-4-B. Verb Conjugation
Helpful Information

Some helpful explanations of terms used in verb conjugations include the following:

1. Conjugation. A conjugation lists a verb's forms by person, number, voice, tense, and mood.

2. Person. English (and most Romantic languages) have six persons – three singular and three plural. They are as follows:

a. First person singular = person speaking *[I]*

b. Second person singular = person spoken to *[you]*

c. Third person singular = person or thing spoken about *[she, he, it]*

d. First person plural = persons speaking *[we]*

e. Second person plural = persons spoken to *[you]*

f. Third person plural = persons or things spoken about *[they]*

3. Number.. English forms of numbers are as follows:
a. Singular. Singular refers to one person in first, second, or third persons.

b. Plural. Plural refers to more than one person in first, second, and third persons.

Number and Person must be congruent with each other, so singular subjects   require single verb forms, and plural subjects require plural verb forms

Mnemonics: Singular subjects or nouns call for verbs ending in an "s" or "es".

Plural subjects or nouns call for verbs without an "s" or "es" ending.

4. Voice. In English, there are two classes of voice – active and passive.

a. Active voice is when the subject is active, does the action, is the doer such as *The athlete set a new record.*

b. Passive voice is when the subject is passive, receives the action, is the receiver such as *A new record was set by the athlete.*

5. **Tense.** Verb tense indicates time of action. There are three time divisions: present, past, and future. English has six tenses: present, past, future, present perfect, past perfect, and future perfect. Only present and past tenses express time by themselves. All other forms use helping, assisting, or auxiliary verbs such as the following to indicate time: future *will*, present perfect *has*, past perfect *had*, and future perfect *will have.*

a. Simple tenses express time relationships as stated: present, past, and future.

1) Simple **present** tense = expresses a current action; e.g., *I sing.*

2) Simple **past** tense = expresses a past action; e.g., *I sang yesterday.*

3) Simple **future** tense = expresses a future action; e.g., *I will sing next Sunday.*

b. Perfect tenses express time relationships other than simple present, past, and future.

1) Present perfect tense = expresses an action that belongs to the past but touches the present; e.g., So far, I have sung solo, duet, trio, quintet, and group arrangements.

2) Past perfect tense = expresses an action completed at some time past; e.g., *In my senior year of college, I had sung close harmony in a mixed quintet.*

3) Future Perfect tenses express an action to be completed at some future time; e.g., *Within the next few years, I will have sung my first CD of original songs.*

4) Future tenses express time by the auxiliaries *will* and *shall.* Future also expresses time by using other forms such as *He is singing tomorrow.* *He is to sing tomorrow.* Or *He is going to sing tomorrow.*

5) Progressive verb tense express an action in progress at a particular time; e.g., *He is singing his first solo.*

6. Emphatic verb forms are used to ask questions, make negative statements, or may provide emphasis; e.g., *Does he sing solos? He does not sing solos.* *He does sing solos.*

7. Sample conjugations of regular and irregular verbs follow:

Notes & Questions

C. Table I-3-4-C-1. Sample Verb Conjugations – Regular Verb: to believe

Simple Present Tense Person	Simple Present Tense	Simple Present Tense
1st person singular	I believe.	I am believed.
2nd person singular	You believe.	You are believed.
3rd person singular	He/she/it believes.	He/she/it is believed.
1st person plural	We believe.	We are believed.
2nd person plural	You believe.	You are believed.
3rd person plural	They believe.	They are believed.
Simple Past Tense Person	**Simple Past - Active**	**Simple Past - Passive**
1st person singular	I believed.	I was believed.
2nd person singular	You believed.	You were believed.
3rd person singular	He/she/it believed.	He/she/it was believed.
1st person plural	We believed.	We were believed.
2nd person plural	You believed.	You were believed.
3rd person plural	He/she/it believed.	They were believed.
Simple Future Tense Person	**Simple Future - Active**	**Simple Future – Passive**
1st person singular	I will believe.	I will be believed.
2nd person singular	You will believe.	You will be believed.
3rd person singular	He/she/it will believe.	She will be believed.
1st person plural	We will believe.	We will be believed.
2nd person plural	You will believe.	You will be believed.
3rd person plural	They will believe.	They will be believed.

Table I-3-4-C-2. Verb Conjugations Regular (continued)

Present Perfect Tense Person	Present Perfect - Active	Present Perfect - Passive
1st person singular	I have believed.	I have been believed.
2nd person singular	You have believed.	You have been believed.
3rd person singular	He/she/it has believed.	He has been believed.
1st person plural	We have believed.	We have been believed.
2nd person plural	You have believed.	You have been believed.
3rd person plural	They have believed.	They have been believed.
Past Perfect Tense Person	**Past Perfect - Active**	**Past Perfect - Passive**
1st person singular	I had believed.	I had been believed.
2nd person singular	You had believed.	You had been believed.
3rd person singular	He/she/it had believed.	It had been believed.
1st person plural	We had believed.	We had been believed.
2nd person plural	You had believed.	You had been believed.
3rd person plural	They had believed.	They had been believed.
Future Perfect Tense	**Future Perfect - Active**	**Future Perfect - Passive**
1st person singular	I will have believed.	I will have been believed.
2nd person singular	You will have believed.	You will have been believed.
3rd person singular	He/she/it will have believed.	She will have been believed.
1st person plural	We will have believed.	We will have been believed.
2nd person plural	You will have believed.	You will have been believed.
3rd person plural	They will have believed.	They will have been believed.

D. Table I-3-4-D. Verb Present and Past Tenses: Regular

Regular verbs form their past tense by adding –d or –ed such as the following:

Present Tense	Past Tense	Present Tense	Past Tense
believe	believed	Talk	Talked
Fish	Fished	Type	Typed
Like	Liked	Walk	walked
Love	Loved	Want	Wanted
Ski	Skied	Wish	wished

E. Table I-3-4-E. Verb Present and Past Tenses: Irregular

Irregular Verbs form their past tense in some individual way such as the following:

Present Tense	Past Tense		Present Tense	Past Tense
Am	Was		Ride	rode
Bear	Bore		See	seen
Beat	Beat		Speak	spoke
Fly	Flew		Swim	swam
Read	Read		Write	wrote

F. Table I-3-4-F. Verb Principal Parts -- Irregular

1. Principal parts: Irregular verbs form their tenses in many ways. Dictionaries usually provide four principal parts of irregular verbs: **present, past, present participle, and past participle.** Here are some examples:

Verb – Present	Past Tense	Present Participle	Past Participle
		{Use with form of *be*}	{Use with form of *have*}
Be *(I am, he is)*	*I was, we/you/they were, he was*	*I am, we/you/they are, he is being*	*I/we/you/they have been, he has been*
Write *(I/we/you/they write; she writes)*	*I/we/you/she/they wrote*	*I am writing; we/you/they are writing; She is writing.*	*I/we/you/they have written; She has written*
Go *(I/we/you/they go. She goes.)*	*I/we/you/she//they went.*	*I am going; we/you/they are going; she is going.*	*I/we/you/they have gone. She has gone.*
Fly *(I/we/you/they fly. She flies.)*	*I/we/you/she/they flew.*	*I am flying. We/you/they are flying; He is flying.*	*I/we/you/they have flown. He has flown.*
Have *(I/we/you/they have He has)*	*I/we/you/he/they had*	*I am having, he is having You/they are having*	*I/we/you/they have had He has had*
Sing *(I/we/you/they sing;He sings.)*	*I/we/you/he/they sang.*	*I am singing. We/you/they are singing. He is singing.*	*I/we/you/they have sung. He has sung.*
Swim *(I/we/you/they swim. She swims.)*	*I/we/you/she/they swam.*	*I am swimming. We/you/they are swimming. She Is swimming.*	*I/we/you/they have swum. She has swum.*
Ride *(I/we/you/they ride. He rides.)*	*I/we/you/he/they rode.*	*I am riding. We/you/they are riding. He is riding.*	*I/we/you/they have ridden. He has ridden.*

G. I-3-4. Verbs - Practice

Name_____/33 = _____%

[90% = proficient.]

Directions: Circle all the verbs; write an HV over helping verbs.
___/15=___%

1. We hold these truths to be self-evident, that all men are created equal, that they are endowed by their Creator with certain unalienable rights, that among these are life, liberty, and the pursuit of happiness.
[US Declaration of Independence, 1776.]

* * * * * * * * *

2. We the people of the United States, in order to form a more perfect union, establish justice, insure domestic tranquility, provide for the common defense, promote the general welfare, and secure the blessings of liberty to our selves and our posterity, do ordain and establish this Constitution for the United States of America.

[Preamble, United States Constitution, 1787.]

* * * * * * * * *

{Check answers with Answer Key at back of book.}

H. More Verb Check-Up

Name_____ /33 = ___%

[90% = proficient.

Directions: In the following sentences, select the correct verb.
___/18 = ___%

1. The road (is, are) cracked from the heat.

2. She (expect, expects) too much for the wages she is paying me.

3. Trucks and buses (has, have) less accidents than cars do.

4. Poplar and aspen trees often (shed, sheds) their bark.

5. (Do, Does) I have ulcers or (does, do) anyone in my family have them?

6. He (march, marches) to the (beat, beats) of a different drum.

7. Do adults or children (need, needs) more protein calories?

8. What (do, does) his arguments prove?

9. The bacteria we are studying (cause, causes) various diseases.

10. Hind-sight (is, are) always 20/20, so they (say, says).

11. (Does, Do) the team (has, have) enough jerseys to (go, goes) around?

12. Neither roses nor a plant (make, makes) her day brighter.

13. Rain, as well as snow, (upset, upsets) travel plans every year.

{Check answers with Answer Key at back of book.}

I-3-5. Adverbs

A. Definitions

1. Adverbs describe, modify, or add to the meaning of verbs, adjectives, or other adverbs usually telling where, how, or when. Here are some examples:

    a. [How?] *She ran quickly.*

    b. [Where?] *She ran inside.*

    c. [When?] *She will run tomorrow.*

    d. [How often?] *She runs frequently.*

    e. [Affirmation] *Certainly, she runs fast.*

    f. [Negation] *She is not running.*

B. Adverb Forms

<u>1. **Adverbs**</u> may be...

    a. **Single words** such as *rapidly, gracefully, etc.;*

    b. **Phrases** such as *in the evening, after the storm, etc.;* or

    c. **Clauses** such as *if the class continues, if the university opens, etc.*

2. <u>**All adverbs**</u> need to be placed closest to the word(s) they add meaning to or describe.

3. <u>**Simple adverbs**</u> are words usually ending in *–ly* such as closely, lately, slowly. Some simple adverbs may be used as adverbs or adjectives such as *much, better, more, fast, early,* and *late.* Beware of Adverbs that split an infinitive.

4. <u>**Split infinitives**</u> place one or more words between *to* and the verb such as *He promised <u>to</u> quickly <u>go</u> home after school.* Better, *He promised <u>to go</u> quickly home after school.*

C. Table I-3-5-c-Adverb-Adjective Confusion

Certain words tend to be used only as adverbs or adjectives. The following tend to cause the most confusion:

Adjective	Meaning	Related Adverb	Meaning
Good	(kind, agreeable, satisfactory)	*well*	(satisfactory, in a desirable way)
Real	(authentic, genuine)	*really*	(actually)
Sure	(firm, secure)	*surely*	(certainly)
Some	(indefinite amount)	*somewhat*	(to a certain extent)

D. I-3-5-d. Adverb Practice

Name_____/25 = _____%

[Need 90% or greater for proficiency.]

Directions: Circle the adverbs. [4 points each]

1. He is very tall, slightly bald, and grossly overweight. [1-2-3]

2. Ricky learns fairly quickly, and he is a very capable student. [4-5-6]

3. John is extremely tall; this certainly helps him to sink basketball shots accurately. [7-8-9]

4. The skier very suddenly and skillfully jumped the moguls. [10-11-12]

5. She artfully crafted Haiku poetry about horrendously dangerous tornados. [13-14]

6. Soccer fans enthusiastically cheered wildly when Christian accurately kicked the goal to win the closely contested title match. [15-16-17-18]

7. Curtis and his brothers play the tuba extremely well. [19-20]

8. Ed and Jan lavishly entertained their dinner guests. [21]

9. Rocky painstakingly spread the very finely chopped mulch around the shrubs. [22-23-24]

10. She gracefully swam several lengths of the pool. [25]

{Check with Answer Key at back of book.}

I-3-6. Prepositions

A. Definitions

1. Pre*positions* are connectors that show the relationship [position] of a noun or pronoun to another word.

2. There are only about 60 prepositions.

3. The **most common ones** include *at, by, in, for, on, to,* and *with;* other commonly used prepositions include *about, off, onto,* and *without.*

4. Group prepositions include by means of, by virtue of, in front of, in place of, in spite of, and with regard to.

B. Functions

1. Pre*position*s usually indicate positional relationship about the following:

    a. **Time...** *before, during, after, until, and following* – imply a time relationship.

    b. Space... *in, out, over, under, around, through, above, below,* etc. – signal spatial relationships. Helpful mnemonic: think of the relationship of a dog to its doghouse or an animal to a fence.

    c. **Structure...** *by, for, about,* and *of* – help structure the ideas but they carry little meaning.

    d. **Associational or positional prepositions...** *against, around, at, from, in, into, like, near, on, out, through, to,* and *toward* -- express an associational or positional relationship between things.

2. Mnemonic to help remember the function of prepositions is...
    a. Focus on the root word of preposition... position.

b. Remember that prepositions signal the positional relation-ship between nouns and pronouns and other words.

C. I-3-6. Preposition Practice:

Name_____/25 = ___%
[90% = proficient.]

Directions: Circle the prepositions and prepositional phrases in the following:

1. We the people of the United States, in order to form a more perfect union, establish justice, insure domestic tranquility, provide for the common defense, promote the general welfare, and secure the blessings of liberty to ourselves and our posterity, do ordain and establish this Constitution for the United States of America. [8]

[U.S. Constitution, 1787.
* * * * * * * * * *

2. I pledge allegiance to the flag of the United States of America and to the Republic for which it stands, one Nation, under God, indivisible, with liberty and justice for all. [8]

[Pledge to the American Flag, 1892, Francis Bellamy]
* * * * * * * * * *

3. Oh, beautiful for spacious skies, for amber fields of grain
For purple mountains' majesties above the fruited plain.
America, America, God shed His grace on thee
And crown thy good with brotherhood from sea to shining sea. [9]
[America the Beautiful, ©1893, Katharine Lee Bates; Samuel A. Ward]
* * * * * * * * * *

{Check answers with the Answer Key at back of book.}

I-3-7. Conjunctions

A. Definitions

Conjunctions join or connect words or groups of words providing a junction or connection. Conjunctions are either coordinating or subordinating in function.

B. Functions

1. Coordinating conjunctions join sentence elements of equal form, weight, or function such as two nouns or two subject plus verb units. Coordinating conjunctions include *and, but, for, nor, or, so,* and *yet.* An example sentence using three coordinating conjunctions is... *Tom **and** Susie went to a beach party **and** a boat ride, **but** the wind was too gusty for the boat ride.*

2. Subordinating conjunctions join and show relationship between two elements of unequal importance. Some subordinating conjunctions include the following: *after, although, as, as long as, because, before, how, however, if, since, that, though, unless, until, when, whenever, where,* and *wherever.* Subordinated units tend to be dependent clauses since they lack a sense of completeness even though they have a subject plus verb unit. An example sentence using a subordinating conjunction is... *John, Dianne, and Ada intensely watched the sunset, **because** the five planets were to appear on the western horizon right at dusk. The clouds soon rolled in from the north, **however**, and blocked their view of the unusual occurrence.*

Mnemonic: The key to understanding the role conjunctions lies in the root word of conjunction... *JUNCTION*; a junction is a joint or joining of two items, in this case -- two clauses or two phrases. So, conjunctions indicate when and where two sentence elements are joined together.

C. I-3-7. Conjunction Practice

Name_____/25 = ____%
[90% = proficient.]

Directions: In the following sentences, circle the conjunctions. The number in brackets[_] indicates the number of words to look for and to circle in that paragraph.

1. *I pledge allegiance to the flag of the United States of America and to the Republic for which it stands, one Nation, under God, indivisible, with liberty and justice for all.* [2] 92, Francis Bellamy, 1892]

2. *You're a grand ole flag, you're a high-flying flag, and forever and peace may you wave. You're the emblem of the land I love: the home of the free and the brave. Every heart beats true 'neath the red-white-and-blue, where there's never a boast or brag. Should old acquaintance be forgot, keep your eye on the grand ole flag.* [3-7] [George M. Cohan]

3. Sharon sent Robert to the store to get some meat, potatoes, fresh vegetables, rolls, and ice cream for dinner; however, he could not find fresh vegetables, so he bought a bag of frozen mixed vegetables instead, and he got some cobbler to go with the ice cream. [8-11]

4. After loading one chair at a time, the large Ferris wheel went around and around and around – up into the air and down to the ground, up in the air, and down to the ground – round and around for at least three minutes before unloading and reloading one chair at a time; so, we rode for nearly ten minutes. [12-19]

5. Although she transferred in with 24 credits, Sonia still had to take several core courses, because she had not taken math nor a lab science nor U.S. History nor speech, and she needed a P.E. credit. [20-25]

{Check answers in Answer Key in back of book.}

I-3-8. Interjections

A. Definition

Interjections are one-word (or very-few-word) exclamations that express strong or sudden emotion. They usually end with an exclamation mark or point. Examples include *My heavens! Ouch! Cheers! Aha! No! Yes! Amen! Whew! Wow! Yippee!*

B. Function

Interjections express emotion most often when writing dialogue that represents spoken English, but rarely are used in formal academic papers.

C. Interjection Practice:

Name_____/25 = ___%
[90% = proficiency.]

Directions: Circle the interjections in the following sentences.

1. Wow! That was a close call! That accident was too close for comfort.

2. As the teacher passed back the papers, a "Yippee!" was heard from one of the students.

3. After reaching the top of the mountain, one climber exclaimed, "Whew! I'm exhausted!" "Me, too!" echoed another. [2]

4. "What a shame!" whimpered the reporter. "Those people have suffered so much loss!"

5. Heavens! I did not think that I did that well on the exam!

6. Aha! So, that's the secret – the more one studies the better the grades.

7. "Can you come to the party next Friday night?" asked Mark. "No!" retorted Sam. "I must study for an exam that I have to take on Saturday."

8. "Yes!!" shouted Sam's mother as he ran the touchdown that won the game.

9. "I do declare! Someone banged into my car while I was shopping!"

10. "Ah! That iced tea hits the spot on a hot day!"

11. "Mmm! Mom's apple pie always tastes great!"

12. "Yes, Sir!" responded the new recruit to the Officer of the Day.

13. "Watch out!" warned Dad.

14. "Run!" exclaimed the police officer trying to help evacuate the building.

15. "All right!" exclaimed the basketball player as he sunk a free throw.

16. "Run, boy, run!" exclaimed the football coach to the 8-year-old player.

17. "Sink it!" shouted the crowd as Jordan readied a free-throw shot.

18. "Yea, Team! We won!" cried the girls on the championship team.

19. "Thank Heavens, I passed the test!" yelled the student.

20. Mom said, "Congratulations, John! You did a super job mowing the lawn."

21. "Yikes! That snake scared me!"

22. "Oops! I spilled the milk."

23. "Look Out! The train is coming!"

24. "Wow! That car almost hit us!"

{Check answers in Answer Key in back of book.}

I-3-Parts of Speech
Mastery Check-Up-1

Name_____/50 = ____%
[90% = proficient]

Directions: Indicate the part of speech of every word on the line above the word.

        N   V ADV
For example, Dean ran rapidly.
Use the following codes: N (noun), PN (pronoun), ADJ (adjective), ART (article), V (verb), HV (helping/assisting verb), ADV (adverb), PRE (preposition), CON (conjunction), and INT (interjection).

1. *I pledge allegiance to the flag of the United States of America and to the Republic for which it stands – one nation under God, indivisible, with liberty and justice for all.*

[1892, Francis Bellamy] __/31 = ___%

2. Super job! Each team ingenuously demonstrated its part of speech—meeting different learning modalities and the eight multiple intelligences. __/19 = ___%

3. The students all worked hard to prepare their parts of speech presentations. [___/12]

4. Team five illustrated how adverbs add to verbs, adjectives, and other adverbs. [___/12]

5. Team six cleverly demonstrated prepositions showing positional relationships between words. [___/10]

6. Team one presented nouns as the names of persons, places and things. [___/12]

7. Team three involved everyone in a game to match adjectives to nouns. [___/12]

8. Team four engaged the class to actively demonstrate verbs through some skits. [___/12]

9. Team two vividly depicted pronouns taking the place of nouns. [___/10]

[Practice: ___/80 = ___%]

{Check answers in Answer Key at back of book.}

Chapter 4

Easily Confused Words-I: Homonyms, Homophones, and Homographs

A. Rationale

Because the English language utilizes many words from other languages and inherently offers irregular sound and spelling patterns, many words are easily confused. Homonyms – words with the same name – include homophones and homographs. Homophones sound alike but have different spellings and meanings, and homographs are spelled the same but have different meanings and origins. Often, only the way the word is used in a given sentence context clarifies the most appropriate word choice or meaning.

B. Definitions

1. Homonyms. Coming from Greek *"homos"* (same) plus *"onyma"* (name), *Homonyms* literally means words that have the same name. They include homophones, homographs, and seem-a-likes.

2. Homophones. Coming from Greek *"homos"* (same) plus *"phonos"* (sound), *Homophones* have the same phonetic sounds but have different spellings and meanings. Examples include *cite/site, there/their/they're, to/too/two, capital/capitol,* and *assent/ascent.* More examples follow later in this chapter.

3. Homographs. Rooted in Greek *"homos"* (same) plus *"graphos"* (writing), *Homographs* look alike – are spelled alike -- but have different meanings and origins. Examples include *record*(n)/ *record*(v), and *chaps*(n-friends)/*chaps*(n-cowboy leather leggings)/ *chaps*(v-dries out). More examples follow later in this chapter.

4. Seem-A-Like Homonyms. Other homonyms seem alike but differ in meaning. Only the way the word is used in a given sentence context clarifies the most appropriate word choice.

Notes & Questions

C. I-4-1. Homonym Check-Up

NAME_____/20 = ____%

[90% = proficient]

Directions: Select the correct word for each space. Write the letter A or B or C or D or E in the blank in the right-hand column. Some may be used twice. Some may not be used at all. No words starting sentences are capitalized.

1. _____   1) The baseball players took their __1__ shoes __2__
               the lockers, __3__.

2. _____   A. to   B. too   C. two

3. _____

4. _____   2) __4__ going to be late to __5__ class if you don't
               hurry up.

5. _____   A. your   B. you're   C. youre

6. _____   3) __6__ a shame that the computer lost __7__ memory.

7. _____   A. it's   B. its   C. its'

8. _____   4) It pleases __8__ that my friends and __9__ went to the
               movies together.

9. _____   A. I   B. me   C. my

10. _____   5) __I __10__ the notes on the desk, because I needed to
               __11__ down for a nap.

11. _____   A. lay   B. lie   C. laid   D. lied
               E. layed

12. _____   6) __12__ going to __13__ seats over __14__.

13. _____   A. their   B. there   C. they're

14. _____

15. _____   7) __15__ threw the ball to __16__? I missed the
               double play.

16. _____ A. who   B. whom   C. whoever   D. whomever

17. _____ 8) __17__ __18__ you going after class?

18. _____ A. were   B. where   C. wear   D. whir

19. _____ 9) How did the cold weather __19__ the plants outdoors?

20. _____ A. affect   B. effect

21. _____ 10) How did the icy roads __20__ school closings?
                                 A. affect   B. effect

{Check answers with Answer Key in back of book.}

D. I-4-2. Homophones Word List --
Homophones = Sound-A-likes

Homophones. Homophones sound alike but have different spellings and meanings. Examples of homophones include the following. For a more complete listing of the various meanings and nuances of these words, consult an up-to-date dictionary.

Aid... (verb) provides help; (n) help received

Aide... (noun) an assistant or an officer

Already... (adverb) previously

All ready... (adverb plus adjective) completely, totally ready

All together... (adverb plus adjective) in a group

Altogether... (adverb) completely, entirely

Altar... (noun) a place for religious rites or activities

Alter... (verb) to change or make different

Aural... (adjective) listening

Oral... (adjective) verbal, aloud

Born... (verb) birthed

Borne... (verb) carries; past participle of *to bear*

Cent... (noun) a penny; 1/100 of a dollar

Scent... (noun) a smell, fragrance, odor

Sent... (verb) to move something away from its present locale

Chord... (noun) a string; three or more musical notes sounded together

Cord... (noun) a woven rope; an anatomical structure (spinal cord)

Coarse... (adjective) rough, crude, not fine

Course... (noun) systematic plan of action, study, travel, etc.

Complement... (noun) something that completes; (verb) to make complete

Compliment... (noun) expression of flattery or praise; (verb) to congratulate

Dear... (adjective) adored, loved, precious

Deer... (noun) animal

Desert... (noun) dry, arid land relatively free of water; (verb) to forsake, leave or abandon

Dessert... (noun) final course of a meal (usually pie, cake, etc.)

Discreet... (adjective) cautious, prudent, wise

Discrete... (adjective) distinct, individual, separate

Homophones (continued)

Flew... (verb) past tense of *fly*

Flu... (noun) an illness with aches, pains, and fever

Flue... (noun) a passage for air in a chimney or smokestack

For... (preposition) in place of; instead of; with regard to; (conjunction) because

Fore... (adjective) first or near the front

Four... (noun) 4

Formally... (adverb) in a standard or conventional manner

Formerly... (adverb) earlier in time

Foreword... (noun) introduction to a book

Forward... (adjective) movement toward the front

Forth... (adverb) forward, onward

Fourth... (adj) 4th

Grate... (verb) to annoy or irritate; (n) metal frame or fireplace

Great... (adjective) unusual, large, of high rank or value

Hear... (verb) to perceive sound

Here... (adverb) in this place

Dianne M. Haneke, Ph.D.

Idle... (adjective) inactive; (verb) engine running

Idol... (noun) image of a god

Its... (pronoun) possessive pronoun for *it*

It's... (pronoun plus verb) contraction for *it is*

Lead... (noun) a heavy metal

Led... (verb) guided; past tense of *lead* (to guide or direct)

Lessen... (verb) makes less

Lesson... (noun) an exercise or activity for learning

Passed... (verb) gone beyond; succeeded (on a test); past tense of *pass*

Past... (adjective) of former time gone by or ended; before now; (adv) beyond point in time or space

Principal... (adjective) most important in rank; (noun) a school administrator

Principle... (noun) a fundamental law or truth; rule of logic, action, conduct, etc.

Their... (pronoun) possessive pronoun of *them*

There... (adverb) at or to that place

They're... (pronoun plus verb) contraction for *they are*

Homophones (continued)

To... (preposition) preposition expressing movement forward

Too... (adverb) also, as well

Two... (noun) number 2

Vain... (adjective) unsuccessful; excessive and unwarranted pride

Vane... (noun) wind direction indicator

Vein... (noun) blood vessel returning blood to heart

Ware... (noun) merchandise or manufactured goods

Wear... (verb) clothe in

Where... (adverb) at what place?; (conjunction) in or at the place

Who's... (pronoun plus verb) contraction for who is

Whose... (pronoun) possessive pronoun meaning of whom

Yore... (adverb) long ago; (noun) time long past

Your... (pronoun) possessive pronoun for *you*

You're... (pronoun plus verb) contraction for *you are*

More Homophones

Dianne M. Haneke, Ph.D.

E. I-4-3. Homographs Word List -- Homographs = Look-A-Likes

Homographs. Homographs look alike – are spelled alike -- but have different meanings and origins. Examples of seem-a-likes include the following; for a more complete listing of the various meanings and nuances of these words, consult an up-to-date dictionary.

Angle... (noun) math term; There are three angles inside a triangle.

Angle... (verb) to fish; Tom enjoys angling for trout.

Axes... (noun) plural of *axis*; The graph has both x and y axes.

Axes... (noun) plural of *ax.* The lumberjacks used axes to lop off the branches.

Ball... (noun) formal dance; The teens dressed up for the junior ball.

Ball... (noun) round object; Throw the football to me.

Bear... (noun) large, wild animal

Bear... (verb) to carry or to support; Joshua had to bear the heavy load.

Cleave... (verb) to hold on to; In the flood waters, Sue had to cleave to the tree branch.

Cleave... (verb) to cut; Robert had to cleave the large steak into three pieces.

Crow... (noun) Native American Indian tribe

Crow... (noun) large black bird

Crow... (verb) rooster's loud cry

Die... (noun) plural of dice; Sol rolled the die to see who would start the game.

Die... (noun) tool; Mrs. Jones used the die cut machine to make the decorations.

Die... (verb) stop living; Usually, people die when they get older.

Does... (noun) plural of female deer, *doe*

Does... (verb-present tense) to do; Amanda does her math homework first.

Fair... (noun) farm goods show; David entered his rabbits in the 4-H fair.

Fair... (noun) bazaar, carnival, festival; Wayne sold his trinkets at the fair.

Fair... (adjective) honest, just, impartial, objective; Debbie is a fair judge.

Fair... (adjective) lovely, beautiful; Ada has such fair skin.

Fair... (adverb) mediocre, average; Mark did fair on his project.

Fly... (noun) special kind of insect

Fly... (verb) to move through the air using wings

Grave... (noun) a burial site

Grave... (adjective) serious, very important; The severe storm left some grave problems.

Hide... (noun) animal skin

Hide... (verb) to keep from being seen, to conceal

Like... (verb) to enjoy or be pleased with; I like pizza.

Like... (adjective) similar; Sam looks a lot like John.

Minute... (noun) sixty seconds

Minute... (adjective) very small; Rose tended to the minute details of the party.

Pitcher... (noun) a baseball player who throws the ball for the batter to hit

Pitcher... (noun) a container that allows you to pour liquids

Read... (verb-present tense) I like to read books.

Read... (verb-past tense) Yesterday, I read the newspaper.

Record... (noun) This is a record of our family's vacation.

Record... (verb) Today, Alexandra will record our vacation's happenings.

Run... (noun) a snag; There is a run in the knit sweater.

Run... (verb) to move fast on foot; Joseph likes to run in the marathon.

Run... (verb) to allow to flow; Please let the water run to water the trees.

Saw... (noun) a hand tool for cutting wood; Mary used the saw to cut the board.

Saw... (verb) to cut wood; Ed had to saw the board into two pieces.

Saw... (verb-past tense of *to see*) Jan saw the dogs in the park.

Tear... (noun) a drop of water or liquid from an eye

Tear... (verb) to rip apart

Wind... (noun) air moving faster than usual; The wind was blowing and gusty.

Wind... (verb) to twist or turn around and around; It's time to wind the grandfather clock.

Yard... (noun) three feet in length

Yard... (noun) an area surrounding a house; Children play in the yard.

More Homographs

F. I-4-4. Seem-A-Like Homonyms Word List

Seem-A-Like Homonyms. Other homonyms seem alike but differ in meaning. Often, only the way the word is used in a given sentence context clarifies the most appropriate word choice. Examples of seem-a-likes include the following; for a more complete listing of the various meanings and nuances of these words, consult an up-to-date dictionary.

Accept... (verb) takes, receives

Except... (verb) to leave out, exclude, or omit; (preposition) leaving out or omitting; (conjunction) were it not true

Access... (noun) entrance, admission; (verb) to gain or have access to

Excess... (noun) surplus, overabundance; (adjective) more than usual; (verb) do away with the position

Accidentally... (adverb) by chance; unexpectedly and unintentionally

Incidentally... (adverb) casually

Advice... (noun) opinion or counsel

Advise... (verb) to give advice to

Affect... (noun) feeling; (noun) to influence or to act upon

Effect... (noun) result; (verb) to cause or bring about a result

Allusion... (noun) indirect hint, reference, or suggestion

Illusion... (noun) unreal image; false idea or conception

Amend... (verb) to alter, change, make better, improve

Emend... (verb) to correct by editing

Among... (preposition) involves more than two, e.g., ...*among the four of us*...; in company of,   surrounded by

Between... (preposition) space or time separating two; e.g., ...*between the two of us*; (adv) intermediate space

Angel... (noun) a heavenly spirit or messenger from God

Angle... (noun) shape made by two straight lines; (verb) to fish or scheme; to move or bend at an angle

Ante-... a prefix meaning *before, in front of*; functions as an adjective.

Anti-... a prefix meaning *agains;* functions as an adjective.

Appraise... (verb) to evaluate, assess, judge quality or worth

Apprise... (verb) to advise, teach, or inform

Ask... (verb) to request information; inquire of

Ax or axe... (noun) tool with blade to cut wood; (v) to trim, split, cut off

Can... (helping-verb) has the ability to do it; (v) to preserve; (n) container

May... (helping-verb) has permission to do it

Must... (helping-verb) is obliged to do it

Capital… (noun) city/town seat of state govt.; money available for investment

Capital…(adjective) punishable by death

Capitol… (noun) building where state or national government meets

Cause… (noun) producer producing an effect;

Effect… (noun) product; (verb) to bring about

   [**Mnemonic**: the cause usually follows the *because*…]

Censor… (noun) critic with power of censorship or stopping something

Censer… (noun) incense vessel

Censure… (noun) strong disapproval; (v) to express strong disapproval

Compare… (verb) to show similarities and likenesses

Contrast… (verb) to show differences and dissimilarities; (n) a difference

Conscience… (noun) sense of right wrong

Conscious… (adjective) aware of one's surroundings

Conscientious… (adjective) scrupulous; honest; done according to what one knows to be right; painstakingly showing care and precision

Consul... (noun) an official in a foreign service of a country

Council... (noun) a group of persons, often governing

Counsel... (noun) discussion deliberation; (verb) to give or take advice

Costume... (noun) style of dress; (verb) to dress or put on a costume

Custom... (noun) usual or habitual practice; (adjective) made or done to order

Decent... (adjective) proper fitting

Descent... (noun) descending, coming down or going down

Dissent... (noun) disagreement; (verb) to disagree

Desert... (noun) dry, arid wasteland; (verb) to leave or abandon

Dessert... (noun) final course at a meal

Device... (noun) a contrivance or something built for a specific plan

Devise... (verb) terbo plan, invent, or scheme

Disinterested... (adjective) impartial, unbiased

Uninterested... (adjective) not interested, indifferent

Effective... (adjective) having proven capacity to do something; producing a result

Strong... (adjective) powerful, robust; (adverb) in a strong, greatly severe manner

Elicit... (verb) to draw out

Illicit... (adjective) unlawful

Elusive.. (adjective) hard to catch

Illusive... (adjective) misleading

Emigrate... (verb) to leave one's (homeland) country to settle and live in another

Immigrate... (verb) to come into another country to settle and live

Eminent... (adjective) well-known; rising above; high and lofty

Imminent... (adjective) impending, threatening, likely to happen without delay

Envelop... (verb) to surround

Envelope... (noun) wrapper for a letter

Ethic... (noun) a principle of right or good moral conduct

Ethics... (noun) study of the nature of morals

Ethos... (noun) fundamental values, spirit, and mores of a group or culture

Ethnic... (adjective) pertaining to a social, racial, religious, cultural, or national group

Explicit... (adjective) specific, directly stated

Implicit... (adjective) implied but not directly stated

Extant... (adjective) still existing, not extinct

Extent... (noun) amount, size, length, breadth

Farther... (adjective) more distant (referring to actual distance)

Further... (adjective) more distant (usually the choice for all meanings other than actual distance)

Human... (adjective) pertaining to mankind; (noun) a person

Humane... (adjective or adverb) bearing best qualities of human beings: kind, tender, merciful, etc.

In... (preposition) contained, within, inside of; (adv) from point outside to inside; (adj) person in power

Into... (preposition) motion toward a point inside

Infer... (verb) to draw a conclusion from or arrive at by reason

Imply... (verb) to hint or suggest meaning indirectly

Ingenious... (adjective) clever

Ingenuous... (adjective) straightforward, candid, open, honest

Instance... (noun) case or example; (verb) to show or exemplify by means of an instance

Instants... (noun) moments; (adjective) urgent, pressing, imminent

Indexes... (noun) guides (plural of index)

Indices... (noun) alternate plural of index

Indicia... (noun) plural variation of indicators: signs or things that reveal

Lay... (verb) to put or set something down or to place something

Lie... (verb) to recline

Learn... (verb) to acquire or gain knowledge or skill

Teach... (verb) to provide instruction enabling others to gain knowledge or skill

Loose... (adjective) not tight, free; (verb) to make less tight or set free

Lose... (verb) to misplace, to suffer loss, or to be deprived of; not win

Moral... (adjective) ethical, right conduct; (noun) a moral implication or lesson taught by a fable or event

Morale... (noun) psychological-emotional state of feeling well or badly; strong spirit in the face of adversity

Picture... (noun) a drawing or photograph

Pitcher... (noun) a baseball player

Pitcher... (noun) container used to pour liquids

Precede... (verb) to go before

Proceed... (verb) to advance, continue, or move onward

Pretend... (verb) to make believe; Maria pretends she is a queen.

Portend... (verb) to provide a sign that something will happen; Animals portend earthquakes.

Quality... (noun) a characteristic element, attribute, basic nature of something or someone

Quantity... (noun) an amount or portion determined by measurement

Quiet... (adjective) still, silent, not noisy

Quit... (verb) to stop or give up

Quite... (adverb) very, somewhat, or completely

Receipt... (noun) a statement that a bill was paid

Recipe... (noun) a plan of action for cooking or preparing food

Stationary... (adjective) cannot be moved

Stationery... (noun) writing paper

Than... (conjunction) used in comparison

Then... (adverb) at that time; next in order of time

Thorough... (adjective) complete; Samantha did a thorough job of cleaning house.

Through... (preposition) from start to finish, beginning to end, by means of; It went through the tunnel.

Used… (verb-past tense) to employ something; Juan used the saw.

Used…(adverb) He got used to using that saw.

Used… (adjective) second-hand, previously owned; Pablo bought a used bike.

Way…(noun) a path taken; Which way did he go?

Weigh…(verb-present tense) to check how heavy something is; How much does it weigh?

Weight…(noun) the amount of how heavy something is; It's weight is 10 pounds.

More Homonyms Notes

G. I-4-3. Easily Confused Words – Post Checkup/Test – 1

NAME_____/20 = ____%

[90% = proficient]

*Directions: Select the correct word for each space. Write **A** , **B, C, D,** or **E** in the blank at the left. Words may be used twice or not at all. No words to start sentences are capitalized.*

___1. The brothers went _1_ the store; their friend went, _2_.

___2.   A. to   B. too   C. two

___3. You were _3_ taught how to write _4_ for academic purposes.

___4.   A. formally   B. formerly   C. familiarly

___5. _5_ a shame that the computer lost so much of _6_ memory.

___6.   A. it's   B. its   C. its'

___7. Between you and _7_, _8_ am pleased that _9_ friends came to see me.

___8.   A. I   B. my   C. me   D. mine

___9.

___10. _10_ car is double parked? _11_ owns it needs to move it before it gets towed.

___11.   A. who   B. whose   C. who's   D. whoever

       E. whomever

___12. 6) _12_ going to _13_ car that is parked over __14_.

___13.   A. their   B. there   C. they're   D. they's

       E. thare

___14.

___15. 7) Please __15_ me so that I can __16_ the greatest __17_ on my students.

___16. A. advice   B. advise   C. affect   D. effect
        E. advize

___17.

___18. 8) Simple logic, __18__, helps you know that the __19__ building is located

___19. in the __20__ city.

___20. A. then   B. than   C. capital   D. capitol

{Check with Answer Key at back of book.}

Notes & Questions

H. I-4-4. Easily Confused Words –
Check-up/Post Test - 2

NAME_____20 = _____%

[90% = proficient]

Directions: Select the correct word to appropriately complete the sentence.

_____1. The heavy rains (a-affected, b-effected) flooding in the river valleys and mudslides in the mountains.

_____2. Many lives were (a-affected, b-effected) by all the flooding.

_____3. The (a-principals, b-principles) worked with the site-based team of teachers to lead the school to Blue Ribbon status.

_____4. The school faculty and staff valued the high moral (a-principals, b-principles) and virtues of honor and respect for all persons.

_____5. The principal (a-complemented, b-complimented) the site-based team's choice for Teacher of the Year.

_____6. The administration and the faculty (a-complement, b-compliment) each other with their personal strengths and weaknesses.

_____7. The professor (a-implicitly, b-explicitly) addressed the talking issue by kidding about it.

_____8. The professor (a-implicitly, b-explicitly) addressed the talking issue by asking the students to curtail unnecessary conversations during his instructions.

_____9. More persons (a-emigrate, b-immigrate) into the United States of America than

_____10. persons (a-emigrate, b-immigrate) out of the USA.

____11.   (a-Altogether, b-All together) ten people arranged the Homecoming activities.

____12.   Homecoming was (a-altogether, b-all together) exciting.

____13.   She is (a-all ready, b-already) here, and

____14.   she is (a-all ready, b-already) to go to the airport.

____15.   The executor of the will wondered if he could (a-excess, b-access)

____16.   the (a-excess, b-access) assets of the estate.

____17.   President Bush could (a-accept, b-except) the furnishings in the oval office

____18.   (a-accept, b-except) the drab olive green bookcase.

____19.   Is "tell the truth, no matter what" an (a-ethnic, b-ethic) issue?

____20.   His (a-ethnic, b-ethic) background encourages him to be "street-wise."

{Check answers with Answer Key in back of book.}

Notes & Questions

I. I-4-5. Easily Confused Words –
Check-up/Post Test - 3

NAME_____ _____/20 = ___%
[90% = proficient]

Directions: Select the word that best completes each sentence. Write its letter on the line at left.

___1. (a-Can, b-May) I borrow your car to run to the store?

___2. (a-Can, b-May) I do 100 push-ups? No way, Jose.

___3. Did you have to wait (a-a while, b-awhile) for the plane to arrive?

___4. I spent quite (a-a while, b-awhile) shopping in the bookstore while waiting for your delayed flight to arrive.

___5. The nurse's (a-aid, b-aide) assisted the nurse in caring for the patient.

___6. The bright light was a tremendous (a-aid, b-aide) to the doctor during the surgery.

___7. The spinal (a-chord, b-cord) is an anatomical "rope" of many nerve fibers.

___8. The piano (a-chord, b-cord) is a combination of three or more notes that provide harmony.

___9. The teacher (a-allowed, b-aloud) the children to talk

___10. (a-allowed, b-aloud) during small group or cooperative learning projects.

___11. The window (a-pane, b-pain) did not feel the stinging

___12. (a-pane, b-pain) of the sleet hitting the window during the storm.

Dianne M. Haneke, Ph.D.

___13. For healthy living, one cannot (a-beet, b-beat) juicing carrots and

___14. a fresh (a-beet, b-beat) for a refreshing, healthful drink.

___15. Diamonds are rated in terms of a (a-carat, b-caret, c-carrot).

___16. A symbol to indicate that a word is added is called a (a-carat, b-caret, c-carrot).

___17. A healthy vegetable to eat raw is a (a-carat, b-caret, c-carrot).

___18. The teacher shortened the (a-lessen, b-lesson) to enable students to finish.

___19. The governor (a- discreetly, b- discretely, c-descreetly) presented

___20. the (a-discreet, b- discrete, c- descreet) facts under the tense circumstances.

{Check answers with Answer Key at back of book.}

Additional Notes About Homonyms -- Easily Confused Words –

Chapter 5

Easily Confused Words-II:
Plurals and Possessives

A. Rationale

Plurals and possessives can be confusing. Usually, both word forms involve adding an *s*. The following information and guidelines may make it easier for you to use appropriately each form.

B. Definitions

Often, plurals and possessives can be confusing for both readers and writers. The following definitions hopefully help clear up the confusion:

1. Plurals. Plurals indicate more than one of a noun; for example, *one cow, two cows; one deer, two deer; one horse, two horses; one house, two houses; one lady, two ladies; etc.*

2. Possessives. Possessives indicate that the noun or pronoun owns or possesses something(s); for example, *John's horse; Ty's three fish; James' rabbits; Mark's dolphins; etc.*

C. Overview

Chapter 5 focuses on two skills: plurals and possessives, and has six parts: a) a Check-Up on plurals, b) a Check-Up on possessives, c) guidelines on plurals, d) guidelines on possessives, e) a post-test on plurals, and f) a post-test on possessives. Take both Check-Ups, then do only the work that you need to review.

D. Objective

This chapter clarifies the similarities and differences between plural and possessives and .presents opportunities to work with both kinds of easily confused words.

Notes & Questions

E. I-5-1. Check-Up on Plurals

Name_____/12 = ____%
[90% = proficient]

Directions: Select the correct plural form of the word at the left. Write A, B, C, D, or E in the left-hand column blank space.

___1. lady   A) ladies   B) ladies'   C) ladys   D) lady

___2. man   A) mans   B) men   C) mens   D) man

___3. company   A) companys   B) companies   C) companyes   D) company

___4. student   A) student's   B) students   C) studentes   D) studenties

___5. family   A) family's   B) families   C) families'   D) family

___6. radio   A) radios   B) radioes   C) radios'   D) radio

___7. potato   A) potatos   B) potatos'   C) potatoes   D) potato

___8. hero   A) heros   B) heroes'   C) heroes   D) hero

___9. self   A) selfs   B) selfes   C) selves   D) selves'

___10. half   A) halfs   B) halfes   C) halves   D) halves'

___11. church   A) churchs   B) churches   C) church   D) church's

___12. belief   A) beliefs   B) beliefes   C) believes   D) belief

{Check with Answer Key at back of book.}

F. I-5-2. Check-Up on Possessives

Name_____/12 = _____%
[90% = proficient]

Directions: Select the correct possessive form for each word on the left. Writ
A, B, C, D, or E in the left-hand column.

BEWARE! Do not change the initial word; just make the first word possessive
whether it is currently singular or plural.

___1. lady	A) ladie's	B) ladies'	C) lady's	D) ladys'
___2. men	A) mans'	B) men's	C) mens'	D) man's
___3. company	A) companys'	B) companie's	C) company's	D) companies'
___4. students	A) student's	B) students	C) students'	D) studente's
___5. families	A) family's	B) familie's	C) families'	D) familys'
___6. radio	A) radios'	B) radioe's	C) radio's	D) radioes'
___7. potato	A) potato's	B) potatos'	C) potatoe's	D) potatoes'
___8. hero	A) hero's	B) heros'	C) heroe's	D) heroes'
___9. selves	A) self's	B) selfs'	C) selve's	D) selves'
___10. half	A) halfs'	B) half's	C) halve's	D) halves'
___11. church	A) churchs'	B) churches'	C) churchies'	D) church's
___12. belief	A) belief's	B) beliefes'	C) believes'	D) beliefs'

{Check with Answer Key at back of book.}

G. I-5-3. Guidelines on Plurals: Rules and Guidelines to Form Plurals

Eleven rules guide the formation of plurals in the English language. The first three rules explain the most commonly regular plural formations.

1. Most nouns regularly form a plural by adding —s to the end of the singular word form: e.g., desk — desks; lesson — lessons; objective — objectives; teacher — teachers; piano — pianos.

2. When the singular word form ends in *–ch, –s, -sh, -x, or –z*, form the regular plural by adding *–es* to the end of the word: e.g., *church — churches; class— classes; dish — dishes; fax —faxes; buzz — buzzes.*

3. When the singular word form ends in a consonant followed by a --y, form the regular plural by changing the *-y* to *-i* and adding *–es*: e.g., *candy — candies; city — cities; university — universities; variety — varieties.*

The other eight rules explain ways and means of handling variations:

4. When the singular word form ends in a vowel followed by a *–y*, form the plural by adding *–s*: e.g., *day — days; key — keys; boy — boy; buy — buys.*

5. When the singular word ends in a consonant followed by an *–o*, form the plural by adding *–es*: e.g., *hero — heroes; potato — potatoes; tomato — tomatoes; zero — zeroes.*

6. When the singular word ends in a vowel followed by an *–o*, form the plural by adding *–s*: e.g., *patio — patios; radio — radios; video — videos.*

7. For most nouns ending in *–f* or *–fe*, form the plural by adding *–s*: e.g., *belief — beliefs; cliff — cliffs; roof — roofs; gulf — gulfs; café — cafes; cuff — cuffs.*

8. For some words that end in *–f* or *–fe*, form the plural by changing the *–f* to *–v* and adding *–es*: e.g., *leaf — leaves; bookshelf — bookshelves; half — halves; life — lives.*

I-5-3. Plural Guidelines (continued...)

9. For singular compound words, form the plural by making the base noun or second noun plural – following the guidelines above: e.g., *mother-in-law* > *mothers-in-law; playground — playgrounds; teacher-aid — teacher-aides; room-mother— room-mothers.*

10. Some words use the same form for both singular and plural: e.g., *bass, rye, corps, salmon, deer, series, dozen, sheep, elk, trout, fish, wheat.*

11. Some words form the plural by irregularly altering the singular word form: e.g., auto — autos; axis — axes; basis — bases; child — children; crisis — crises; criterion — criteria; datum — data; die — dice; focus — foci; foot — feet; goose — geese; index— indices; louse— lice; man — men; medium — media; mouse — mice; oasis — oases; ox — oxen; parenthesis — parentheses; piano — pianos; radius — radii; solo — solos; stimulus — stimuli; tooth— teeth; woman — women.

H. Reminders About Plurals and Possessives

1. The lists are intended only to illustrate the rule and are not intended to be all-inclusive or exhaustive.

2. Most dictionaries list nouns in the singular form and list only the unusual and irregular plural forms for that word. Therefore, learn these guiding rules for forming plurals and cross-check with your up-to-date dictionary.

3. Do the same for forming possessives.

4. When in doubt, check it out!

Notes on Plurals

I. I-5-4. Guidelines About Possessives

1. Rules and Guidelines to Form Possessives

Possessive forms of nouns always require an apostrophe. Six rules govern the formation of possessives. The first two cover singular word forms; the next two cover plural word forms; and the last two cover unusual forms. These illustrative rather than exhaustive lists provide examples of each rule as follows:

a. Form the possessive case of singular nouns by adding an apostrophe and an *s* *('s)* e.g., *the boy's book; the girl's pony tail; the teacher's desk; the school's gyms.*

b. Form the possessive case of singular nouns with more than one syllable and ending with an */s/* or */z/* sound by adding only the apostrophe. This is optional but avoids too many */s/* sounds: e.g., *the trapeze's bar, the trapezes' bars; Frances' new car; Charles' new bik;, the princess' newborn son; Moses' ten commandments, Jesus' birth.*

c. Form the possessive case of plural nouns ending in –*s* by adding just an apostrophe: e.g., *the students' recess; the teachers' lounge; the girls' locker-room; the boys' club; the potatoes' skins* and *the families' reunions.*

d. Form the possessive case of plural nouns not ending in –*s* by adding an apostrophe and an *s* *('s)*: e.g., *the children's story hour; the sheep's wool; the mice's tails, the men's Bible study..*

e. Form the possessive of a hyphenated noun through using the above guidelines to alter the part following the last hyphen: e.g., *My sister-in-law's business address is local. My sisters-in-law's reunion plans are being finalized. The student-of-the-day's picture hangs on the bulletin board. The students-of-the-day's pictures hang on the bulletin board.*

f. Form the possessive of nouns joined by *and* as follows:

f-1) Show individual possession by applying the above rules to each individual so that each noun shows possession: e.g., *Lois' and Kent's trips were to exotic paradise islands.*

f-2) Show joint possession by applying the above rules to the noun that follows the last *and* so that the last noun shows the possession: e.g., *Lois and Kent's trip was to an exotic paradise island.*

Notes & Questions

J. I-5-5. Plurals – Post Check-up Test

NAME_____/12 = _____/100 [90% = proficient]

Directions: Select correct plural for each word. Write A, B, C, D, or E in the blank at left.

____1. child   A) childs   B) child's   C) children   D) childrens'

____2. woman   A) womans   B) woman's   C) women   D) womens'

____3. sheep   A) sheep   B) sheeps   C) sheep's   D) sheeps'

____4. deer   A) deers   B) deer's   C) deer   D) deers'

____5. shelf   A) shelfs   B) shelf's   C) shelves   D) shelves'

____6. school   A) schools   B) schooles   C) school's   D) schools'

____7. class   A) class'   B) classes   C) classes'   D) class's

____8. piano   A) pianos   B) pianoes   C) piano's   D) pianos'

____9. valley   A) valley's   B) valleys   C) valleys'   D) vallies

____10. louse   A) louse's   B) louses'   C) louses   D) lice

____11. student   A) students   B) student's   C) studentes   D) students'

___12. chalk   A) chalkes   B) chalk's   C) chalks   D) chalkies

{Check answers with Answer Key at back of book.}

K. I-5-6. Possessives – Post Test/Check-up

NAME_____/12 = _____/100
[90% = proficient]

Directions: Select correct possessive form for each word. DO NOT change the first word at the left; just indicate its possessive form by writing an A, B, C, or D in the blank.

1. children	A) childs	B) childrens	C) childrens'	D) children's
2. woman	A) woman	B) woman's	C) women	D) womens'
3. sheep	A) sheep's	B) sheeps'	C) sheeps	D) sheeps's
4. deer	A) deer	B) deer's	C) deers	D) deers'
5. shelf	A) shelf's	B) shelfs	C) shelves	D) shelves'
6. schools	A) school's	B) schools	C) schooles	D) schools'
7. class	A) class'	B) class	C) classes'	D) class'es
8. pianos	A) pianos	B) piano's	C) pianos's	D) pianos'
9. valley	A) valley	B) valley's	C) valleys'	D) valleys's
10. louse	A) louse's	B) louse'	C) lice	D) lices'
11. board	A) boards	B) board's	C) boards's	D) boards'
12. chalks	A) chalks	B) chalks'	C) chalkes'	D) chalk's

{Check answers with Answer Key at back of book.}

Chapter 6

Three Kinds of Vocabulary: Antonyms, Synonyms, and Analogies

A. Rationale

Effective writing requires proficient use of a variety of powerful, descriptive, active words – nouns, verbs, adjectives, and adverbs. Expanding one's vocabulary provides a greater choice of options for communicating more efficiently with various readers. Exploring antonyms, synonyms, and analogies extends understanding of the relationships between words, increases one's vocabulary, and thereby, enhances word choices when writing. A good, up-to-date dictionary and a recently-published thesaurus aid these explorations. Often, antonyms, synonyms, and analogies appear in academic potential tests, academic achievement tests, and language drills.

B. Ways to Increase Vocabulary

There are many ways to increase one's vocabulary. First-hand experiences provide new words or familiar words in new contexts, but since a person can experience first-hand only a limited amount of life and the world, other means more frequently increase one's vocabulary. A person best appreciates how to acquire new vocabulary or how to expand one's vocabulary when he or she studies a foreign language. To really learn the language's vocabulary and sentence syntax, a person enrolls in an "immersion" experience where nothing but that language is written, spoken, or read for a specific period of time. During that time, a person watches TV, reads newspapers, shops in stores, and travels using only that language – doing a variety of life activities to more thoroughly learn the language. Reading books, magazines, and newspapers expands vocabulary. Listening, speaking, and writing the language increase vocabulary. But in all of these language activities, it helps to think about and to use antonyms, synonyms, and analogies or word relationships to expand the vocabulary of any language. The remainder of this chapter deals with English antonyms, synonyms, and analogies as sources for better understanding and making use of a variety of words when writing.

C. Definitions

1. Antonyms. Antonyms mean the opposite or nearly the opposite. They help draw comparisons and describe contrasts. They also assist in remembering a variety of synonyms. Beware: an antonym may be for only one meaning of a word with several meanings. Since antonyms are easier for children to grasp, they should be introduced first. A list of some examples follows these definitions and Check-Ups, but a simple example is... *hot:cold*.

2. Synonyms. Synonyms mean the same or similar. Dictionaries often employ synonyms in their definitions. Synonyms help draw comparisons and may enhance contrasts. Synonyms may or may not assist in remembering antonyms. Beware: a synonym may be for only one meaning of a word with several meanings. Since synonyms are harder for children to grasp, they should be explored after introducing antonyms. A list of some synonym examples follows these definitions and Check-Ups, but a simple example is *hot:warm*.

3. Analogies. Analogies are useful for teaching and testing the relationships between words and their various meanings. Primarily, analogies are based on synonyms and antonyms, but analogies may also be based on cause and effect, sequence, numerical relationship, degree, grammatical relationship, part-whole relationship, member-group relationship, object-action, object-class, object-description, object-place, object-use, object-user, and other relationships. A list of some analogy examples follows these definitions and the Check-Ups, but a simple example is *hot:cold::*

warm:cool, read as "*hot is to cold as warm is to cool*"; this is an example of an antonym analogy. Using the same words, *hot:warm:: cold:cool* reads as "*hot is to warm as cold is to cool*"; this is an example of a synonym analogy. Another analogy is… *burn:hot::numbness: cold;* this is an example of an effect-cause analogy.

Notes & Questions

D. I-6-1. Antonym Check-Up

Name_____/12 = _____%

[8 points each; 90% = proficient.]

Directions: Select the best word that means the opposite of the word in the list. When two answers seem plausible, which one is more often linked as an opposite of the first word?

___1. hot   A) cold   B) cool   C) warm   D) tepid
                E) chilly

___2. cool   A) cold   B) warm   C) tepid   D) hot
                E) boiling

___3. above   A) over   B) under   C) below   D) top
                E) beside

___4. close   A) shut   B) nearby   C) secure   D) open
                E) afar

___5. fail   A) flunk   B) pass   C) success   D) lose
                E) repeat

___6. in   A) outside   B) out   C) enter   D) inside
                E) amid

___7. yes   A) okay   B) maybe   C) nay   D) affirmative
                E) no

___8. up   A) down   B) risen   C) ascending D) airborne
                E) under

___9. wet   A) damp   B) dry   C) moist   D) humid
                E) soggy

___10. tall   A) brief   B) little   C) short   D) large
                E) lofty

___11. win   A) victory   B) overcome   C) lose   D) lost
               E) tied

___12. wild   A) tame   B) domestic   C) unrestrained   D) calm
               E) natural

Bonus...

___13. more   A) most   B) greater   C) less   D) further
               E) additional

{Check answers with Answer Key in back of book.}

Notes & Questions

E. I-6-2. Synonym Check-Up

Name_____/12 = _____%
[7 pts each; 90% = proficient.]

Directions: Select the best word that means the same as the word in the left list. When two answers seem plausible, which one is more often linked as a pair with the first word?

___1. all   A) entire   B) some   C) none   D) one
              E) nearly

___2. border   A) center   B) corner   C) edge   D) top
              E) middle

___3. city   A) state   B) country   C) village   D) borough
              E) town

___4. energy   A) endeavor   B) effort   C) power   D) weakness
              E) listless

___5. faith   A) trust   B) weak   C) fearful   D) positive
              E) independence

___6. gift   A) loss   B) present   C) donor   D) loan
              E) wrap

___7. happy   A) sad   B) hatred   C) glad   D) gloomy
              E) elate

___8. idea   A) dream   B) thought   C) conscious   D) pensive
              E) meditate

___9. listen   A) spoken   B) hearing   C) hear   D) hearken
              E) heed

___10. need   A) beg   B) require   C) like   D) lacking
              E) missing

Grammar Improves Writing

___11. terrify A) frighten   B) calm   C) hostage   D) scream
               E) surprise

___12. thaw   A) iced   B) cold   C) melt   D) warm
               E) heat

Bonus...

___13. sell   A) buy   B) purchase   C) vendor   D) vend
               E) retail

{Check answers with Answer Key in back of book.}

Notes & Questions

F. I-6-3. Analogies Check-Up

Name_____/20 = ____%

[5 pts each; 90% = proficient.]

Directions: Select the best word to fill in the blank. Consider 1) which word is related to which word [1:2 and 3:4 or 1:3 and 2:4]? 2) How are these words related: antonyms, synonyms, etc.? 3) When two answers seem plausible, which one is more often linked as a pair? THERE MAY BE MORE THAN ONE CORRECT ANSWER FOR MOST OF THESE; it depends upon which relationship you perceive and how many synonyms for that word might fit the analogy.

Antonyms...

____1. up:down::open: ____   A) entry   B) close   C) free
D) slam

Synonyms...

____2. thin: slim::close-by:____   A) near   B) far   C) distant
D) here

Cause -Effect relationships...

____3. fertilize: grow::wash:__   A) scrub   B) harvest   C) cleanse
D) clean

____4. rain:wet::sun:____   A) hot   B) burn   C) cloudy
D) bright

Sequential relationships...

____5. plant:harvest::sleep:____   A) dream   B) awake   C) night
D) day

____6. one:three::six:____   A) two   B) twelve   C) eight
D) nine

Numerical relationships…

___7. 8:4::4:___   A) 1   B) 2   C) 3
                             D) 4

___8. ten:twenty::six:___   A) twelve   B) sixty   C) three
                             D)sixteen

Degree relationships…

___9. intelligent:brilliant:: hungry:___

                             A) smart   B) thirsty   C) starving
                             D) full

__10 lower:lowest::higher:___   A) tallest   B) highest   C) shortest
                             D) taller

Notes & Questions

F.I-6-3. Analogy Check-Up (continued)

Grammatical relationships...

___11 she:her::you:___   A) your   B) yours   C) his
D) hers

___12. our:ours::they:___   A) theirs   B) them   C) us
D) yours

Part-whole relationships...

___13. toe:foot::page:__   A) screen   B) book   C) play
D) stage

___14. wheel:car::wing:___   A) bird   B) airplane   C) train
D) helicopter

Member-group relationships...

___15. teacher:faculty::student:__   A) home   B) school   C) class
D) team

___16. sailor:navy:soldier:___   A) army   B) air force   C) marines
D) toy

Object-Action relationships...

___17. clock:tick::bell:__   A) tock   B) school   C) bellfry
D) ring

___18. drum:beat::horn:___   A) pound   B) blow   C) car
D) carry

Object-Class relationships...

___19 . poodle:dog::hymn:__   A) cat   B) music   C) song
D) choir

Bonus...

___20.   rose:flower::dog:___   A) hound   B) plant   C) animal
                                      D) barks

Object-Use relationships...

___21.   stove:cook::plane:__   A) travel   B) trip   C) pilot
                                      D) airport

___22.   truck:drive::plane:___   A) ride   B) fly   C) sit
                                      D) race

{Check answers with Answer Key in back of book.}

Notes & Questions

G. Table I-6-4. Vocabulary: Antonyms – Word List

Since there is an antonym for nearly every word imaginable, the following list is illustrative, not exhaustive. Antonyms seem easier for children to learn than synonyms, and sometimes, writers find the exact word they desire by first thinking of its opposite. This list is illustrative -- not exhaustive. Consult your dictionary or thesaurus for antonyms of specific words.

above – below	active - resting	add – subtract
after – before	agile – clumsy	alive – dead
all – none	beautiful – comely	beginning – ending
boy – girl	brother – sister	burning – freezing
busy – still	children --- adults	clean – dirty
closing – opening	coldest – hottest	created – destroyed
crooked – straight	dark – light	day – night
deep – shallow	different – same	dishonor – honor
disobey – obey	dullness – brightness	down – up
far – near	fast – slow	faster – slower
fat – skinny	fathers – mothers	first – last
gentleman – lady	good – bad	greater – lesser
group – individual	hard – soft	hardness – softness
high – low	higher – lower	hot – cold
ignorance – knowledge	illiterate – literate	impolite – polite

indoors – outdoors	inside – outside	left – right
longer – shorter	man – woman	many – few
messy – neat	mother – father	no – yes
older – younger	parts – wholes	peaceful – stressful
poor – rich	problems – solutions	respect – disrespect
short – tall	sister – brother	stronger – weaker
sweet – sour	teacher – learner	teacher – student
warm – cool	wet – dry	you -- me

Notes & Questions

H. Table I-6-5-H. Vocabulary: Synonyms – Word List

Since there is at least one synonym for nearly every word imaginable, the following list is merely illustrative, not exhaustive. Consult a dictionary or thesaurus for synonyms of specific words.

action – motion	add – sum	adequate – enough
answer – response	aroma – smell	ask – query
beautiful - lovely	begin – start	beginning – starting
brook – creek	building – constructing	calm – peaceful
comforting – easing	country – nation	daily - everyday
demonstrate - show	dish – plate	drawing – sketch
elasticity – flexibility	ended – finished	eternal - everlasting
fighting – battling	final – last	frequently – often
gentlest - kindest	give – donate	growing – maturing
helped – assisted	high – tall	honest – sincere
honor – respect	joined – united	loud – noisy
low – short	lyrics – words	married – wedded
music – tune	new – unused	nothing – zero
ocean – sea	orderly – organized	oscillate – turn
photo – picture	power – strength	powerful – strong

rivulet – stream	round – spherical	scrub – cleanse
shrub – bush	steady – regular	true - real
truth – fact	useful – helpful	vista - view
void – nullify	want – wish	waterfall - cascade
wish - dream	yacht - boat	yak - bison

Add Additional Analogies

gorilla - ape		

Notes & Questions

I. Table I-6-6 Vocabulary-Analogies-Word List

First, determine the relationship of the first pair of words; then, find a second pair of words with the same relationship. Read the analogies like this: IN:OUT::HOT:___ or IN is to OUT as HOT is to ___. Reasoning process: since IN and OUT are antonyms (opposites), I need an antonym for HOT; the most common pairing that I recall is HOT:COLD, so, I look for COLD or something similar. Analogies are based on a variety of relationships of words -- the most common two of which are antonyms and synonyms. Note the relationship categories and examples below. There is no simple reference or listing of analogies; generating analogies happens as one explores the relationships of words. For illustrative and comparison purposes, the various relationships of *HOT: COLD* are presented throughout the following examples.

Notes & Questions

Table I-6-6-I Vocabulary–Analogies–Word List

Relationship	Example 1	Example 2
Antonyms:	hot:cold::warm:cool	in:out::up:down
Synonyms:	hot:steaming::cold:freezing	right:correct::far:distant
Cause/Effect:	hot:boil::cold:chill	happy:smile::tired:sleep

Table I-6-6-I Vocabulary-Analogies–Word List (Continued)

Relationship	Example 1	Example 2
Degree:	warm:hot::cool:cold	jog:run::master's:doctorate
Grammatical:	its:it's::his:he's	hot:hottest::cold:coldest
Member-Group:	principal:adminstration:: teacher:faculty	Scout:BoyScouts:: laborer:union
Object-Action:	stove:heat::freezer:chills	hand:clap::foot:tap
Object-Class:	stove:cooker::freezer:cooler	algebra:math::apple:fruit
Object-Description:	fire:hot::ice:cold	class:learning::exam:testing
Object-Place:	fire:stove::icecube:freezer	fish:sea::bird:sky
Object-Use:	stove:cook::freezer:chill	drum:beat::piano:melody
Object-User:	stove:chef::cooler:butcher	plane:pilot::ship:sailor
Part-Whole:	elbow:arm::knee:leg	toe:foot::finger:hand
Sequential:	heat:hot::chill:cold	workout:sweat::cold:shiver
Other:	top:bottom::left:right	read:listen::write:speak

Add Additional Analogies

Relationship	Example 1	Example 2

Dianne M. Haneke, Ph.D.

J. I-6-7. Vocabulary: Antonyms
– Posttest 1

NAME_____/12 = ____%
[8 pts each; 90% = proficient.]

Directions: Look for most commonly linked pairs of words; write letter of best answer on line.

___1. hot   A) cold   B) warm   C) cool   D) tepid

___2. cold   A) hot   B) warm   C) cool   D) chilly

___3. greater   A) small   B) great   C) smallest   D) smaller

___4. disobeys   A) mindful   B) obeys   C) sneaky   D) cooperates

___5. partial   A) complete   B) almost all C) some   D) incomplete

___6. heterogenous
                  A) mixed   B) opposites   C) likenesses D) homogenous

___7. problem   A) query   B) answer   C) solution   D) investigation

___8. donate   A) give   B) hoard   C) contribute D) generous

___9. teachers   A) learners   B) experts   C) facilitators D) coordinators

___10. united   A) joined   B) divided   C) fallen   D) separations

___11. boy   A) man   B) girl   C) lady   D) lad

___12. dog   A) cat   B) kitten   C) puppy   D) pet

{Check answers with Answer Key in back of book.}

Improve Your Writing 137

K. I-6-8. Vocabulary: Synonyms
– Posttest 2

NAME_____/12 = _____%
[8 pts each; 90% = proficient.]

*Directions: Look for most commonly linked pairs of words; write letter of be[s]
answer on line.*

___1. students   A) learners   B) teachers   C) facilitators   D) coordinators

___2. loving   A) disliking   B) caring   C) helpers   D) bossing

___3. nation   A) city   B) county   C) country   D) continent

___4. skimming   A) writing   B) reading   C) speaking   D) listening

___5. language   A) culture   B) ethnic   C) words   D) environment

___6. brook   A) river   B) creek   C) stream   D) inlet

___7. finish   A) ending   B) starting   C) middle   D) beginning

___8. elastic   A) stretch   B) flexible   C) fabric   D) limited

___9. maturing   A) taller   B) bigger   C) growing   D) aged

___10. intra-personal
                 A) internal   B) external   C) alone   D) interpersonal

___11. boy   A) female   B) girl   C) male   D) man

___12. cold   A) chilly   B) hot   C) ice   D) warm

{Check answers with Answer Key in back of book.}

L. I-6-9. Vocabulary: Analogies
– Posttest/Checkup 3

NAME_____/12 = ____%
[8 pts each; 90% = proficient.]

Directions: Look for most commonly linked pairs of words; write letter of best answer on line.

Analogies… *[Think of familiar pairs; whether likes, opposites, or otherwise related.]*

___1. hot:warm::cold:___   A) tepid   B) cool   C) icy

___2. hot:cold::summer:___   A) winter   B) fall   C) spring

___3. piano:music::canvas:___   A) painting   B) palette   C) artist

___4. workout:sweat::chilled:__   A) cool   B) shiver   C) icy

___5. algebra:math::physics:__   A) subject   B) English   C) science

___6. plane:pilot::ship:__   A) captain   B) seaman   C) sailor

___7. them:you::their:___   A) yours   B) your   C) our

___8. hand:claps::head:___   A) nods   B) bows   C) bobs

___9. university:dean::school:__   A) aide   B) teacher   C) principal

___10. top:bottom::front:__   A) entry   B) back   C) side

___11. smarter:wiser::smartest:__   A) wise   B) wisest   C) wiseguy

___12. snake:reptile::whale:__   A) fish   B) mammal   C) mollusk

Bonus:

___13. dog:walks::bird:__   A) hops   B) hovers   C) flies

{Check with Answer Key in back of book.

Part II

Basic Sentence Structures: English Grammar and Usage

A. Table II-intro-1. References for Review
References for Review

Topic in Workbook	ARCO...	Grammar	Help Yourself	Writing	Survival Kit
II-A: Sentences	pp. 49-52	pp. 47-65	pp. 29-50	pp. 21-	
II-B: subjects & predicates	pp.17-24; pp. 45-51	pp. 47-65	pp. 29-50		
II-C-1: fragments	pp. 49-50		pp. 33-35		p. 207
II-C-2: run-ons	pp.51		pp. 165-182		p. 209
II-C-3: punctuation	pp. 54-62; pp. 78-82; pp. 88-94	pp. 115-126	pp. 183-244	pp. 20	
II-D: subject-Verb agreement		pp. 79-87	pp. 77-94	p. 7	pp. 192-197
II-E: verb tenses		pp. 11-14; pp. 68-73	pp. 51-74		pp. 219-221
II-F: parallel construction			pp. 265-280		
II-G: active & passive voice		pp. 107-108	pp. 287-296	pp. 22	
II-H1: misplaced, dangling modifier		pp. 74-78	pp. 243-264		p. 218
II-H-2: awkward, choppy, wordy		pp. 88-106	pp. 281-286 pp. 297-320		

Reference List

Lerner, M. (1994). <u>The Princeton review: Writing smart: Your guide to great writing.</u> NY: Random House.

Mattson, M., Leshing, S., Levi, E. (1993). <u>Help yourself: A guide to writing and rewriting</u> (3rd ed.). New York: Macmillan. [out of print]

Muschla, G. R. (1991). <u>The writing teacher's book of lists: With ready to use activities and worksheets.</u> Paramus, NJ: Prentice Hall.

Muschla, G. R. (1993). <u>Writing workshop survival kit</u>. West Nyack, NY: The Center for Applied Research in Education.

Pulaski, M.A.S. (1982). <u>Step-by-step guide to correct English (2nd ed.)</u>. NY: Macmillan.

Staff of the Princeton Review. (1996). <u>The Princeton review: Grammar smart: A guide to perfect usage.</u> NY: Random House.

Basic Sentence Structures -- Grammar and Usage

A. Introduction

Grammar is a language's system of rules for constructing sentences. Understanding grammar enhances a student's ability to effectively select appropriate words and construct informative sentences. Section I reviews the basic building blocks of writing – words. Selecting the most descriptive, active, appropriate words is basic to constructing effective sentences.

Section II – Sentences – presents opportunities for students to develop greater expertise in sentence construction by reviewing the following: Chapter 7-Four Kinds of Sentences, 8-Two Parts of Sentences (subjects and predicates), 9-Three Incomplete Sentences (fragments, run-ons, and punctuation,) 10-14-Sentence Agreement in subject-verb; in verb tense; in parallel construction; in active or passive voice; and 15-Two Sentence Flaws (misplaced modifiers and awkward sentences). Writers convey meaning by effectively employing appropriate words to generate and construct powerful and thought-provoking sentences.

As in Section I, learners' needs (knowledge-gaps) vary throughout the concepts and skills covered in Section II; so, the onus for the mastery of these principles is on the learners for reviewing these sentence concepts, assessing needs, mastering various kinds of sentences, eliminating sentence problems through study, and moving on to the next constructs.

Learning effective selection of appropriate words leads to constructing more efficient sentences (Part I). Based on effective word selection, learning how to generate and construct efficient sentences (the topic of this Part II) leads to the construction of well-organized, more powerful, and more informative paragraphs (the topic of Part III).

Additional Notes

Chapter 7

Four Kinds of Sentences

A. Introduction

One or more words expressing a complete thought form a sentence. A sentence must make sense. Four types of sentences communicate the process and results of "making sense" or "constructing meaning" of one's world: 1) declarative, 2) interrogative, 3) exclamatory, and 4) imperative.

B. Definitions

These four kinds of sentences are defined as follows:

1. Declarative Sentence. A declarative sentence makes a statement, gives information, or tells what happens. Most declarative sentences place the subject first and the predicate second. All declarative sentences begin with a capital letter and end with a period *(.)*. Examples of declarative sentences include the following: *The boy ran.* Or *The President alluded to the impact of international trade on the American economic status.*

2. Interrogative Sentence. An interrogative sentence asks a question; it usually gives part of the verb, then the subject, then the rest of the verb. All interrogative sentences begin with a capital letter and end with a question mark *(?)*. Examples of interrogative sentences include the following: *How long will this rain last?* Or *Why did the U.S. Congress defeat the much-needed piece of legislation?*

3. Exclamatory Sentence. An exclamatory sentence shows strong emotion or feeling; it usually begins with the subject and ends with the verb. All exclamatory sentences begin with a capital letter and end with an exclamation mark/point *(!)*. Examples of exclamatory sentences include the following: *Wow!* Or *The retirement dinner party really surprised her immensely!*

4. Imperative Sentence. An imperative sentence gives a command – telling someone to do something; it usually begins with the verb because the subject (you) is understood; sometimes, the subject is stated. Imperative sentences begin with a capital and end with a period *(.)*. Examples of imperative sentences include the following: *Pass the salt and pepper. Please pass the salt and pepper.* Or *John, please pass the salt and pepper.*

C. Uses

These four types of sentences may be used in any combination in any writing project as long as the sentence type matches the sentence meaning. That is, interrogative sentences must be used when asking questions; exclamatory sentences must be used when making exclamations; etc. Using a variety of sentence structures makes any text more enjoyable to read.

D. Practice – Four Kinds of Sentences

Directions: Write one sentence for each of the four types of sentences.

1. [declarative]_____
_____
_____

2. [interrogative]_____
_____
_____

3. [exclamatory]_____
_____
_____

4. [imperative] _____
_____
_____

Notes & Questions

II-7-E. Four Kinds of Sentences – Check-Up

Name_____/25 = ____/100
[4 pts each; 90% = proficient]

Directions: _Indicate each kind of sentence; use_ **D** _(**declarative**),_ **IN** _(**Interrogative**),_ **E** _(**exclamatory**), or_ **IM** _(**imperative**)._

____1.   Where are you from?

____2.   We're from Texas.

____3.   Wow! The Grand Canyon is so majestic!

____4.   Have you ever seen anything as beautiful as the Grand Canyon?

____5.   No, I haven't.

____6.   How many times have you visited the Grand Canyon?

____7.   This is my sixth visit.

____8.   Watch your step; there's quite a drop-off at the Rim.

____9.   Yikes! I see what you mean! It just drops off for thousands of feet!

____10.   Are you camping, staying in an RV, or staying in a motel?

____11.   We drove our motor home RV to the Canyon.

____12.   And you?

____13.   We're staying in the Grand Canyon Inn on the South Rim.

____14.   I want to get a souvenir video of the Canyon.

____15.   I also want to take the airplane ride over the Canyon.

____16.   Me, too.

____17.   This has been a fantastic vacation!

Dianne M. Haneke, Ph.D.

_____18.   I agree with you about that.

_____19.   Have a great day!

_____20.   You, too!

_____21.   That surely was a friendly traveler!

_____22.   Which one?

_____23.   The one that just chatted with me at the Rim – she was really friendly.

_____24.   Is she staying at the campground or at the hotel?

_____25.   She's staying in her motor home at the South Rim Campground.

{Check answers with Answer Key in back of book.}

Additional Notes

Chapter 8

Two Parts of Sentences: Subjects and Predicates

A. Introduction

One or more words telling a complete thought comprise a sentence. Two essential elements of any sentence are 1) a subject – who/what the sentence is about – and 2) a predicate – what the subject is doing. Together, these two parts of a sentence must make sense. That's why reading and writing are often considered to be "making sense" or "constructing meaning of one's world."

B. Definitions

1. Simple Subject. Who or what the sentence is about is the simple subject; the simple subject is a noun, a pronoun, or a *you* (understood), and the simple subject is usually a single word unless the subject is a multi-word proper noun. For example, *The tall, good-looking **athlete** skillfully **swished** a three-point basket to tie up the game and send the game into overtime.* Who or what is the sentence about? The a*thlete*, so *athlete* is the simple subject in this example. The simple subject is located by answering the question, *Who or what performed the action?* When studying sentence structures, identify a simple subject by drawing a circle around it.

2. Simple Predicate. The simplest word telling what the subject is or did is the simple predicate; the simple predicate is usually a verb or verb clause. In the above sentence, what did the athlete do? The athlete *swished...* so, *swished* is the simple predicate in this example. The simple predicate is located by answering the question, *What did the subject do?* When studying sentence structures, drawing a box or a double circle identifies the simple subject .

3. Compound Subject. Two or more subjects doing the same action – using the same verb – make up a compound subject. For example, in the sentence -- *Horses, burros, and goats grazed in the same pasture* -- *Horses, burros,* and *goats* comprise the compound subject and *grazed* is a simple predicate. When studying sentence structures, indicate compound subjects by drawing a circle around all the subject words.

4. Compound Predicate. Two or more actions (verbs) done by the same subject constitute a compound predicate. For example, in the sentence -- *During the summer, children play all day and sleep all night* -- *children* is the simple subject and *play* and *sleep* comprise the compound predicate. When studying sentence structures, indicate compound predicates by drawing a box around the words.

5. Complete Subject. The complete subject refers to the simple or compound subject (noun or pronoun) and all the describing modifiers. For example, in the sentences used above, *The tall, good-looking athlete...; Horses, burros, and goats...;* and *children...* are each the complete subject of their respective sentences. When studying sentence structures, a <u>single underline</u> indicates the complete subject, and a single vertical line *(|)* separates the complete subject from the complete predicate.

6. Complete Predicate. The complete predicate refers to the simple or compound predicate (verb) and all the describing modifiers. When studying sentence structures, a <u>double underline</u> indicates the complete predicate, and a single vertical line *(|)* separates subject and predicate.

C. Examples

The tall, good-looking athlete...// = complete subject

...skillfully swished a three-point basket to tie up the game and sent the game into overtime. = complete predicate.

Horses, burros, and goats... // = complete subject

... grazed in the same pasture. = complete predicate

During the summer, children... // = complete subject

... play all day and sleep all night. = complete predicate

Notes & Questions

D. Simple, Complete, and Compound Subjects and Predicates – Check-Up

Name_____/20 = _____%

[5 pts each; 90% = proficient]

Directions: In the first eight sentences, do the following:
[___/40 points]

a) Draw a circle around the Simple Subject.

b) Draw a box around the Simple Predicate.

c) Draw one vertical line between the subject and predicate.

d) Draw one line under the Complete Subject.

e) Draw two lines under the Complete Predicate.

1. The tall, lanky farm boy ran quickly across the field chasing the horse.

2. Rebecca, Mary, and Joan studied together for their chemistry final exam.

3. The tired, weary policeman carefully guided motorists around the scene of the horrible accident.

4. Stately Dean Smith sternly called the four sophomore men into his office to reprimand them for their behavior.

5. Mom and Dad came gladly to the Parents' Weekend and Homecoming activities, because they are proud alumnae.

6. Last night, Thomas, Britt, and Bill tried out for the varsity basketball team.

7. Researching professors often talk over the heads of their undergraduate students.

8. A caring principal usually makes all the difference in the world.

{Check answers with Answer Key in back of book.}

156 Dianne M. Haneke, Ph.D.

E. Chapter 8 -- Check-Up Part B: [___/30]

Directions: In the following 6 sentences, circle the compound subject.

9. Loretta, George, Tom, and Susan went out for pizza and sodas tonight.

10. Upon entering the restaurant, Robert and Sharon ran into Sam and Kelly.

11. Tennis and swimming are my favorite sports and past-times.

12. James and Mary attended Troy and Sue's party last night.

13. While skiing, Rob and Laura lost sight of their friends Rick and Sharon.

14. Dennis and Charlene attended Smiths' party last night though the weather was windy and rainy.

F. Chapter 8 Check-Up Part C: [___/30]

Directions: In the following 6 sentences, box the compound predicate.

15. Loretta, George, Tom, and Susan ate pizza and drank sodas tonight.

16. Upon entering the restaurant, Robert and Sharon ran into Sam and Kelly and greeted John and Dianne.

17. I play tennis, walk a mile, or swim laps for daily exercise.

18. James and Mary bought a gift and attended Troy and Sue's party last night.

19. While skiing, Rob and Laura missed a turn and lost sight of their friends Rick and Sharon.

20. For daily exercise, Ricky swims, plays basketball, or jogs two miles.

{Check answers with Answer Key in back of the book.}

Chapter 9

Incomplete Sentences:
Fragments, Run-ons, and Punctuation

A. Introduction

Rule: Every sentence must contain at least one subject plus verb unit and should communicate a sense of completeness or a complete thought.

Three types of incomplete sentences tend to plague writers: fragments, run-ons, and misuse of punctuation. A brief review of the definitions, some basic principles, and some possible remedies can eliminate this writing malady.

B. Fragment Definitions and Remedies

1. Defining Fragments. Fragments are incomplete sentences – sentences lacking either a subject or a predicate or lack both. Examples might include the following:

Just a little while ago. [This adverbial phrase lacks both a subject and a verb or predicate; who or what did what just a little while ago?]

Running through the gooey mud. [This predicate lacks a subject; who or what was running through the gooey mud?]

All the kings' horses and all the kings' men. [This subject lacks a predicate; what did the kings' horses and kings' men do or not do?]

That among these are life, liberty, and the pursuit of happiness. [This dependent clause by itself is incomplete; it lacks a subject and a predicate or verb; who or what did what? How does this clause tie to what?]

2. Identifying Fragments. Fragments are easily identified by asking, *Who or what did what?* If either part is missing, the phrase or clause is an incomplete sentence and, as such, is a fragment. The other cue to fragments is, *Does this make sense? Does this sound complete?* If not, there's a good chance it is a fragment, so look for the basic part missing – subject or verb.

3. Remedying Fragments. Among remedies for sentence fragments are the following:

Directions: Correct sentence fragments…

a. **lack a subject**… by adding a subject (noun or pronoun).

b. **lack a verb**… by adding a verb.

c. **lack a sense of completeness**… by adding one or more words to make sense; by removing word such as "that"; by combining it with an adjoining, related sentence; or by rewriting.

C. Run-on Definitions and Remedies

1. Defining Run-ons. Run-ons are two or more sentences not correctly connected. Two or more sentences joined to form a longer sentence must be connected correctly (by one of the following four means) so as not to confuse the reader: 1) a semicolon *(;)*; 2) a comma *(,)* plus a coordinating conjunction; and/or 3) a semicolon *(;)* plus a conjunctive adverb plus a comma *(,)*; or 4) separate sentences. Run-ons are also called *comma faults, comma blunders, fused sentences,* and *run–together sentences.*

2. Coordinating conjunctions include *and, but, for, not, or, so,* and *yet;* for example, *It was a hot day, so I stayed inside.*

3. Conjunctive adverbs include the following: *accordingly, also, anyhow, besides, consequently, furthermore, however, indeed, moreover, nevertheless, otherwise, still, then,* and *therefore;* for example, *It is a hot day; however, I must go to the store to get some groceries.*

4. Identifying Run-ons. The three kinds of run-on sentences are as follows:

a. A run-on having a comma but no connective between the sentences (also known as the *comma splice*).

b. A run-on having a connective but no punctuation between sentences

c. A run-on having neither a connective nor punctuation between sentences.

5. Remedying Run-ons. Each type of run-on has its own remedies.

a. The following illustrate three remedies for correcting a **comma splice run-on** – a run-on having a **comma but no connective**: *The northern cold front came in last night, the winds blew, the horses ran wildly around the pasture, all my joints ached.*

1) Change the comma(s) to semicolon(s): *The northern cold front came in last night; the winds blew; the horses ran wildly around the pasture; all my joints ached.*

2) Add a coordinating conjunction after the comma: *The northern cold front came in last night, the winds blew, the horses ran wildly around the pasture,* **and** *all my joints ached.*

3) Make each independent clause stand as a separate sentence. *The northern cold front came in last night. The winds blew. The horses ran wildly around the pasture. All my joints ached.*

b. The following illustrate three remedies for run-ons with **connective(s)** but no punctuation for the sentence: *The dog jumped up on the stranger however the owner did not reprimand the dog.*

1) Add a comma before the connective conjunction to the same sentence as follows: *The dog jumped up on the stranger, however the owner did not reprimand the dog.*

2) Add a semicolon before the connective conjunction and a comma after the connective for the same sentence as follows: *The dog jumped up on the stranger; however, the owner did not reprimand the dog.*

3) Separate run-on into separate sentences for the same sentence as follow: *The dog jumped up on the stranger. However, the owner did not reprimand the dog.*

c. The following illustrate four remedies for **run-ons with neither connective nor punctuation** for the following sentence: *The dog jumped up on the stranger the owner reprimanded the dog.*

1) Add a comma and a coordinating conjunction for the same sentence as follows: *The dog jumped up on the stranger, and the owner reprimanded the dog.*

2) Add a semicolon for the same sentence as follows: *The dog jumped up on the stranger; the owner reprimanded the dog.*

3) Add a semicolon, a conjunctive adverb (see preceding page), and a comma for the same sentence as follows: *The dog jumped up on the stranger; however, the owner reprimanded the dog.*

4) Divide the run-on into separate sentences for the same sentence as follows:. *The dog jumped up on the stranger. The owner reprimanded the dog.*

II-9-D. Punctuation Definitions and Remedies

1. Defining Punctuation. Punctuation marks are like "road signs" the writer provides for the reader. Punctuation marks appropriately employed provide guidance to complete ideas and clarify meaning, whereas, punctuation marks used inappropriately confuse the audience or reader. Twelve punctuation marks typically are used in the English language.

a-b-c. Period (.), Question Mark (?), and Exclamation Point (!). These signal the reader to stop and pause briefly before continuing. They are parallel to the red light on a traffic signal.

d-e. Comma (,) and Semicolon (;). These signal the reader to slow down and proceed slowly, with caution. They are parallel to the yellow or amber light in a traffic signal, or they are parallel to a speed bump in the road.

f. Colon (:) This signals the reader to continue without a pause, tells the reader what follows the punctuation further explains what precedes the punctuation, and is parallel to the green light in a traffic signal.

g. Dash (--). A dash signals a sharp change in the flow of ideas and tone of voice or separates parenthetical elements for emphasis. Often, dashes are used erroneously or in excess. Two continuous hyphens cover the approximate width of an "M," constitue an "em-dash," and are stronger than a single dash.

h-i-j. Parentheses ( ), Block Parentheses [ ], and Curly Parentheses { }. These signal the reader whatever is in the parentheses further explains what precedes the punctuation, but it is not essential to or necessary for understanding the basic communication of the sentence.

k. Quotation Marks. Quotation marks *("Yes!")* signal the reader he is reading a conversation or quoted material. Double quotes are used when there is a quotation of conversation or previously written text. Single quotes ('yes!') are used for quotations within quotations such as Mark asked, "So, what did he say?" Dad replied, "I thought I heard him say, 'Yes!' at lunch."

1. Ellipses (…). Ellipses signal that words are intentionally left out. Ellipses in front of a word or phrase means preceding words are omitted such as *…that among these are life, liberty, and the pursuit of happiness.* When words are omitted in the middle, the ellipses have a space on each side to so indicate such as *…our fathers brought forth on this continent….* When ending words are omitted, the ellipses follow the last word such as *Four score and seven years ago:*

2. Punctuation Summary. Standard conventions of print for the language you are writing usually dictate the use of most punctuation marks. This is especially true of terminal punctuation. However, in English, punctuation selection is ultimately up to the author, and his or her options should be based on helping his or her audience to make the most accurate and appropriate sense of the written text. The greatest latitudes of choices seem to lie with the use of commas, dashes, and parentheses. A good "rule of thumb" to follow is punctuation should facilitate reading fluency and enhance a "smooth ride" throughout the written text. Punctuation usage poses "speed bumps" or provides a "bumpy ride" should be altered or avoided.

E. Punctuation Guidelines.

1. Apostrophe ('). Use an apostrophe:
a. To show the possessive case of nouns and certain pronouns as follows:

1) Nouns and indefinite pronouns not ending in *s* take an apostrophe and an *s*.

2) Plural nouns ending in an */s/* or a */z/* sound take just an apostrophe.

3) Singular nouns ending in an */s/*, */sh/*, or */z/* sound may take either an apostrophe and an *s* or an apostrophe by itself… *Mr. Jones' home.*

4) When showing ownership or a similar relationship, only the last noun takes the possessive form such as ...*my mother and father's anniversary...*

5) When showing separate ownership or similar relationship, each noun takes the possessive form such as ...*my brother's and sister's friends...*

6) When constructing compounds, the apostrophe and *s* are added to the part immediately preceding the modified word such as ...my brother-in-law's boat...

b. To show certain special plurals as follows:

1) Abbreviations written with both internal and final periods usually take an apostrophe plus *s: Ph.D.'s, M.D.'s.*

2) Figures may take either an apostrophe and *s* or just an *s... 1900s or 1900's.*

3) Letters and words referred to as such usually take an apostrophe plus *s.*

c. To indicate the omission of letters or figures in contractions as follows: *aren't, isn't.*

d. To show inflected forms of verbs made up of abbreviations as follows: *OK'd.*

2. Brackets [ ] Use brackets in pairs:
a. To enclose editorial corrections, explanations, or comments within a quoted passage.

b. To indicate parentheses within parentheses.

3. Colon [:]. Use a colon:
a. Between hours and minutes in expressions of time and between chapter and verse in Biblical citations as follows: *10:30 PM Romans 8:28.*

b. Following the salutation of a business letter... *Dear President Bush.*

c .When introducing a formal statement, a long quotation, or a speech in a play.

d. When introducing an illustrating or amplifying item or series of items.

4. Comma [,]. Use a comma:

a. Before coordinating conjunctions such as *and, but, or, for,* and *nor* when they join the clauses of a compound sentence.

b. To separate an introductory clause or phrase from the main clause.

c. To set off words like *yes* and *no,* mild interjections, words in direct address, transitional words and phrases, and absolute phrases... *Yes, I plan to attend Homecoming.*

d. To set off contrasted sentence elements... *Pizza, not hot dogs, is her favorite food.*

e. To set off sentence elements out of natural order.

f. To set off a question at the end of a statement... *You are coming, aren't you?*

g. To set off main elements in an address; a title following a person's name; and the year if the month and day are given. If only the month and year are given, use no comma.

h. To indicate an omitted word or words in parallel constructions.

i. To separate coordinate adjectives modifying the same noun. (If the word *and* can be substituted for the comma, the adjectives are coordinate.)

j. To separate words, phrases, and clauses in a series.

k. To set off a nonrestrictive phrase or clause from the rest of the sentence. (A non- restrictive clause or phrase is one is not essential to the meaning of the sentence.)

l. To set off a clause or phrase disrupts the main clause.

m. To separate figures of five or more digits; insert a comma after each group of   three digits counting from the right.

n. To set off direct quotations from such expressions as *he said* and *she replied.*

o. To separate inverted names, phrases, etc., as in a bibliography, index, or catalog.

p. Following the salutation of a personal letter and the closing phrase of either a personal or business letter.

5. Dash [--]. Use a dash:
a. To indicate an abrupt change in thought or a break in the sentence flow.

b. To introduce a clause or phrase summarizing what has gone before.

c. To set off an appositive or parenthetical expression, especially when commas are needed for minor divisions within the expression or when a complete sentence is interpreted within another.

d. There are actually three dashes used in print: *hyphen dash, en dash,* and *em dash.* Fine lines of distinction guide their use. For more information about all three consult other references such as the internet.

6. Ellipsis […]. Use an ellipsis – three periods, also called suspension points:
a. To show material has been omitted from a quotation. Use four periods when the omission comes at the end of a declarative statement.

b To show a statement or series could be continued beyond what is given (when sed in place of *etc., and so forth,* or a similar expression.

7. Exclamation Mark [!]. Use an exclamation mark after a particularly forceful interjection or an imperative sentence.

8. Hyphen [-]. Use a hyphen:

a. Between elements of regularly hyphenated compounds such as *sixty-one, half-hour.*

b. Between some base words and prefixes, suffixes, or similar forms joined to the base or   root words either to change their meanings or to create now words.

c. Between the elements of temporary compounds – phrases thought of as a unit and   sometimes hyphenated to prevent ambiguity such as *a foreign-coin dealer.*

d. To indicate the continuation of a word divided at the end of a line.

Beware: Do not insert a hyphen in the following instances:

a. A suffix of fewer than three letters ordinarily is not separated from the rest of the word.

b. A word should not be divided so only one letter stands at the end of a line.

c. Whenever possible, hyphenated words should be divided only at the hyphen.

d. Words of more than one syllable should be hyphenated only between syllables.

e. Words of one syllable should not be hyphenated.

9. Parentheses [( )]. Parentheses are used in pairs:

a. To enclose figures and letters indicating enumerations within a text.

b. To enclose material that is explanatory, supplementary, or illustrative.

10. Period [.]. Use a period:

a. After declarative sentences, indirect questions, and most imperative sentences.

b. After many abbreviations.

c. After most polite requests phrased as questions... *Would you please send me a copy of your book.*

11. Question Mark [?]. Use a question mark:

a. After direct questions.

b.After an interrogative element within a sentence (though not after an indirect question.)

c. After each query in an unnumbered or unlettered series.

d. To express editorial doubt.

12. Quotation Marks (" "). Use double quotation marks in pairs:

a. To enclose direct quotations short enough to be run into the text. (Quotations of three or four lines or more usually appear without quotation marks but are set off from the text by space, indention, block indention, etc.

----Use single quotation marks to enclose a quotation within another quotation.

b. To enclose titles of poems, essays, short stories, articles, lectures, chapters of books, songs, and radio and TV programs.

c. To enclose words referred to as words, used in special senses, or given particular emphasis – or use italics in such cases.

13. Semicolon [;]. Use a semicolon:

a Between independent clauses not joined by a coordinating conjunction *(and, but, or* etc.)

b. Between independent clauses joined by a conjunctive adverb *(however, indeed, therefore).*

c. Between independent clauses of a compound sentence if the clauses are very long or are themselves subdivided by commas, or if a more definite break is desired than marked by a comma.

d. To replace a comma in separating elements in a series if the elements themselves contain commas.

14. Double Punctuation [." ,"]. Regarding double punctuation usage:

a. Period and comma always go inside closing quotation marks.

b. Colon and semicolon go outside closing quotation marks.

c. Question mark and exclamation mark go inside closing quotation marks if they apply to the quoted material; outside if they apply to the whole sentence.

d. When a complete sentence within a parentheses stands alone (not as part of another sentence), terminal punctuation goes inside closing parenthesis.

e. When a complete declarative sentence within parentheses is part of another sentence, a period goes inside closing parenthesis only if last word is an abbreviation taking a period. A parenthetical question or exclamation may end with a question mark or an exclamation point. (A parenthetical sentence of whatever kind does not begin with a capital letter unless the first word is regularly capitalized.)

f. A period indicating an abbreviation is not omitted before any mark of punctuation unless the mark is a period at the end of a declarative sentence or similar construction.

g. When a word, clause, or phrase within parentheses is part of a sentence,

h. A comma, semicolon, or period does not go before the closing parenthesis.

i. A question mark or exclamation mark goes before the closing parenthesis if it applies to the parenthetical material.

j. A comma, semicolon, or period goes after the closing parenthesis only if the sentence without the parenthetical material requires such punctuation there.

k. Except as noted above, a mark of punctuation ordinarily is not used in combination with another mark at the same location within a sentence. When two marks are called for, usually retain only the stronger mark.

[These notes were taken from <u>Webster's New World College Dictionary (4th ed.), 2000.</u>]

Notes & Questions

F. Sentence Structures: Fragments -- Check-Up

Name_____ /33 = ___%
[3 pts each; 90% = proficient]

Directions: For the first eleven sentences, write F for fragment or C for complete sentence. [Some inappropriate punctuation is used to not give away the answer.]

___1. The basketball player ran.

___2. Though it is hot out.

___3. Ran faster and faster until he caught up.

___4. How could he have missed that play?

___5. On the last night of the tournament.

___6. He studied for hours and hours but to no avail.

___7. Without a vision people lack direction and perish.

___8. Do unto others.

___9. Over and over again until she was sick of rehearsing.

___10. Practice makes perfect, or so they say.

___11. Four score and twenty years ago.

{Check answers with Answer Key in back of book.}

G. Sentence Structures: Run-ons -- Check-Up

Name_____/33 = _____%
[3 pts each; 90% = proficient]

*Directions: For next 11 sentences, write **RO** for **run-on** or **C** for **correct**.*

____12.　John came home he had dinner he went shopping with a friend.

____13.　John came home. He had dinner. He went shopping with a friend.

____14.　Her umbrella blew away in the wind; she ran after it.

____15.　Her umbrella blew away in the wind she ran after it.

____16.　My dog wanted me to play I stopped writing and we played.

____17.　My dog wanted me to play. I stopped writing, and we played.

____18.　All we saw was smoke; then suddenly we saw the flames.

____19.　All we saw was smoke then suddenly we saw the flames.

____20.　She hates writing she seldom turns in a written assignment she often fails.

____21.　She hates writing. She seldom turns in a written assignment. She often fails.

____22.　She hates writing, seldom turns in a written assignment, and often fails.

{Check answers with Answer Key in back of book.}

H. Sentence Structures:
Punctuation -- Check-Up

Name_____/44 = ___%
[4 pts each; 90% = proficient]

Directions: For these 11 sentences, write **C** *for* **correct***, and write* **I** *for* **incorrect** *regarding punctuation and capitalization. If it is incorrect, change the punctuation so it is correct. Look for proper use of periods, questions marks, exclamation marks, commas, colons, semi-colons, and capitals. [Each sentence is worth 4 points: 2 for C/I and 2 points for corrections, if needed.]*

___1. which of the following is correct: donuts, or doughnuts?

___2. Julie said, "My dog is a chestnut brown Healer mix."

___3. "My dog is a chestnut brown Healer mix" said Julie.

___4. "Where is my cap?" asked John.

___5. how did I forget such a simple thing on the midterm.

___6. My favorite foods are pizza, vegetable lasagna, and quesadillas.

___7. My favorite restaurants are Macaroni Grill, Red Lobster, Olive Garden, and El Chico.

___8. Where does your dad work? Mine works for Dell Computer.

___9. These days, most students work their way through college.

___10. where were you born I was born in san Francisco

___11. Which grades and which subjects do you want to teach.

{Check answers with Answer Key in back of book.}

Chapter 10

Sentence Agreement:
Subject-Verb Agreement in Number

A. Introduction

Another writers' plague is the agreement of the sentence subject with the verb regarding number – singular or plural. General Rule: Subject and verb must agree in number.

B. Rules and Guidelines

A number of rules guide writers and users of the English language toward subject-verb agreement in number such as the following:

Rule 1. A singular subject (noun or pronoun) requires a singular verb form.

Rule 2. A plural subject (noun or pronoun) requires a plural verb form.

Rule 3. The subject and the verb must agree in number even when separated from each other by other parts of the sentence; e.g., *The tallest tree in the whole forest of Redwoods was struck by lightning. The tallest tree... was struck...*

Rule 4. A singular collective noun referring to a single unit requires a singular verb form; e.g., *The women's basketball team plays a home game tonight. ...team plays...*

Rule 5. A singular collective noun referring to the members of a group as individuals requires a plural verb form; e.g., *The woodwind quintet play various instruments. ...quintet* (5 persons) *play ...instruments.*

Rule 6. A plural collective noun requires a plural verb form; e.g., *The scene casts rehearse daily for the pageant.* The *casts rehearse...*

Rule 7. Usually, the following words are singular, and when used as the subject, they require singular verb forms: *any, anybody, anyone, each, either, everybody, everyone, everything, neither, nobody, nothing, one, somebody, someone,* and *something;* e.g., *Each of us fulfills his own destiny. Each... fulfills...* e.g., *Neither of these responses is correct. Neither... is ...*

Rule 8. *All* requires a singular verb form when *all* means *everything,* when *all* is followed by a singular noun, or when *all* is followed by a singular noun or pronoun; e.g., <u>*All*</u> *is done.* <u>*All*</u> *the painting* <u>*is*</u> *dry.*

Rule 9. *All* requires a plural verb form when *all* means all the people, places, or things or when *all* is followed by a plural noun or pronoun; e.g., *All were upset with the tragedy. All public servants were touched by the tragedy.*

Rule 10. *None* requires a singular verb when *none* means no one; e.g., *None was found alive.*

Rule 11. *None* requires a plural verb when *none* means not any; e.g., *None have been located.*

Rule 12. With *either...or, neither...nor, or not only...but also,* when both parts of the subject are singular, use a singular verb form, and when both parts are plural, use a plural verb form. However, when one part of the subject is singular and the other part is plural, THE VERB AGREES WITH THE PART OF THE SUBJECT NEAREST THE VERB; e.g., *Neither the doctor nor the* <u>*nurses*</u> <u>*were*</u> *ready to help the patient in crisis. e.g., Not only they but I am cold.*

Rule 13. Expressions such as *with, along with, as well as* – do not change the number of the subject; e.g., *Ada, along with Jan and Ed, is coming to dinner tonight. Ada...is...*

Rule 14. In sentences beginning with *There is* or *There are,* the subject follows the verb. *When the subject is singular, use a singular verb; when the subject is plural, use a plural verb;* e.g., *There are several ports of call on our cruise. ...are...ports...; There is one of the ports that is my favorite. ...is...one...*

C. Helpful Mnemonic

1. When the noun ends in –*s* (typically a plural subject), the verb usually does not end in –*s* (typically a plural verb form).

2. When the noun does not end in –*s* (typically a singular subject), the verb usually does end in –*s* (typically a singular verb form).

Notes & Questions

D. SENTENCE STRUCTURES -- Agreement: Subject/Verb - Pretest

Name_____/20 = ___%
[5 pts/sentence; 90% = proficient]

*Directions: Indicate if the subject and verb agree in number – singular or plural. Write **AN** for agree in number and a **DN** for disagree in number.*

___1. There's three parts to a paragraph: introduction, body, and conclusion.

___2. There are three parts to a paragraph: introduction, body, and conclusion.

___3. They were going to the basketball game last night.

___4. They was going to the basketball game last night.

___5. We was late to class on Monday.

___6. We were late to class on Monday.

___7. There are five classes held on campus last night.

___8. There was five classes held on campus last night.

___9. There were five classes held on campus last night.

___10. There is five classes held on campus last night.

___11. Five cars are involved in Tom's accident last week.

___12. Five cars is involved in Tom's accident last week.

___13. Five cars were involved in Tom's accident last week.

___14. Five cars was involved in Tom's accident last week.

___15. Engines run better when weather is neither too hot nor too cold.

___16. Engines runs better when weather is neither too hot nor too cold.

___17. Honesty, justice, and truth are desirable virtues.

___18. Honesty, justice, and truth is desirable traits to have.

___19. We was on our way to the grocery store when the big storm hit.

___20. We were on our way to the grocery store when the big storm hit.

{Check answers with Answer Key in back of book.}

Notes and Questions
About Subject-Verb Agreement

Chapter 11

Sentence Agreement:
Pronoun Antecedents and Referents

A. Introduction

Another difficult area for writers to master focuses on the agreement of pronouns with their antecedent (comes before, precedes) referent (noun the pronoun refers to). This agreement must be in number (singular or plural), in person (first, second, or third), and in gender when third person singular (*he, she, it*).

B. Definitions

1. A **pronoun antecedent** is the word or group of words a pronoun stands for, refers to, or replaces. Since *antecedent* means going or coming before in time, order, or logic; prior, previous, preceding -- a *pronoun antecedent* is literally the word preceding the pronoun the pronoun replaces. Antecedent Example: *When the helicopter flew over, it made a lot of noise. Helicopter* is the antecedent for the pronoun *it.*. It is a pronoun antecedent because the noun the pronoun refers to precedes the pronoun.

2. The **pronoun referent** is the noun (word, phrase or clause) the pronoun refers to. The reference linking of the pronoun to the noun for which it substitutes must be clear to the reader to avoid miscommunication of information. Generally, the pronoun refers to the last or closest noun preceding it. Other nouns in between the pronoun and the noun it refers to cause confusion for the reader. Referrent Example: *When playing their best, the Texas Longhorns are unbeatable.* It is a pronoun referent because the noun the pronoun refers to comes after the pronoun.

3. **Mnemonic: Mnemonic: When noun precedes pronoun it is an antecendent; when noun follows pronoun it is a referent. In practicality, the terms "*pronoun referent*" and "*pronoun antecedent*" often are used interchangeably, though this is technically incorrect.**

C. Rules

General Rule: Pronouns and their antecedents (they refer to must agree in number (singular or plural), tense (past, present, future), and gender (when third person singular).

Rule 1: Singular antecedents require singular pronouns whether the antecedent and pronoun are in the same or adjacent sentences.

Rule 2: Singular antecedents may be collective nouns.

Rule 3: Two antecedents (one singular and one plural) combined in a neither-nor or either-or phrase, the pronoun agrees with the antecedent nearer the pronoun.

Rule 4: Plural antecedents require plural pronouns whether the antecedent and pronoun are in the same or adjacent sentences.

Rule 5: Plural collective nouns that are antecedents require plural pronouns.

Rule 6: Singular collective nouns (referring to a group as a unit) that are antecedents may require plural pronouns. E.g., *The basketball team practiced their free throws.*

Rule 7: Pronoun references must be clear to the reader to avoid confusion or ambiguity. A noun coming between an antecedent and its pronoun may be mistaken for the antecedent and cause confusion. E.g., *One of the Board members continued his argument after the meeting adjourned.* [Since *members* appears between the subject noun *One* and the pronoun *his*, a reader might select a plural pronoun such as *their*, thinking it should refer to *members.*]

D. Mnemonic

The closeness or proximity of the pronoun to the referent (noun it references) is the key to clarity for the reader. Pronouns should refer to nearest noun -- the previous or the following noun. The easiest way to check for clarity of pronoun referents is to circle the pronoun and draw an arrow to the noun it references. If the nearest noun preceding or following is the noun referred to, the reader will understand clearly; if the nearest noun preceding or following the pronoun is not the noun referred to, the reader may experience some confusion.

Notes & Questions

E. Pronoun-Antecedent Agreement – Pretest/Checkup

Name_____/25 = _____%
[4 pts/sentence; 90%= proficient]

Directions: Underline the subject. Circle the most appropriate pronoun. Draw an arrow from the pronoun to the noun it references.

1. The girls went off campus for lunch; (they, them) ate at Jason's Deli.

2. The men's baseball team played (their, its) last game for the season

3. The class all turned in (its, their) papers on time this semester.

4. My friend and I went to the movies. (We, Us) saw a great film.

5. John left early for work, but a traffic jam made (he, him) late.

6. Julie just got promoted. (She, Her) now manages a branch office.

7. Bob and Corey are eating (his, their) Doritos.

8. Neither Bob nor Corey is eating (his, their) Doritos.

9. Each of the girls is eating (her, their) enchiladas.

10. Everyone should eat (his, their) share of the pizza.

11. Nancy arrived early, but (she, her) rental car was not ready yet.

12. Airports are so busy planes cannot get to (its, their) gates on time

Directions: Underline the subject. Circle the most appropriate pronoun. Draw an arrow from the pronoun to the noun it references.

13. Did you find (your, your's) luggage on the baggage conveyor belt?

14. Several passengers from the flight were missing (his, their) luggage.

16. The crewmen carried (its, their) luggage off the spaceship.

17. The City Council made (its, their) decision public the next morning.

18. The City Council members made (its, their) opinions known in the local paper.

19. The firemen put on (its, their) helmets before entering the blazing building.

20. John and Mark put on (his, their) swimsuits to go swimming.

21. Debbie, Erik, and Allyssa ate (his, her, their) pizza in a hurry.

22. Ricky's family gathered for (its, his, their, our) family reunion.

23. Marie and Dominick danced at (his, her, their) wedding reception.

24 John and Dianne enjoyed the three-week trip in (his, her, their) motor home.

{Check answers with Answer Key at back of book.}

Chapter 12

Sentence Agreement: Verb Tenses

A. Introduction

Chapter 12 covers verbs and their various tenses. It reviews the agreement of verbs and their tenses in relation to number – singular or plural.

B. Rule

Rule: Verbs should agree in tense throughout the sentence and with adjoining sentences. Occasionally, the meaning requires a change or shift in tense, but remaining in the same tense is an important goal for writers. You may want to review verb tenses in Chapter 3.

C. Helpful Tips

Tip 1.   Meaning is the key to choice of tense.

Tip 2.   Preferably, use present tense as much as possible. Avoid shifting back and forth between tenses -- past, present, and future – unless it is critical to the meaning being communicated. Likewise, avoid shifting between simple, progressive, and perfect tenses – unless it is critical to the meaning.

Tip 3.   Use active voice and action verbs of simple past, present, or future tenses to keep the reader actively engaged with your text.

Tip 4.   Use helping or assisting verbs sparingly. Helping verbs often are employed with progressive and perfect tenses, and they tend to offer speed bumps to slow down the reader and hinder understanding.

D. II-12-D. Verb Tense Agreement – Pretest/Checkup-1

Name_____ ____/46 = ____%
[2 pts; 8 free; 90% = proficient]

Directions: Indicate if the subject and verb agree in number and verb tense. Write AN=agree in number, DN=disagree in number, AT=agree in tense, DT=disagree in tense.   # Tense

___ ___ 1.   There's three parts to a paragraph: introduction, body, and conclusion.

___ ___2.   There are three parts to a paragraph: introduction, body, and conclusion.

___ ___3.   They were going to the basketball game last night.

___ ___4.   They was going to the basketball game last night.

___ ___5.   We was late to class on Monday.

___ ___6.   We were late to class on Monday.

___ ___7.   There are five classes held on campus last night.

___ ___8.   There was five classes held on campus last night.

___ ___9.   There were five classes held on campus last night.

___ ___10.   There is five classes held on campus last night.

___ ___11.   You is going to need a jacket tonight; it will be cold.

___ ___12.   You are going to need a jacket tonight; it will be cold.

{Check answers with Answer Key in back of book.}

188 Dianne M. Haneke, Ph.D.

Directions: *Indicate if the subject and verb agree in number and verb tense.*
Write **AN**=*agree in number,* **DN**=*disagree in number,* **AT**=*agree in tense,*
DT=*disagree in tense.* **# Tense**

___ ___13.　　Five cars are involved in Tom's accident last week.

___ ___14.　　Five cars is involved in Tom's accident last week.

___ ___15.　　Five cars were involved in Tom's accident last week.

___ ___16.　　Engines runs better when weather is neither too hot nor too cold.

___ ___17.　　Engines run better when weather is neither too hot nor too cold.

___ ___18.　　Honesty and truth are desirable virtues.

___ ___19.　　Honesty and truth is desirable virtues.

___ ___20.　　Diamonds is a girl's best friend – or so they say.

___ ___21.　　Diamonds are a girl's best friends – or so they say.

___ ___22.　　The display of five planets in an arc is spectacular last night.

___ ___23.　　The display of five planets in an arc was spectacular last night.

Check answers with Answer Key in back of book.}

G. Notes on Verb Tenses and Verb Tense Agreements

Chapter 13

Sentence Agreement: Parallel Construction

A. Introduction

Parallel construction in writing can be subtle and harder to recognize; therefore, parallelism can elude the author. Parallel construction requires expressing parallel ideas of a series in a like manner. The writer must use similar kinds of words, phrases, or clauses (groups of words) to express parallel (a series of) ideas. Notice the parallel construction of each of the following series:

[words] ...*Children like running, jumping, hopping, and skipping*. {all –ing forms}

[phrases] ...*Julie likes to play clarinet, to sing alto, and to listen to country music*. {to- forms}

[clauses] ...*Because of the severe weather, roads were flooded, electricity was knocked out, and trees were blown over*. {all past tense forms}

B. Rules

The following rules foster sentence agreement by parallel construction:

Rule 1: Words in a series expressing parallel ideas should be parallel in construction; e.g., ...*Baseball, basketball, football, and soccer are Ricky's favorite sports*.

...*Planes arrive, stay a while, and depart again*.

...*Professionals include doctors, lawyers, merchants, chiefs, teachers, and nurses*.

Rule 2: Phrases (groups of words used as units) in a series expressing parallel ideas should be parallel in construction. Prepositional phrases should be parallel when expressing parallel ideas; e.g.,

> ...Dianne likes *to swim laps, to play tennis, to walk a mile, and to shoot hoops*.

> ...Mark travels *by plane, by train, by car, or by bus*.

> ...John camps anywhere he can -- *on the seashore, in the mountains, or at the lake*.

> ...Luci *plays tennis, swims laps, and walks a mile* to stay physically fit.

Rule 3: Clauses (groups of words containing subject plus verb units) in a series expressing parallel ideas should be parallel in construction; e.g.,

> ...Because of the heat wave, *workers drank more water, athletes took precautions, and homes used more AC*.

> ...*She graduated from college, taught school, earned a master's, and earned a doctorate* while *her husband graduated from college, worked with computers, retired, and worked as a technical trainer*.

> ...During the severe storm, *the tornado blew down some homes, the winds knocked over some trees, and the hail dented some cars*.

C. Recap

As a writer, conscientiously pursue parallel construction any time you include a series in your writing -- whether a series of nouns, a series of verbs, a series of prepositional phrases, or a series of parallel clauses. Parallelism makes your text more readable and more understandable for others. It is not hard; it just takes some focused effort on your part as the writer.

13-D. Parallel Sentence Construction – Pretest/Checkup

Name_____/24 = _____%
[5 points; 5 free; 90% or better to pass]

*Directions: In the 20 sentences, indicate **P** for parallel or **NP** for not parallel on the line to the left. If it is not parallel, underline the non-parallel phrase and rewrite it in parallel form using a caret [^] above the sentence part to be revised.*

_____1.　Julie liked to read, to sing, and play sports.

_____2.　Tom bought an amplifier, tuner, and two large speakers.

_____3.　Emily is neither a diver nor can she swim very well.

_____4.　My friend owns a ski lodge, a mountain cottage, and a condominium.

_____5.　My husband painted the garage, built a fence, and planted a garden.

_____6.　Mark likes to swim, scuba dive, and to travel.

_____7.　Tommy plays the drums, tuba, and saxophone.

_____8.　Betty plays a clarinet, an oboe, a bassoon, and the piano.

_____9.　The accident held up traffic, forced me to be late, and making me anxious.

_____10.　After back surgery, Luci had to relearn how to walk, to run, and to sit.

_____11.　The hunter claimed to have shot a deer, elk, antelope, and a buffalo.

_____12.　Ada and Sol planted a tree, terraced the back yard, and repainted the house trim.

H. II-13-D. Parallel Sentence Construction – Pretest/Checkup

Directions: Indicate P for parallel or NP for not parallel on the line to the left. If it is not parallel, underline the non–parallel phrase and rewrite it in parallel form using a caret [^] above the sentence part to be revised.

____13.　The fishermen caught two salmon, yellow tuna, and blue marlin this trip.

____14.　Nancy had trouble trusting God, others, or herself.

____15.　Delighted, with excitement, and without fear she started the new job.

____16.　The toddler had learned to crawl, stand, and walk.

____17.　The storm dumped 5 inches of rain, blew down trees, and closed roads.

____18.　Ricky runs track, likes to play basketball, and enjoys footballs, too.

____19.　John understands computers hardware, writes computer software, and trains trainers to repair computer servers.

____20.　Debbie likes living on the beach, loves to travel, and paints landscapes.

____21.　Antonio is a smart boy, enjoys racecars, likes to fish, and plays soccer.

____23.　Erik likes to run on the beach, ride on the ferris wheel, and hunt for seashells.

____24.　Debbie is a good artist, a great mom, and a loving daughter.

{Check answers with Answer Key in back of book.}

Chapter 14

Sentence Agreement:
Active and Passive Voice

A. Introduction

Another issue for writers constantly to be aware of is voice. Since every sentence has a subject plus a verb, **voice** is the verb form telling whether the subject does the action (active) or receives the action (passive). Whichever voice you choose to use, be consistent.

B. Definitions

1. Active voice. Active voice indicates the subject is doing the action – the subject is the doer. The active voice emphasizes who or what is performing the action. For example, in *The boy ran across the field.* – the subject, the boy, is doing the action; the boy is running. In *The graduate student studied hard to prepare for his oral exams.* – the subject, the student, is doing the action; the student studied.

2. Passive Voice. Passive voice indicates the subject receives the action – the subject is passive. The passive voice shifts emphasis away from the doer of the action and onto the receiver of the action. Passive voice helps when it is less important who or what does the action and more important who or what receives the action. For example, in *The boy was chased across the field by the bull.* – the subject, the boy, passively receives the action of being chased. In *The graduate student was urged to study hard to prepare for his oral exams.* – the subject, the student, passively receives the action of being urged. In this situation, who did the urging is not important.

C. Rules

The following rules support sentence agreement regarding active and passive voices.

1. Use the active rather than the passive voice for stronger, more powerful, more direct, and more effective writing.

2. Use the active voice to emphasize who or what does the action.

3 Use the passive voice to emphasize who or what receives the action.

4. Though a sentence may contain both an active and a passive verb, such a shift in voice is correct only when it strengthens the writing or when it is essential to the meaning; thus, this practice is not too common and generally should be avoided.

D. Tips

The following tips assists writers to retain agreement throughout their writings:

1. Use active voice for more powerful, more effective writing.

2. Be consistent throughout any specific writing or paper.

3. Avoid shifting back and forth between active and passive voice.

4. Consider your audience – your reader – and what meaning they will construct from reading your text. How does voice affect or impact communication?

5. How does voice effect or carry out communication?

Notes & Questions

I. II-14-E. Active/Passive Voice – Pretest/Checkup

Name_____/25 = ____%
[4 points; need 90% or greater to pass]

Directions: Indicate A for active voice and P for passive voice on the line to the left of the sentence.

___1.   The paper was written in a hurry by Jim.

___2.   The paper came together in a hurry for Jim.

___3.   The ball was hit hard enough to be a home run.

___4.   The batter hit the ball hard enough to be a home run.

___5.   Who or what the sentence is about is called the subject.

___6.   Subjects tell who or what the sentence is about.

___7.   The predicate states what the subject does or what action the subject takes.

___8.   What the subject is or does is called the predicate.

___9.   The flood destroyed many homes.

___10. Many homes were destroyed by the flood.

___11. The university senior barely passed the teacher certification exams.

___12. The teacher certification exams were barely passed by the university senior.

___13. After poor attendance, the manager closed the theatre for three months.

___14. The theatre was closed by the manager for three months after poor attendance.

___15. We have been thought of and prayed for by many.

___16. Many have thought of and prayed for us.

___17. The men working on the fly-over wear safety harnesses.

___18. Safety harnesses are worn by the men working on the new fly-over.

___19. George W. Bush was elected President of the United States in 2000.

___20. In 2000, George W. Bush became the President of the United States.

___21. Rocky dug up the small shrub so he could transplant it.

___22. The small shrub was dug up by Rocky so he could transplant it.

___23. Dennis hit a home run over the center field fence to tie the score.

___24. A home run over the center field fence was hit by Dennis to tie the score.

___25. The writer wrote so well her readers could vividly imagine being right there.

Bonus...

___26. Her writing was so well written her readers could vividly imagine being right there.

{Check answers with Answer Key in back of book.}

Chapter 15

Two Sentence Flaws: Misplaced Modifiers and Awkward Sentences

A. Introduction.

In English, the meaning of a sentence depends extensively on word order or the position of words in a sentence. Sometimes, this is called syntax. Two sentence flaws often slip by writers: misplaced modifiers and awkward sentences. Misplaced modifiers usually create awkward sentences. Misplaced modifiers include dangling modifiers, squinting modifiers, and other misplaced modifiers. Awkward sentences include choppy sentences, stringy sentences, and wordy sentences. These sentence flaws complete our consideration of sentence structures as basic building blocks for writing paragraphs, papers, and other writings.

I. Misplaced Modifiers

B. Definitions

1. Modifiers. A modifier is a word or groups of words adding something specific to the meaning of the word it describes, modifies, relates to, or applies to.

2. Misplaced modifiers. Misplaced modifiers are words not applying or relating clearly or accurately to the specific word or words you want them to modify or describe. Misplaced modifiers often attach themselves to the wrong words and thereby promote ambiguous or more than one meaning for the sentence.

The most easily misplaced modifiers include the following words: *almost, either/or, even, ever, hardly, just, merely, more, most, nearly, only, rather, and very.*

3. Dangling modifiers. Dangling modifiers (**dangling participles**) "dangle" when there is no clearly logical word for the "dangler" to modify; e.g., *Lying on the beach, the sun burned our legs.* [Who or what was lying on the beach? Who or what does the phrase modify or describe – the sun? legs? Since a modifying word or phrase modifies the nearest word, current sentence construction states the sun was lying on the beach, but neither makes logical sense.]

4. Squinting modifiers. Squinting modifiers are either-or modifying words standing in the middle of the sentence and can apply to either what precedes or what follows it in the sentence, and this produces ambiguous meaning for the reader. For example, *Arriving in Tennessee before sunset we found a campsite.* [Did we arrive before sunset? Or did we find a campsite before sunset? As currently structured, it is not clear the case. Neither placement nor nearness helps us here.]

5. Word Placement. Notice how the placement of a one-word modifier alters the meaning of the following sentences:

Just an 18-wheeler drove safely through the low-water crossing during the flooding.

An 18-wheeler **just** drove safely through the low-water crossing during the flooding.

An 18-wheeler drove **just** safely through the low-water crossing during the flooding.

An 18-wheeler drove safely **just** through the low-water crossing during the flooding.

An 18-wheeler drove safely through **just** the low-water crossing during the flooding.

An 18-wheeler drove safely through the low water crossing **just** during the flooding.

An 18-wheeler drove safely through the low-water crossing during **just** the flooding.

Rule: Position each modifier in the sentence so it clearly and accurately applies to the specific word or words you want it to modify. A modifying word or phrase modifies the nearest word (for better or worse).

2. Awkward Sentences

C. Definitions

Writers get tangled up in several kinds of awkward sentences including unclear awkward sentences, wordy sentences, choppy sentences, and stringy sentences.

1. Awkward Sentences: Awkward sentences usually do not present readily identifiable errors or they are simply written poorly. Awkward sentences are confusing, illogical, unclear, or obscure. Awkward sentences should be rewritten considering carefully the basic elements and structures of sentences

a. Rule: Avoid writing awkward sentences.

b. Helps...

Who or what is the sentence about? That is the subject.

What is the subject doing? That is usually the verb.

When, where, why, and how questions help you describe the subject, elaborate on the verb, and/or think clearly about what you desire to write.

2. Wordy sentences. Wordy sentences use more words than necessary – more words than the meaning and style of writing assignment require. Unnecessary words cloud the meaning and weaken the impact of the statement. Wordiness is also called *repetitiousness, redundancy, padding, or tautology.* Repetition can be avoided by using synonyms. (Consult your Thesaurus.)

a. **Rules:**

Rule 1: Avoid writing wordy sentences. (Get to the point.)

Rule 2: Avoid needless repetition of words or phrases. (Get to the point.)

Rule 3: Avoid needless repetition of ideas. (Get to the point.)

Rule 4: Avoid padding – intentional inclusion of material simply increases the length of a paragraph or paper without adding anything of importance or consequence to the meaning. (Get to the point.)

Rule 5: Avoid wordy sentences, they weaken your writing. Get to the point in fewer words.

b. More **Avoids...**

1) Avoid *There is... There are... There was... There were...* constructions whenever possible; helps you get to the point in fewer words.

2) Avoid the passive voice; allows you to get more quickly to the point.

3) Avoid words added for emphasis – *very definitely, certainly, absolutely, really,* etc. or use judiciously; helps you stick to the point.

4) Avoid *I think... I feel...*whenever possible; enables you to get to the point. [Reader assumes what you say is what you think or feel, so get to the point.]

5) Avoid unnecessary use of helping verbs ...*are going to be going...;* gets to the point and avoids "couchy language use."

3. Choppy sentences. Choppy sentences are several short sentences following one another with abrupt starting and stopping not strengthening the writing. [This gets to the point too quickly without considering the flow of ideas.] Examples of choppy sentences include the following: *It rained last night. Many streets flooded. The Police Chief declared an emergency. I was scared.*

Rule: Avoid writing choppy sentences unless they strengthen what you are writing.

4. Stringy Sentences. Stringy sentences occur when writer s ignore logical stopping   places and tie together ideas that should be expressed in separate sentences.   Usually, stringy sentences can be rewritten as separate ideas. Remember, each sentence should represent an idea. An example of a stringy sentence might be the   following: *Last night, it rained four inches in one hour and our streets were   flooded and police had to rescue people from the swollen creeks and a state of   emergency was declared by the Emergency Control Center in our town and the   t o r n a d o siren went off and I was scared because our dog got so scared that she shook violently and she jumped into bed with me and I didn't know what to do but   I sure was glad when the rain stopped.*

Rule: Avoid writing stringy sentences.

D. General Tip

Construct sentences that are active enough to be interesting, long enough to cover the details, and short enough to get to the point. More is not necessarily better!

J. II-15-E. Misplaced Modifiers – Pretest/Checkup

Name/#_____/20 = ____%
[5 pts each; 90% = proficient]

*Directions: If the sentence is correct as is, write **C** on the line. If there is a misplaced modifier, circle the misplaced modifier, draw an arrow to word that it modifies, and write **MM** on the line.*

___1.　　Pulling the bow-string, the arrow shot off.

___2.　　When I pulled the bow-string, the arrow shot off.

___3.　　Running at top speed in the marathon, her wig flew off.

___4.　　As she was running at top speed in the marathon, her wig flew off.

___5.　　She was running at top speed in the marathon when her wig flew off.

___6.　　While driving down the highway, my cell phone rang.

___7.　　While I was driving down the highway, my cell phone rang.

___8.　　The hikers stopped feeling the earthquake plodding up the mountain.

___9.　　The hikers stopped feeling the earthquake as they were plodding up the mountain.

___10.　　The spacecraft's camera photographed the comet hurtling through space.

___11.　　Hurtling through space, the spacecraft's camera photographed the comet.

___12.　　While she was playing the piano, the doorbell rang.

___13.　　The doorbell rang while playing the piano.

____14. When the tornado siren went off, it was "pouring cats and dogs."

____15. While it was "pouring cats and dogs," the tornado siren went off.

____16. When Tom approaches the accident intersection, he gets in the center lane.

____17. Tom gets in the center lane approaching the accident intersection.

____18. The bird stops to take a drink from the birdbath while flying.

____19. While flying the bird stops to take a drink from the birdbath.

____20. Avoiding misplaced modifiers makes a writer "healthy, wealthy, and wise."

{Check answers with the Answer Key in back of book.}

K. Awkward/Choppy/Stringy/Wordy Sentences – Pretest/Checkup

Name/#_____ /20 = ____%
[5 pts each; 90% = proficient]

*Directions: In the next 20 sentences, on the line to the left, write **OK** for okay, **AWK** for awkward, **CH** for choppy, **S** for stringy, or **W** for wordy, and circle the part of the sentence that is awkward, choppy, stringy, or wordy.*

___1. When my professor writes *awkward* in the margin of my paper is because she says she is confused by it.

___2. We had a great time at the dinner party; there was plenty of fun, food, and fellowship.

___3. The game started. Hill scored. Jones made a free-throw.

___4. Bob played piano. John played drums. Sue played guitar.

___5. A true grammarian is hard to find, because there are so few persons, you know, who conduct advanced research studies of language and language-related issues so as to determine what is the most appropriate phrasing to use when writing sentences so they are comprehensible by persons trying to read them.

___6. There are very few, if any, students who truly know what financial aid services are available to them as undergraduate students.

___7. His opinion is Corinthian columns are more beautiful than Doric columns.

___8. Carotene deficiency is the cause of some visual problems including blindness.

___9. England has been invaded by the Romans, the Saxons, and the Normans.

L. Awkward... Sentences – Pretest/Checkup
(continued)

*Directions: Write **OK** for okay, **AWK** for awkward, **CH** for choppy, **S** for stringy, or **W** for wordy; circle the part of the sentence that is awkward, choppy, stringy, or wordy.*

___10.   Our house will be in need of a new air conditioning unit next summer.

___11.   There are three new courses the School of Education now requires of all its students at every level.

___12.   The window was left open. Rain dripped in. Every thing got soaked.

___13.   A spark flew. The carpet ignited. The fire spread. The house burned down.

___14.   I went to the movies. I fell asleep. A loud bang wakened me.

___15.   Uppermost in my mind is I believe today's government does not care very much about individual citizens.

___16.   There are at least five things that can be done to im prove the program.

___17.   I personally feel this is the case.

___18.   Much of the camp was ruined due to the fact of the flooding river.

___19.   On first walking into the dentist's office, the picture scared me.

___20.   Every morning Sharon runs a mile after her shower.

{Check answers with Answer Key in back of book.}

Part III:

Basic Paragraph and Text Structures: Process Writing

Table III-Intro A. References for Review

Topic In Workbook	Arco: Step by Step	Help Yourself	Writing Smart	Other Resources
IV-22: audiences, styles, purposes, parts, & processes			pp. 10, 52; 75+, 84-93	
IV-24: APA format				Syllabus guideline APA Manual
IV-25: peer reviews & feedback				
IV-25: revising			pp. 32-35	
IV-25: editing & proofreading			pp. 29-39 55, 62, 93	
IV-26-27: abstract, summary, précis				
IV-28: action research; IV-29 review of literature			pp. 74-81 142-152	
IV-30: compare/ contrast				
IV-31: evaluation, critique, analysis			pp. 74-81	
IV-32: editorial, personal opinion, reflection, position paper			pp. 52-72	

Grammar Improves Writing

B. Reference List

Behrman, C. H. (2000). <u>Writing skills problem solver: 101 Ready-to-use-writing process activities for correcting the most common errors.</u> West Nyack, NY: The Center for Applied Research in Education.

Bryant, T. (1998). <u>Writing skills flipper: A basic flip-guide to writing and speaking.</u> South Bend, IN: Christopher Lee Publications.

Fry, E. B., Kress, J. E., Fountoukidis, D. L. (2000). <u>The reading teacher's book of lists (4th ed.).</u> Englewood Cliffs, NJ: Prentice-Hall.

Lerner, M. (1994). <u>The Princeton Review: Writing smart: Your guide to great writing.</u> NY: Random House.

Mattson, M., Leshing, S., Levi, E. (1993). <u>Help yourself: A guide to writing and rewriting (3rd ed.).</u> New York: Macmillan. [out of print]

Muschla, G. R. (1991). <u>The writing teacher's book of lists: With ready to use activities and worksheets.</u> Paramus, NJ: Prentice Hall.

Muschla, G. R. (1993). <u>Writing workshop survival kit.</u> West Nyack, NY: The Center for Applied Research in Education.

Part III

Basic Paragraph and Text Structures: Process Writing

A. Introduction

Building upon the foundations of mastering word selection and mastering sentence construction, we are now ready to improve writing paragraphs. But first, three considerations enable you to write effective paragraphs: Process Writing, Graphic Organizers, and Basic Text and Paragraph Structures.

Writing is a process. Some view writing as a five-step process and others as a seven-step process. However, to emphasize the need for both personal and peer reviews for the revising and editing steps, we commend to you an eight-step writing process. Chapter 16 explains the eight-step writing process in detail.

Graphic Organizers help writers get started. Used as part of the pre-writing step, graphic organizers enable writers to graphically identify the key points or main ideas and to cluster supporting details with each main idea. Chapter 17 explains in detail getting started with some Graphic Organizer options.

B. Six Text and Paragraph Structures

Children learn to read and to write narrative, story, or descriptive text from pre-school through college. However, six text structures dominate readings and writings people deal with daily in school and in everyday life: 1) summary/abstract/précis text; 2) descriptive/narrative text; 3) sequential/how-to text; 4) compare/contrast text; 5) cause/effect text; and 6) problem/solution text. Chapters 18 through 23 explain in detail each of these text structures.

C. Definitions

1. Summary/Abstract/Précis Text. A Summary, Abstract, or Précis text concisely recaps the key points of a story, an article, a speech, or a book. A summary or abstract is the basis of most if not all expository text structures. For example, the writer must generate at least a summary list of key points and supporting details to write a sequential/how-to, a compare/contrast, a cause/effect, or a problem/solution paragraph or paper. We will discuss this further in Chapter 18.

2. Descriptive/Narrative Text. Narrative text describes a situation or tells a story with lots of detail possibly including some conversation or dialogue. Creative writing assignments, most often requested in an English class, use narrative text style. Chapter 19 provides more details and some practice for writing descriptive/narrative text.

3. Sequential/How-to Text. This type of text presents steps for doing something such as how to make a model airplane or brownies. Sequential text covers step by step – first, then, and finally – issues in history or scientific experiments. It is observed in history, science, or math classes, and it is most often requested for assignments in history (timeline), science (scientific process), or math (formulas). A flow chart or time line graphic organizer helps organize this kind of text. Chapter 20 affords more details and some practice in writing this type of text or paragraph.

4. Compare/Contrast Text. Compare/contrast text explores the likenesses and differences of two or more people, place, things or events. They are observable in English (literature: character studies), social studies/history (people, places, things, events), math (geometric shapes, angles), and science (genus, species; phenomena) and compare/contrast writing assignments are most likely requested in these classes. A Venn diagram helps organize ideas for this kind of text. More details and some practice writing compare/contrast text and paragraphs are in Chapter 21.

5. Cause/Effect Text. Cause/effect text structures enable the reader to grasp cause-effect relationships. These are observable in history and science texts; this type of text is most likely required for social studies and science writing assignments such as lab experiment reports. A cause/effect flow chart helps organize ideas for this type of writing. Chapter 22 illustrates and gives you practice writing cause and effect text and paragraphs.

6. Problem/Solution Text. This structure helps the reader identify the problem and explore possible solutions. It is observable in social studies and science texts when viewing causes of the Revolutionary War or factors causing water to change its state of matter to steam. The problem-solution flow chart graphic organizer helps organize ideas for a problem/solution paper. For more information and practice writing this type of text, consult Chapter 23.

D. Essential Basics of Paragraphs

As stated earlier, every paragraph needs the following basic components of an introduction (to state the main idea or key point of the text or paragraph), a body (to present in a logical order at least three supporting details of the main idea), a summary (to recap the essence or key points of the paragraph), and a conclusion (to draw a conclusion answering *"So what?"* from presented data).

These points follow the Haneke Handy Model for writing. The thumb represents the introduction of the main idea sentence; the middle three fingers represent the minimum key detail sentences supporting the main idea; and the little "pinkie" represents the summary and the conclusion sentences. Every paragraph, paper, chapter, or book needs these four components. Let these basics guide you when writing the paragraph assignments in Part III and the one-page paper assignments in Part IV. Organization of the basic ideas and essential parts – using graphic organizers, organizing the presentation of ideas, using appropriate text structures and paragraph structures and following the eight-step writing process -- are important keys to effective writing.

E. Paragraph Evaluation

Name_____ Sp Su ___
Total ___/100 = ____% (90%=proficient)

Table III-intro-E-Paragraph Evaluation

Paragraph	Match Goals (/5)	Organize Flow of Ideas (/5)	Sentence Structure (/5)	Spelling Grammar (/5)	Total Score (/20)
Summary/ Abstract/ Précis	/5	/5	/5	/5	/20
Descriptive	/5	/5	/5	/5	/20
Sequential/ How-to	/5	/5	/5	/5	/20
Compare/ Contrast	/5	/5	/5	/5	/20
Cause/ Effect	/5	/5	/5	/5	/20
Problem/ Solution	/5	/5	/5	/5	/20
Total Scores:	/25	/25	/25	/25	/100

First Impressions:

Are the following paragraph components clearly identifiable?

Introduction/thesis statement?	[Y, N]
Body (at least three details)?	[Y, N]
Summary/recap of essence?	[Y, N]
Conclusion (so what?) ?	[Y, N]

Overall Perceptions:

1) Well done. Proceed to next level. _____

2) Adequate, but would benefit from more work. _____

3) Definitely needs more review and practice. _____

4) Rank order of skills from stronger to weaker:

   a) Matching goals for paragraph _____

   b) Organization & Flow of ideas _____

   c) Sentence Structure _____

   d) Spelling, grammar, & mechanics _____

Suggestions for Improvement:

1) Use Graphic Organizers to organize ideas. _____

2) Use Outline to organize flow of ideas. _____

3) Follow KISS principle: keep it simple; tighten it up. _____

4) Consider presentation; Is it inviting to reader? _____

5) Is it easy for reader to identify your key points? _____

Additional Comments

Chapter 16

Writing: An Eight-Step Process

A. Introduction

Writing is a process. Some view writing as a five-step and some as a seven-step process, but emphasizing the need for both personal and peer reviews for the revising and editing steps, we recommend an eight-step writing process. Graphic Organizers help writers identify main ideas and cluster supporting details for key points. The Eight-Step Writing Process and Graphic Organizers in this chapter prepare you for writing papers of any kind.

B. Eight Steps

Definitions and explanations of each of the eight process steps of writing follow:

1. Pre-writing. (Before writing a paragraph or paper.) Brainstorm about your ideas.

2. Organize Ideas. "Dump" or jot down ideas on a graphic organizer. Logically order the key points. Generate an outline. More details and practice with Graphic Organizers are provided in Chapter 17 and later in this chapter.

3. Writing First/Rough Draft. (First writing.) Using your outline, type a first draft. For a paragraph, include an introduction sentence, at least three body sentences, a summary sentence, and a conclusion sentence. For a paper, include an introduction paragraph (telling what key points you cover), at least three body paragraphs (covering your key topics), a summary paragraph (telling how many key points you covered and relate them to the overall topic), a conclusion paragraph (answering the questions, "So what? Why is this important information?") This is a rough draft (not polished) so focus on the organization and flow of ideas and not so much on the mechanics, spelling, etc.

4. Revision. (Both you and a peer will review and revise your writing.) Focus on the organization of ideas, the purpose for/of your writing, and the intended audience.

> **4-a. Personal Review Revision.** Did you clearly identify the overall topic? Do you have at least three main ideas? (You may have more.) Does each main idea have at least three supporting details? (Again, you may have more.) Does your writing address the purpose for which you are writing? Does your writing addressyou're your intended audience? Can another person read and easily outline your writing? A paragraph and a paper both require the same basic components and processes. More information and practice revising is in Chapter 27 and later in this chapter.

> **4-b. Peer Review Revision.** (Someone else reads your paragraph or paper as a cross-check of your revisions.) Have a classmate or a friend look primarily at the flow of ideas. Ask your peer reviewer to make recommendations about the flow of the main ideas and details; are they identifiable? Can she or he outline your writing? Ask your peer reviewer to jot a brief handwritten outline of the key ideas. Ask your peer reviewer NOT to focus on grammar, spelling, or mechanics just yet.

5. Rewrite. Rewrite and rewrite until you feel comfortable with the flow of main ideas and supporting details —— considering what you your peer reviewer noticed and suggested.

6. Editing. Address mechanics, spelling, sentence structure, agreement, parallelism, etc.

> **6-a. Personal Editing.** Focus on grammar, spelling, punctuation, and mechanics. You are polishing your writing - preparing for publication or posting publicly. This is one of the

last steps of the writing process; not every piece of writing makes it to this step.

6-b. Peer Review Editing. Ask a classmate or friend to read your rough draft looking at the mechanics, spelling, punctuation, etc. Ask for help; then rewrite to make corrections.

7. Final Draft. Focus on the aesthetic presentation of your writing for others to read. Technical aspects of margins, borders, spacing, etc. are addressed at this point. Not every piece of writing makes it to this final stage in the writing process.

8. Publishing. Your writing is placed for others to read such as on a bulletin board, in a class booklet, in a publication, or for grading as a class assignment.

When you teach children to write, teach them the steps of process writing. Keep in mind not every piece of writing makes it to publication, and therefore, not every piece of writing needs to be polished or graded. Real authors "table" or file many of their writings for reconsideration at a later time, and when real authors select a piece they really want to work on, they polish it, and eventually, they publish it. Allow children and students to make such choices as well. DO NOT GRADE EVERY WRITING —-your own writings or the writings of others.

C. Revising Practice
[For more about revising, see Chapter 27.]

Directions: Revise the following paragraph to better organize the ideas:

Reading and writing go hand in hand. Good readers usually write well, and good writers usually read well. Reading is a receptive language skill, whereas writing is an expressive language skill. I don't think reading and writing use the same basic skills, but I'm not sure. There are three steps in reading: pre-reading (getting ready), reading, and post-reading (reflecting on what you read). There are eight steps in writing. So, there are some similarities between the reading and the writing processes. I enjoy both reading and writing; I find them relaxing. I really like to share ideas by writing.

D. Editing Practice
[For more about editing, see Chapter 27.]

Directions: Edit the following paragraph to correct spelling, grammar, and punctuation:

"all we can do is hang on to our colons punctuation is bound to change like the rest of language punctuation is made for man not man for punctuation a good sentence should be intelligible without the help of punctuation in most cases and if you get in a muddle with your dots and dashes you may need to simplify your thoughts and shorten your sentence " [Philip Howard.] What questions would you like to ask mr howard what bothers you about his paragraph quoted above sure it is a long sentence but can you write a better one effectively illustrating the need for punctuation of various kinds i think that might be a difficult task for most people because many people are afraid of punctuation many are afraid of run-ons and fragments.

E. Peer Review and Feedback Practice
[For more about peer reviews, see Chapter 27.]

Succinctly provide peer review feedback to the writer of either paragraph 1 or 2 above. Provide at least one positive comment. Focus on not more than three (3) points.

_____

_____

_____

_____

_____

Grammar Improves Writing

F. Writing as a Process: Check-Up

Name/#_____
[90% = proficient]   _____/10 = ____%

A. Directions: Order the following five basic steps of Process Writing by num bering them.

____   revising

____   writing draft(s)

____   brainstorming/pre-writing

____   publishing/final draft

____   editing

Name_____   _____/5

B. Directions: Write the matching letter on the line to the left of the process step

____1. publish/final draft

____2. editing

____3. brainstorming/pre-writing

____4. revising

____5. write draft(s)

A. Check flow and re-organizing ideas; cohesiveness

B. Best copy; ready for others to view

C. Check for spelling, punctuation grammar, mechanics

D. Choose topic; select main ideas dump/jot down ideas; outline; use graphic organizer

E. Write organizing main ideas and supporting details into paragraphs

{Check answers with Answer Key in back of book..}

Chapter 17

Getting Started: Graphic Organizers

A. Introduction

Graphic organizers help to cluster and organize ideas pictorially – main ideas and supporting details – for various writing tasks. Following are samples of graphic organizers. These may be photocopied and used to organize your ideas and details for writing assignments for this course and other courses as well as for teaching writing organizational skills to children for various writing assignments. Various uses for the various graphic organizers — all stepping stones to generating an outline — follow:

B. Organizers and Their Recommended Uses

Some of the Graphic Organizers offer rather specific uses whereas others afford a variety of uses.

1. **Bubble Charts** cluster main ideas and their supporting details. They are useful at all ages for brainstorming ideas for writing assignments -- for organizing paragraphs or entire papers of any kind.

2. **Sequential Time Lines** are a flow chart for health, history, or scientific development over time. These help students organize ideas for any sequential or how-to writing tasks in mathematics, history, science, home economics, shop, and other areas.

3. **Venn Diagrams** help a writer explore likenesses and differences of two or more people, places, or things. Log likenesses in the overlap of the circles and log differences on respective sides of the circles. These help organize ideas for compare/contrast papers in mathematics, science, social studies, history, sociology, psychology, and any other topic.

4. Cause-Effect Flow Charts help organize causes and effects for cause-effect papers. List the causes and their effects. These charts can be used in mathematics, science, social studies, history, health, and most other areas.

5. Problem-Solution Flow Charts help writers organize problems and possible solutions. List the problem and offer several solutions. These charts can be useful with mathematics, science, history, geography, health, or any topic.

6. Concept Maps help organize ideas in a manner preparing for developing the three-level outline. List the overall topic in the square at the top. List the main ideas or key points in the larger boxes at the top of the diagram. List at least three supporting details under each main idea. To set up a logical flow of ideas, number the main ideas in the order you want to address them. Then number the supporting details under each main idea in the order you want to present them. Now you are ready to transfer this information to a Three-Level Outline. The Concept Chart can be useful for any topic.

7. Strengths-Weaknesses Tables assist the writer in listing strengths and weaknesses for a critique or analysis of an article. Under strengths, list the strengths (as you see them). List weaknesses under weaknesses. This chart is good for any subject.

8. Haneke's Handy Model uses the hand to remind people about basic paragraph and paper structure -- organizing the main idea and supporting details of any paragraph, chapter, or paper for any type of writing. The thumb represents the overall topic, the three middle fingers represents the main ideas or the supporting details for a main idea, and the pinkie represents the summary and conclusion sentences or paragraphs. This handy model is useful for any subject, any paragraph, and/or any paper.

These eight graphic organizers facilitate organization of the ideas you want to share. They help organize the main ideas and the supporting details for any writing. They also enable you to address the purposes and goals of the writing.

9. Create Your Own Graphic Organizer. Another idea, you can create your own graphic organizer more relevant to the actual topic of your writing. You can draw a tree; the trunk can be the main idea; the large branches can be the key points; and the smaller branches off the main ones can be for the supporting details -- for a family tree project or branches of language writing project. You could draw a trumpet for a musical writing – with the bell being the main idea and the three valves the key points. Just brainstorm about what graphically relates to your topic. Allow your creativity to use the above graphic organizers as spring boards to generate your own graphic organizers for your writings. Otherwise, you are more than welcome to use the graphic organizers provided. They will assist you in most if not all writing projects.

C. Graphic Organizers.

Do not write on these graphic organizers in the book; make copies so you have them to work on various writing projects at home, at school, or at work. Modify any of these to meet your needs – retaining the basic essentials – or create one of your own relating more closely to your topic.

Table. III-17-C. Graphic Organizers

The following Graphic Organizers are helpful when used during the pre-write step. They are useful for dumping ideas and clustering the ideas as a pre-step to generating an Outline to organize the flow of ideas for any paragraph or paper. Readers are invited to create their own Graphic Organizers as long as they accomplish the same purpose.

Notes & Questions

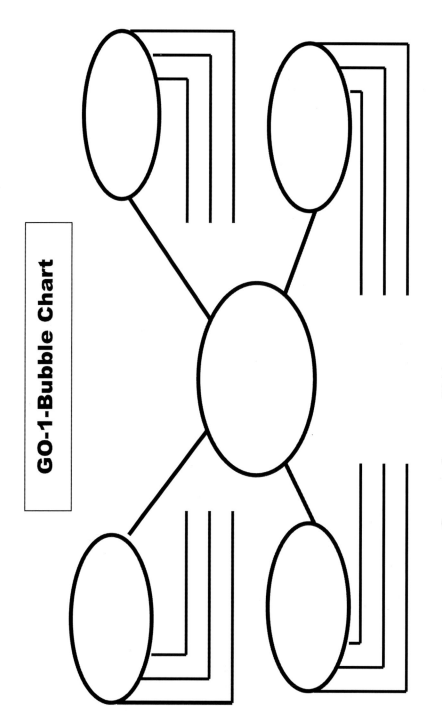

GO-1-Bubble Chart

GO-2-Time Line

Key points of Sequence:

1)

2)

3)

4)

5)

6)

7)

8)

GO-3-Venn Diagram -- Compare/Contrast

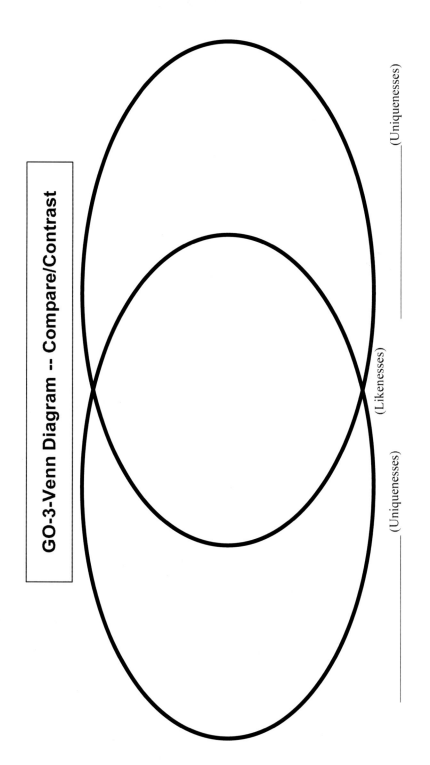

(Uniquenesses)

(Likenesses)

(Uniquenesses)

GO-4-Cause & Effect Flow Chart

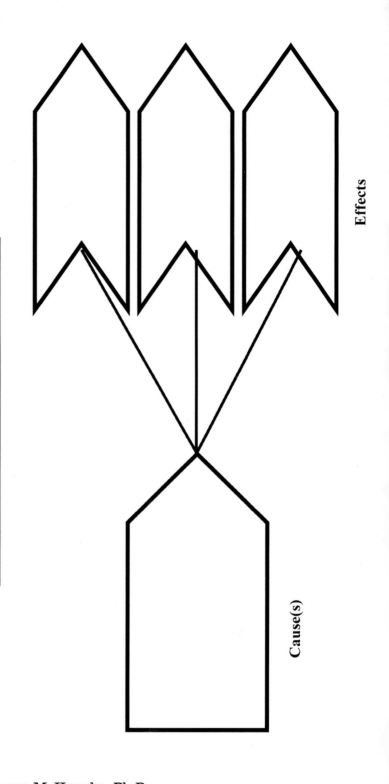

Effects

Cause(s)

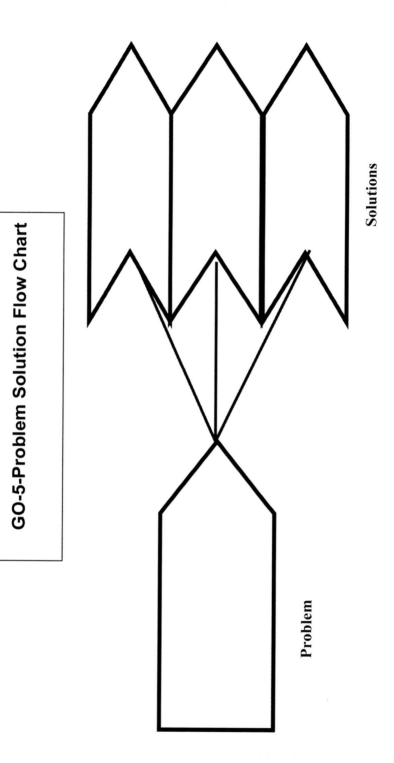

GO-5-Problem Solution Flow Chart

Solutions

Problem

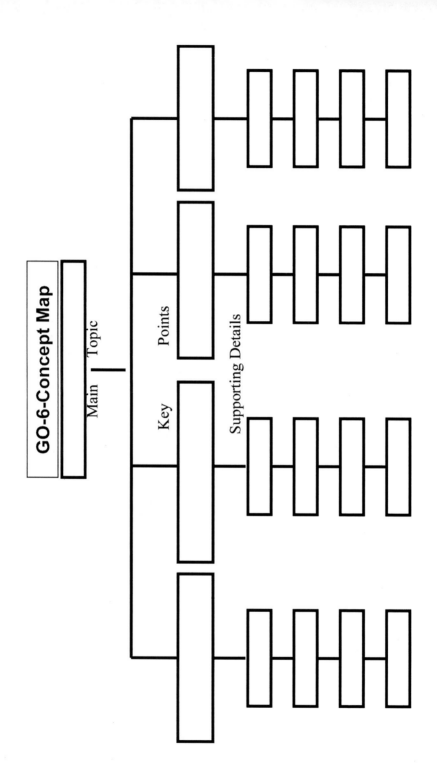

GO-6-Concept Map

Main Topic

Key Points

Supporting Details

GO-7-Strength/Weakness Table
Critique/Analysis/Evaluation

Strengths	Weaknesses	Comments
1-	1-	1-
2-	2-	2-
3-	3-	3-
4-	4-	4-
5-	5-	5-
6-	6-	6-

D. Three-Level Outline/Table of Contents Practice

Directions: Write a 3-level outline on the topic of your choice.

This becomes the Table of Contents for your paper. Be sure the body has at least three main points each supported by at least three details; remember, you may have more key points and more details. On your outline, be sure to include the introduction, summary/conclusion, and reference list/bibliography headings. Remember use words or brief phrases – no sentences.

Overall topic:_____

I.   Introduction

II. Body/ Overall topic:_____

    A. Main idea one:_____

    1. Supporting detail:_____

    2. Detail:_____

    3. Detail:_____

    B. Main idea two:_____

    1. Detail:_____

    2. Detail:_____

    3. Detail:_____

III. Summary:_____

IV. Conclusion:_____

V. Personal Opinion:_____

VI. Bibliography or Works Cited (if applicable)

VII. Graphic Organizer (attached)

VIII. Articles Attached (if applicable)

E. Introduction Paragraph Practice

Directions: Write an introductory paragraph for your topic outlined in D above.

_____

_____

_____

_____

_____

_____

F. Body Paragraphs Practice

Directions: Write a (brief) body of at least three paragraphs, each clearly having a main idea and at least three supporting details.

_____

_____

_____

_____

_____

_____

_____

_____

_____

_____

_____

_____

_____

_____

_____

_____

_____

_____

_____

_____

_____

_____

_____

_____

_____

_____

_____

_____

G. Summary Paragraph Practice

Directions: Write a brief (1-2 sentences) summary of your writing above.

_____

_____

_____

_____

_____

_____

H. Conclusion Paragraph Practice

Directions: Write a brief conclusion (1-2 sentences) about your writing above.

_____

_____

_____

_____

_____

_____

_____

I. Personal Response Paragraph Practice

Directions: Write a brief personal response (1-3 sentences) about your writing.

_____

_____

_____

_____

_____

J. Which do I use?

Directions: Look up these words. List what each is. State briefly when you might use it.

Bibliography:_____

_____

References:_____

_____

Works Cited:_____

_____

Chapter 18

Writing Paragraph 1: Summary/ Abstract/Précis

A. Introduction

Probably the most critical skill to master for effective writing is writing a summary whether a summary of a paragraph, a page, an article, a paper, or a book. It is really much simpler than most people think, but this important skill is the basis of most writings and is the basis of all the various writings in this text.

B. Definitions

1. Summary. *Summary* comes from the Latin (*summa)* meaning *sum*. It presents the main idea in a brief form – a *summarizing*; a *concise*; a *condensation*. A summary presents the key points; sometimes it is also referred to as a *digest*; an *abridgment*; a *compendium*.

2. **Abstract.** An *abstract* is a brief statement of the contents of a writing, a book, a speech, etc. It is also known as a *summary*.

3. **Précis**. A *précis* is a concise or brief *abridgment*; a *summary*; or an *abstract*.

C. Processes

1. Identify the overall main topic.

2. Identify the main ideas or key points.

   a. There are usually three to five key points, though there may be more.

   b. There are usually several supporting details for each main idea.

   c. Ask yourself, Does this point support another point or are there other details supporting this point?

   d. If at least three (3) details support it, it is probably a main idea or key point.

   e. If only one or two details support it, the point is probably a supporting detail for another key point rather than being a main idea or key point.

3. Write a summary paragraph writing one sentence for each of the following:

   a. Introduction: Introduce overall topic.

   b. Body: Write one sentence each to introduce your reader to the key points covered. This should be at least three (3) sentences.

   c. Summary: Write one sentence pointing out ___ (number) of points are covered or addressed in this passage, writing, speech, book, etc.

   d. Conclusion: Write one sentence stating the significance of this coverage of this topic. Answer the questions, "So what? Of what significance is this information?"

   e. (optional) Personal Perspective: Write one sentence stating your impression or opinion of the material presented.

   f. Note: Add no new information in the summary or conclusion statements. Somewhat new information is found only in your opinion statement of the summary, abstract, or précis.

D. Practice

The following activities afford you practice in every aspect of writing this kind of paragraph:

Directions: Write a brief, concise summary, abstract, or précis of each of the following passages.

1. Summary Paragraph 1...

Today is a beautiful day. The sun is shining brightly – dancing in and out around the large billowy white clouds. I even had to wear my sunglasses while driving and while working out in the yard. The temperature has dropped a few degrees this week, so it is not as hot as it has been. Matter of fact, there is a bit of a chill in the air. It is not raining and there is no rain in the five-day forecast according to last night's evening news. It is a beautiful day for flying – in a hot air balloon, a glider, or an airplane – since visibility is almost fifty miles. There is a slight breeze helping the hot air balloons get where they want to go. It is also a nice day for traveling by car, bus, motorcycle or RV. Kids are playing outside – riding their bikes, skating, skateboarding, playing ball games, and climbing on the playscape in the park. It is a beautiful day for taking photographs of scenery, homes, flowers, animals, or just about any thing. I really enjoy and am grateful for beautiful days like this. It is neat and it is inspiring. It inspires me to want to paint or to photograph a variety of things.

    a. Summary/Abstract/Précis:

      1. Overall topic: _____

_____

      2. Main Ideas: _____

_____

    b. Write a brief, concise summary of this paragraph.

_____
_____
_____

_____

_____

_____

_____

2. Paragraph 2:

Directions:

a. Select a topic of your choice (like a sport, a hobby, etc

Overall Topic: _____

b. Select at least three but not more than five main ideas you want to address.

Main Ideas (3-5):_____

_____

_____

_____

c. Write a brief, concise paragraph that is a summary, an abstract, a précis of your overall topic. Use the pattern above to gather your information.

_____

_____

_____

_____

_____

_____

_____

_____

_____

Chapter 19

Writing Narrative Paragraph 2: Descriptive/Elaboration

A. Introduction

Narrative or descriptive text elaborates or describes a person, place, or thing, so careful selection of adjectives is key to writing this kind of paragraph and/or paper. The following exercise guides you through the 7-step writing process -- step by step – to write a descriptive paragraph. A bubble chart or concept map graphic organizer helps organize main ideas and supporting details for this kind of writing. This paragraph should have at least five but not more than ten sentences. Consult the Paragraph Evaluation Rubric in Part III Introduction for things to be evaluated. After you revise and edit it on the computer, turn it in for evaluation.

B. Definition

A Descriptive or Elaboration Narrative paragraph or paper simple describes and provides details about the people, places, and things in a narrative or story format.

C. Practice Assignment

The following activities afford you practice in every aspect of writing this kind of paragraph:

1. **Pre-write** (Brainstorm)… Use a graphic organizer (Bubble Chart) to cluster ideas.

a. Choose TOPIC/main idea:_____

_____

b. List at least three (3) supporting details; (more are fine):

1)_____

2)_____

3)_____

c. Attach your Bubble Chart or Concept Map Graphic Organizer. Circle one you used.

2. **Write first draft**_____

_____

_____

_____

3. Personal Revision: Revise on the computer for ease of block copy moving of text. Focus on ideas and details for coherence. Does the main idea have at least three details to support it? Do the details support the main idea? Are the details ordered logically? Does your paragraph read smoothly and flowing? Is there anything that needs to be changed?

4. Peer Revision: Have one of your peers review your paragraph to make suggestions about flow of ideas.

5. Rewrite the paragraph -- revising logical flow of ideas for coherence.

6a. Personal Edit: Check latest draft for spelling, grammar, punctuation, capitals, and sentence structures, etc. What needs changing?

6b. Peer Edit: Have a peer review your paragraph looking for mechanical errors.

7. Rewrite--Final Draft: Write final, polished paragraph: editing and correcting mechanical errors -- ready-for-publication and **sharing** (#8).

_____

_____

_____

_____

8. Publish: Submit: Turn in your Narrative Descriptive Paragraph for evaluation, attaching printout or disk copy.

Notes & Questions

Chapter 20

Writing Expository Paragraph 3: Sequential/How-To

A. Introduction

Expository text explains people, places, things, and events by relationships – sequence (how-to), compare/contrast, cause/effect, and/or problem/solution; so, careful selection of words and phrases showing relationship is key to writing this kind of paragraph and/or paper. The following exercise guides you through the eight-step writing process -- step by step – to write a how-to or sequence paragraph. This paragraph should have at least five but not more than ten sentences. Consult the Paragraph Evaluation Rubric in Part III Introduction for things to be evaluated. After you revise and edit it on the computer, turn it in for evaluation.

B. Definition

A Sequential/How-to paragraph or paper explains the order in which things occur.

C. Practice Assignment

The following activities provide an opportunity to practice every aspect of writing this kind of paragraph:

1. **Pre-write** (Brainstorm): Use a graphic organizer (time line) to cluster ideas.

    a. Choose TOPIC/main idea:_____

b. List at least three steps/details (more are fine):

1)_____

2)_____

3)_____

2. Attach your Time Line graphic organizer.

3. **Write first draft**:

_____

_____

_____

_____

4a. **Personal Revision**: Revise on the computer for ease of block copy moving of text. Focus on logically reorganizing ideas and details for coherence. Are your details related to your main idea? Are your details ordered logically? What needs re-ordering?

4b. **Peer Revision**: Have one of your peers review your paragraph to make suggestions about flow of ideas.

5. **Rewrite** the paragraph: Revise logical flow of ideas for coherence.

6a. **Personal Edit** : Check latest draft spelling, grammar, punctuation, capitalizations, and sentence structures. What needs changing?

6b. **Peer Edit**: Have one of your peers review your paragraph looking for mechanical errors.

7. **Write Final Draft**: Rewrite the paragraph – editing/correcting mechanical errors.

Write final, polished, ready-for-publication SEQUENTIAL/ HOW-TO paragraph.

_____

_____

_____

_____

_____

_____

_____

_____

8. **Publish**: Submit: Attach a disk or printout copy to turn in your Sequential/How-to Paragraph for evaluation.

Notes & Questions

Chapter 21

Writing Expository Paragraph 4:
Compare-Contrast

A. Introduction

Expository text explains people, places, things, and events by relationships – sequence (how-to), compare/contrast, cause/effect, and/or problem/solution; so, careful selection of words and phrases showing relationship is key to writing this kind of paragraph and/ or paper. The following exercise guides you through the eight-step writing process -- step by step – to write a compare/contrast paragraph. The paragraph should have at least five but not more than ten sentences. Consult the Paragraph Evaluation Rubric in Part III Introduction for what is evaluated. After you revise and edit it on the computer, turn it in for evaluation.

B. Definitions

1. Compare means to look for likenesses or qualities shared in common by two or more persons, place, or things.

2. **Contrast** means to look for differences between or unique qualities of each of two or more persons, places, or things. A compare/ contrast paragraph or paper looks for both the similarities of and the differences between two or more persons, places, or things.

C. Practice

The following activities provide practice for every aspect of your parargraph:

1. Pre-write (Brainstorm): Use a graphic organizer (Venn Diagram) to cluster ideas.

    a. Choose TOPIC/main idea:_____

    b. List at least three compare details; more are fine:

       1)_____

       2)_____

       3)_____

    c. List at least three contrast details; more are fine:

       4)_____

       5)_____

       6)_____

2. Attach your Time Line graphic organizer.

3. **Write first draft**:

4a..**Personal Revision**: Revise on the computer for ease of block copy moving of text. Focus on logically reorganizing ideas and details for coherence. Are your details related to your main idea? Are your details ordered logically? What needs re-ordering?

4b. **Peer Revision**: Have a peer review your paragraph to make suggestions about flow of ideas.

5. **Rewrite** the paragraph – revising logical flow of ideas for coherence.

6a. **Personal Edit**: Check latest draft for spelling, grammar, punctuation, capitalizations, and sentence structures. What needs changing?

6b. **Peer Edit**: Have a peer review your paragraph looking for mechanical errors.

7. **Write Final Draft**-- Rewrite the paragraph – editing/correcting mechanical errors.

Write final, polished, ready-for-publication Compare/Contrast paragraph.

_____

_____

_____

_____

8. **Publish**: Submit a disk or printout copy of your Compare/Contrast Paragraph for evaluation.

D. More Compare/Contrast Practice

Write a 1-page "paper" to compare and contrast having a dog or a cat for a pet. Articulate at least three points comparing the two and at least three contrasting points for each pet. Introduction, summary, conclusion, and personal response should be included.

_____

_____

_____

_____

Notes & Questions

Chapter 22

Writing Expository Paragraph 5:
Cause-Effect

A. Introduction

Expository text explains people, places, things, and events by relationships – sequence (how-to), compare/contrast, cause/effect, and/or problem/solution; so, careful selection of words and phrases showing relationship is key to writing this kind of paragraph and/or paper. The following exercise guides you through the 7-step writing process -- step by step – to write a cause/effect paragraph.

B. Definitions

1. **Cause** means to make something happen; causes may be persons, places, things, or actions.

2. **Effect** means what resulted or what happened; it is usually a noun – person, place, or thing but it may be a responding action. A cause/effect paragraph or paper clearly identifies the cause and the results. [A **helpful mnemonic**: The cause usually follows the word *because*.] The paragraph should have at least five but not more than ten sentences. Consult the Paragraph Evaluation Rubric in Part III Introduction for what is evaluated. After you revise and edit it on the computer, turn it in for evaluation.

C. Practice Assignment

The following activities afford you practice in every aspect of writing this paragraph:

1. **Pre-write** (Brainstorm): 2. Use a **graphic organizer** (Cause/ Effect Flow Chart)) to cluster ideas.

    a. Choose TOPIC/main idea:_____

    b. List at least 1cause and at least three effect details (more are fine):

        1)[cause]_____

        _____

        2)[effect]_____

        _____

        3)[effect]_____

        _____

        4)[effect]_____

        _____

2. Attach your graphic organizer.

3. **Write first draft**:

4a. **Personal Revision** Review: Revise on the computer for ease of block copy moving of text. Focus on logically reorganizing ideas and details for coherence. Are your details related to your main idea? Are your details ordered logically? What needs re-ordering?

4b. **Peer Revision** Review: Haveone of your peers review your paragraph to make suggestions about flow of ideas.

5. **Rewrite** the paragraph: Revise logical flow of ideas for coherence.

6a. **Personal Edit** : Check latest draft for spelling, grammar, punctuation, capitals, and sentence structures. What needs changing?

6b. **Peer Edit** Have a peer review your paragraph looking for mechanical errors.

7. **Write Final Draft**: Rewrite the paragraph – editing/correcting mechanical errors. Write final, polished, ready-for-publication Cause/Effect paragraph.

_____

_____

_____

_____

8. **Publish**: Submit: Attach a disk or printout copy of your Cause/Effect Paragraph for evaluation.

Notes & Questions

Chapter 23

Writing Expository Paragraph 6: Problem-Solution

A. Introduction

Expository text explains people, places, things, and events by relationships – sequence (how-to), compare/contrast, cause/effect, and/or problem/solution; so, careful selection of words and phrases showing relationship is key to writing this kind of paragraph and/or paper. The following exercise guides you through the eight-step writing process —- step by step — to write a problem/solution paragraph.

B. Definitions

1. **Problem** means something needs solving; problems may be persons, places, things, or actions.

2. **Solution** means ways the problem may be taken care of or resolved; solutions tend to be actions but may also be persons, places, or things. A problem/solution paragraph or paper clearly identifies the problem and suggests at least three solutions — like a persuasive paper. The paragraph should have at least five but not more than ten sentences. Consult the Paragraph Evaluation Rubric in Part III Introduction for what is evaluated. After you revise and edit it on the computer, turn it in for evaluation.

C. Practice

The following activities provide practice in every aspect of writing this type of paragraph:

1. **Pre-write** (Brainstorm):

2. Use a **graphic organizer** (Problem/Solution Flow Chart)) to cluster ideas.

    a. Choose TOPIC/main idea:_____

    b. List at least 1 problem and at least 3 solutions/details (more are fine):

        1)[problem]_____

        _____

        2)[solution]_____

        _____

        3)[solution]_____

        _____

        4)[solution]_____

        _____

    Attach your graphic organizer.

3. **Write first draft**:

4a. **Personal Revision** : Revise on the computer for ease of block copy moving of text. Focus on logically reorganizing ideas and details for coherence. Are your details related to your main idea? Are your details ordered logically? What needs re-ordering?

4b. **Peer Revision** Review: Have a peer review your paragraph to make suggestions about flow of ideas.

5. **Rewrite** the paragraph: Revise logical flow of ideas for coherence.

6a. **Personal Edit**: Check latest draft for spelling, grammar, punctuation, capitals, and sentence structures. What needs changing?

6b. **Peer Edit** : Have a peer review your paragraph looking for mechanical errors.

7. **Write Final Draft**: Write final, polished, ready-for-publication Problem/Solution paragraph. Rewrite the paragraph – editing/correcting mechanical errors.

_____

_____

_____

_____

8. **Publish**: Submit: Attach a disk or printout copy of your Problem/Solution Paragraph for evaluation.

Notes & Questions

Part IV

Basic Genres of Writing Papers

A. References for Review – Part IV—Table A

Topic In Workbook	Arco: Step by Step	Help Yourself	Writing Smart	Other Resources
IV-22: audiences, styles, purposes, parts, & processes			pp. 10, 52; 75+, 84-93	
IV-24: APA format				Syllabus guideline APA Manual
IV-25: peer reviews & feedback				
IV-25: revising			pp. 32-35	
IV-25: editing & proofreading			pp. 29-39 55, 62, 93	
IV-26-27: abstract, summary, précis				
IV-28: action research;			pp. 74-81	
IV-29 review of literature			142-152	
IV-30: compare/ contrast				
IV-31: evaluation, critique, analysis			pp. 74-81	
IV-32: editorial, personal opinion, reflection, position paper			pp. 52-72	

B. Reference List for Section IV

Fry, E. B., Kress, J. E., Fountoukidis, D. L. (2000). <u>The reading teacher's book of lists (4th ed.).</u> Englewood Cliffs, NJ: Prentice-Hall.

Lerner, M. (1994). <u>The Princeton Review: Writing smart: Your guide to great writing.</u> NY: Random House.

Mattson, M., Leshing, S., Levi, E. (1993<u>). Help yourself: A guide to writing and rewriting (3rd ed.).</u> New York: Macmillan. [out of print]

Muschla, G. R. (1991). <u>The writing teacher's book of lists: with ready to use activities and worksheets.</u> Paramus, NJ: Prentice Hall.

Pulaski, M.A.S. (1982). <u>Step-by-step guide to correct English.</u> NY: Macmillan.

Part IV

Basic Genres of Writing Papers
Narrative, Expository, Persuasive,
and Academic Texts

A. Introduction

Children from pre-school through college learn to read and write narrative texts. From birth, parents read picture books to children; then, children learn to read picture books, big books, story books, and readers. By third grade, children progress to chapter books and series books, but they are all in narrative, descriptive, story format. Some adults believe because a child can read successfully a story (narrative text) he can read expository text as is found in the content subjects of social studies, science, and mathematics. This is a false assumption. Just because a ten-year-old can read <u>Little House on the Prairie</u> does not necessarily mean he can read efficiently the "Westward Ho" or westward expansion chapter in his social studies textbook.

As stated in Part III on paragraphs, narrative and expository texts are structured differently. The information is packaged differently. For example, within the academic discipline of science, compare a biology text with a chemistry text with a physics text with an earth science text. Do they look the same? Is information presented in the same manner? Even the same word has different meanings in the texts of the various sciences. To illustrate, what does formula mean in biology? In chemistry? In physics? In earth science? Does a formula look the same in each of the sciences? These rhetorical questions highlight the inherent diversity of text within various academic disciplines.

Thus, expository text structure varies or differs from narrative text structure as well as varies or differs from other expository text both inter-disciplinary (between academic disciplines) and intradisciplinary (within a given academic discipline). Similarly, writing narrative text for creative writing or persuasive essays for English is quite different from writing expository text for social studies or history assignments, science assignments, and mathematics assignments. Both narrative and expository text must be taught explicitly — explicit instruction for reading and writing the diverse types of text encountered when studying various subject areas.

B. Definitions

The following definitions clarify the various types of text:

1. Narrative text. Narrative text usually follows the development of a story grammar or story line. Typically, there is a theme, a plot, and main characters who attempt to resolve a problem through a variety of trial and error activities. In the process of problem solving, characters develop and reveal their personalities. Narrative text typically uses a lot of descriptive text as well as some sequential, compare/contrast, and cause/effect structures. A novel is an obvious everyday example of narrative text, but narrative text appears in some sections of most textbooks across the curriculum, so, narrative text can be tailored for any subject area. Since younger students have more experience with narrative text, it is an obvious stepping stone to teaching them how to read and to write expository text… going from the familiar to the unfamiliar.

2. Persuasive text. Persuasive text usually presents a problem or issue, offers a solution, takes a stand or position about the issue, and tries to persuade the reader to see the issue through the eyes of the author. Editorials and position papers are every-day examples of persuasive writing, but persuasive papers may be requested in any coursework in any subject area. A persuasive paper is also a great support to taking a stand in formal debate situations.

3. Expository text. Expository text generally presents information. One of the following formats or structures presents the data: a sequential order, a compare/contrast examination, a cause/effect pattern, or a problem/solution. Most academic textbooks are expository, and they use a mixture of these text structures. For example, consider a biology article or textbook chapter discussing the fauna and flora of the desert. You find narrative text describing the animals and plants. Sequential order may be used when discussing the blooming times of cacti. Compare/contrast may be used to compare and contrast the cacti with other desert flora. The cause/effect may explain how desert storms affect growth cycles of flora. You get the idea.

4. Academic text. Academic text is expository text, and it employs a combination of the following formats: description, sequential/how-to, compare/contrast, cause/effect, or problem/solution. An obvious use of problem/solution is in math; it is also very present in science, social studies, health and other academic areas.

The exercise on the next page gives you an occasion to recognize examples of each of these types of text structures.

Notes & Questions

C. Text Types Refresher Activity

Directions: Identify the following texts: Narrative (N), Expository (E), Persuasive (P), or Academic (A) on the line to the left of the text.

___1. *Once upon a time there were three little bears – Papa Bear, Mama Bear, and Baby Bear. They lived in a den deep in the woods. One day while the Bear family was out hunting for food, a beautiful young girl with long, golden curls discovered the Bear's home. Goldilocks walked into the eating area and found three bowls of soup. She tasted Papa Bear's large bowl, but the soup was too hot. She tasted Mama Bear's middle-sized bowl, but the soup was too cold. Then she tried Baby Bear's small bowl, and the soup was just right, so she ate it all up.*

___2. *There are seven species of bears in the world: brown bears, American black bears, Asiatic black bears, polar bears, sun bears, sloth bears, and spectacled bears. Three kinds of bears inhabit the United States and Western Hemisphere. Brown bears include the world's largest bears -- the Alaskan brown bears (Kodiak bear and peninsula brown bear) and the grizzly bears of western North America. These large bears are easily frightened, and they are very dangerous when annoyed, surprised, or wounded. Alaskan brown bears live in Alaska and the Alaskan islands. Grizzly bears may be the most dangerous animals of North America; they live in the northern Rocky Mountains in Idaho, Montana, and Wyoming. Full-grown Grizzlies are about 8 feet tall when standing on their hind legs, and they weigh about 800 pounds.*

___3. *Bears – all species – need to be protected to avoid extinction. Though they might be dangerous, bears deserve respect from humans. Relocating bears to remote areas of the wilds is a reasonable protective measure for the bears, but back-country hikers and campers must accept and respect bears' territories. Help preserve our bears.*

___4. Some of the most interesting and largest animals are the various species of bears. They are the largest carnivores, though they eat both plants and animals. The Brown Bear (including the Alaskan Brown Bear and the Grizzly Bear) are the largest – often weighing over 1500 pounds. Other bear species in descending order of size are the Polar bear, the American and Asiatic Black Bear, the Sloth Bear, the Spectacled Bear, and the Sun Bear. Campers and residents often see bears in various National Parks as well as in more remote places in the wild. Bears are interesting animals worth investigating more.

Notes on Basic Writing Genres

Chapter 24

Audiences, Styles, Purposes, Parts, and Processes

A. Audiences

Always consider your audience – who do you anticipate will read your writing? When you write for children, you format your presentation differently than when you write for a college class. Part IV prepares you to write more effectively for high school and university level requirements. However, students in middle and high school need explicit instruction in how to write quality academic assignments, too. Pursuing excellence in writing academic assignments is what the remainder of this text is all about.

B. Styles

Part III focuses on narrative and expository styles in terms of six text/paragraph structures: summary/abstract, descriptive, compare/contrast, sequential/how-to, cause/effect, and problem/solution. Part IV introduction presents narrative, persuasive, expository and academic text styles. High-quality academic writing requires a style focusing on a definite audience, emulates one of the expository text structure styles, addresses an explicit purpose, contains all the necessary parts, follows the specific format requested, and gets to the point in a direct manner. Additionally, each writer writes in his or her own unique style – like a unique fingerprint. The words you select, the illustrations you share, your tendency to be more formal or informal, and most uniquely, the logical organization of your data – all comprise your personal writing style.

C. Purposes

Exemplary academic writing addresses the explicit purpose of the assignment as stated by the teacher, instructor, or professor. 1) An assignment to **summarize** the encyclopedia article about Bald Eagles does just that: it summarizes or abstracts the key points presented in the encyclopedia article. 2) An assignment to **describe** eagles does just that: it describes eagles -- their appearance, their homes, their habits, etc. 3) An assignment to explain the lifecycle of the eagle does just that: it explains the **sequential** development of an eagle – its birth, its eaglet stage, etc. throughout its lifespan. 4) An assignment to **compare and contrast** the American Bald eagle with the Golden Eagle does just that: it compares the likenesses and contrasts the differences between the two eagles. 5) An assignment to discuss the **causes and effects** of why the American Bald Eagle has been on the endangered species list does just that: it discusses probable causes and probable effects that precipitated the "endangered" label. 6) An assignment to hypothesize solutions to the **problem** of American eagles being "endangered" does just that: it states the problem of endangered and presents probable **solutions** to the problem. Students address a specific purpose by utilizing appropriate text/paragraph structures to do exactly what is asked of them, and not writing just another freshman composition essay hoping that it suffices.

Additionally, excellent academic writing focuses on the specific type of assignment. Seven types are explicated and required for this class in preparation for all coursework and for teaching students to write different types of assignments. 1) An **abstract, a summary, or a précis** of a narrative piece (poem or story) on the eagles does just that: it briefly recaps or summarizes the main ideas of the poem or story. 2) An expository **abstract, a summary, or a précis** of an article on the eagles does just that: it briefly recaps or summarizes the main ideas of the article. 3) An **action research paper** on sightings of American Bald Eagles on the Colorado River in Texas does just: it relates how many sightings and perhaps briefly describes what the eagles look like one seen. 4) A **review of literature** assignment on eagles does just that: it reviews a specified number of sources and briefly relates the findings – based on brief summaries of the sources consulted. 5) A **compare/contrast paper** does just that: it compares and contrasts the

Bald Eagles with the Golden Eagles – based on brief summaries of the sources consulted. 6) A **critique, analysis, or evaluation** of one of the resources read on eagles does just that: it evaluates whether or not the source relates viable data on the topic – based on a brief summary of the article. 7) An **editorial, personal opinion, or position paper** does just that: it offers the writer's opinion about the topic – eagles – based on brief summaries of sources consulted. Thus, a variety of writing assignments as well as styles and text structures need to be considered when writing any assignment. Also, please note, most writing assignments depend upon a brief summary of the sources consulted, so mastery of how to write an abstract on a source – article, paper, or book – is critical to effective writing.

D. Parts

Five main parts comprise a high-quality academic writing. These explicit details pertain especially to the one-page paper assignments, but just as **"More is not necessarily better…",** if you can write an exemplary one-page paper, you can write an exemplary ten, twenty, or hundred-page paper. The five basic parts of an excellent writing include the following:

1. **Title page.** The title page is the first thing your reader, your teacher, your instructor, or your professor sees. A good title page enhances the presentation of your writing. The title page presents the topic of the paper, for whom the paper is written, the author of the paper, and the date written.

2. **Table of Contents.** The table of contents is really a three-level outline of your paper. It includes I. Introduction, II. Body, III. Summary, IV, Conclusion, V. Personal Response, and Reference List. The body briefly outlines the main ideas and the supporting details for each main idea.

3. **Paper.** The paper follows the outline, and it contains the following seven sections:

    a. Introduction. The introduction introduces the topic of the paper, makes or gives the thesis statement, and briefly states or lists the key points of the paper. The introduction tells what you are going to say.

b. Body. Usually, the body of the paper contains at least one paragraph for each main idea or key point, and each main idea paragraph contains the supporting details. Each supporting detail has at least one sentence of information to support the main idea of the paragraph. Typically, the first sentence of every paragraph states the main idea of the paragraph, and the supporting detail sentences follow. The last sentence of a paragraph is a summary recapping the essence of the paragraph.

c. Summary. The summary paragraph recaps the main ideas/key points of the paper or briefly states what you have said in the paper.

d. Conclusion. The conclusion paragraph states a conclusion you drew from what you read and wrote or says what you conclude from this activity. This paragraph usually answers the questions, "So what? Why is this important?"

e. Personal Response. The personal response paragraph presents your thoughts and opinions about what you read and wrote. [Some teachers allow for this and some do not. As long as you write this paragraph as an addendum to the paper and not part of the body of the paper, most instructors do not object.]

f. Reference List. The reference list is an alphabetical list of sources actually used or referred to in writing the paper. It is alphabetical by authors' last names.

4. Graphic Organizer. The graphic organizer graphically or pictorially presents the main ideas and the supporting details for your paper. Attaching this to your paper shows your reader or teacher how you organized your information.

5. Attached Article(s). The attached article is a photocopy of the article(s) referenced or a computer printout of Internet articles used. Attaching the articles enables your reader to see your original source of data, and helps them help you to avoid plagiarism.

Chapter 26 – Formatting Your Paper – includes more details for these paper components.

E. Processes

Processes for writing a paper follow the basic eight-step writing process presented in Part III. To refresh your memory as you prepare to write the one-page papers, process writing includes the following eight steps:

1. Pre-write/brainstorm ideas using appropriate graphic organizer.

2. Generate a three-level outline of your paper's content.

3. Write first/rough draft.

4a. Personally Revise -- focusing on organization and flow of ideas; Rewrite first draft.

4b. Peer Review Revise – focusing on organization and flow of ideas;

5. Rewrite second draft (and usually rewrite several other drafts).

6a. Personally Edit – focusing on mechanical aspects; Rewrite.

6b. Peer Review Edit – focusing on mechanical aspects; Rewrite.

7. Write Final Draft -- polishing paper to an exemplary status.

8. Publish: share your writing via publishing, printing and circulating, posting, etc.

F. Three-Level Outline Practice

Directions: Select a topic of your own choosing. Brainstorm at least three key points or main ideas and at least three details for each main ideas.

Remember use words or brief phrases – no sentences.

Overall topic:_____

I.   Introduction:

II.   Body/ Overall topic:_____

A. First main idea:_____
_____

    1. Supporting detail:_____
    _____

    2. Detail:_____
    _____

    3. Detail:_____
    _____

B. Second main idea:_____
_____

    1.Detail:_____
    _____

    2. Detail:_____
    _____

    3. Detail:_____
    _____

C. Third main idea:_____
_____

    1.Detail:_____
    _____

    2. Detail:_____
    _____

    3. Detail:_____
    _____

III.   Summary:_____

IV.   Conclusion:_____

V.   Personal Opinion:_____

VI. Reference List, Bibliography or Works Cited (whichever is applicable)

VII. Graphic Organizer (attached)

VIII. Articles Attached (if applicable)

G. Introduction Paragraph Practice

Directions: Write an introductory paragraph for your topic outlined in Section F above.

_____

_____

_____

_____

_____

H. Body Paragraphs Practice

Directions: Write a (brief) body of at least three paragraphs, each clearly having a main idea and at least three supporting details.

_____

_____

_____

_____

_____

_____

_____

_____

_____

_____

_____

_____

_____

_____

_____

_____

_____

_____

_____

_____

_____

_____

_____

_____

_____

_____

_____

_____

I. Summary Paragraph Practice

Directions: Write a brief (1-2 sentences) summary of your writing you wrote above.

_____

_____

_____

_____

_____

J. Conclusion Paragraph Practice

Directions: Write a brief conclusion (1-2 sentences) about your writing you wrote above.

_____

_____

_____

_____

_____

_____

K. Personal Response Paragraph Practice

Directions: Write a brief personal response (1-2 sentences) about your writing you wrote above.

_____

_____

_____

_____

_____

L. Reference List, Bibliography, Works Cited Practice

Directions: Write a sample Reference List including at least three (imaginative but realistic) sources, one being an Internet source. Use APA format. Consult the Appendices and the Bibliography in back of this book for more assistance and examples.

_____

_____

_____

_____

_____

_____

_____

_____

_____

_____

_____

M. APA Citations in Text Practice

Directions: Answer each prompt below to assist you in this practice. More help and examples are presented in the Appendices and Bibliography at the back of this book.

1. How would you provide citation for the following quotation cited in the text of a paper?

   "Give me liberty or give me death!"

   _____

   _____

   _____

2. How would you provide citation for the following general idea cited in the text of a paper

   "Democracy is a government by the people, for the people, and of the people."

   _____

   _____

   _____

N. Revising Practice

Directions: Revise and rewrite the following paragraph to better organize the ideas:

> Reading and writing go hand in hand. Good readers usually write well, and good writers usually read well. Reading is a receptive language skill, whereas writing is an expressive language skill. I don't think that reading and writing use the same basic skills, but I'm not sure. There are three steps in reading: pre-reading (getting ready), reading, and post-reading (reflecting on what you read). There are five steps in writing: 1) pre-writing (brainstorming), 2) First draft, 3) revising, 4) editing, and 5) publishing. I enjoy both reading and writing; I find them relaxing.

_____

_____

_____

_____

O. Editing Practice

Directions: Edit the following paragraph to correct spelling, grammar, and punctuation:

> "all we can do is hang on to our colons punctuation is bound to change like the rest of language punctuation is made for man not man for punctuation a good sentence should be intelligible without

the help of punctuation in most cases and if you get in a muddle

with your dots and dashes you may need to simplify your thoughts

and shorten your sentence " [Philip Howard] What questions would

you like to ask mr howard what bothers you about his paragraph

quoted above sure it is a long sentence but can you write one that

effectively illustrates the need for punctuation of various kinds i

think that might be difficult

Directions: Succinctly provide peer review feedback to the writer of either paragraph 1 or 2 above. Provide at least one positive comment. Focus on not more than three (3) points.

_____

_____

_____

_____

_____

_____

Notes & Questions

Chapter 25

Avoiding Plagiarism

A. Introduction

A critical issue with writing papers is dealing with plagiarism. When children first start writing research papers for school, they tend to copy word-for-word directly from the encyclopedia or other source materials. They feel their voice and words are "not good enough" and, for some reason, it is better to use the words of published authors. Primary elementary school children are concrete thinkers (per Piaget's developmental stages), and they have difficulty rewording information in their own words; it's possibly too abstract for their developmental stage. As a result, children learn early to copy text when writing a paper.

Problem? That is simply and clearly **plagiarism**. Now, teachers do not intentionally train children to plagiarize, but that is exactly what happens. This procedure prevails on up through the grades until sometime in high school, college, or university someone says, "You plagiarized that!" Sometimes baffled, students are not always sure how to go about avoiding plagiarism. Well, that is what this chapter is about, and hopefully, the contents of this chapter will enable you to break the habit of plagiarizing and to know how to avoid it from now on.

B. Definition

Webster's <u>New World College Dictionary (4<u>th</u> ed.)</u> (2000) defines *plagiarism* as, "1) the act of plagiarizing; 2) an idea, plot, etc. plagiarized." The same source defines *plagiarized* as "to take (ideas, writings, etc.) from (another) and pass them off as one's own." These words come from the Latin word *plagiarius* meaning "kidnapper, literary thief."

C. Solution

The solution is so simple, and it needs to be taught explicitly and reinforced overtly as early as possible – perhaps by the fourth or fifth grade – and throughout middle school, high school, and college or university classes. The solution lies in using one's own words. The best way to do use one's own words is to adhere to the following steps:

1. Read the original source document.

2. Briefly, tell someone – in your own words -- the key points you gained from your reading.

3. Write down the key points in your own words on an index card or a graphic organizer.

4. Do the same for all the sources you use.

5. Organize your key points (main ideas) and supporting details on an appropriate graphic organizer depending upon the type of writing assignment you are writing.

6. Organize your key points (main ideas) and key supporting details in a three-level outline.

7. Proceed with the Eight-Step Writing Process and write your paper.

You may use a key word(s) from the original source(s), but do NOT copy down any sentences from the source(s) unless you believe the sentence is so indispensable to the paper you will include it with quotation marks and use appropriate citation format (explained in Part IV of this book.) Even when you get ideas from a source, you are to use the appropriate citation format for borrowing ideas – otherwise, it is plagiarism. Since there is "nothing new under the sun," it is reasonable to expect at least one cited source for every paragraph in the body of a paper. Even rewritten in your own words, the ideas didn't just "fall out of the sky"; they came from somewhere, so tell your reader your source of inspiration for both ideas and words.

D. Summary

Plagiarism is stealing words and ideas from another writer. It is technically illegal. It is best avoided by using your own words to summarize what you read. If and when you borrow ideas or directly quote words from someone or some source, "Thou shalt..." signal such to your reader by using appropriate citation formatting as well as quotation marks when directly quoted from the original source.

Notes on Plagiarism

Chapter 26

Formatting Your Paper

A. Introduction

Pursuing excellence to format your paper, you will be pleased with the results of employing the parts and processes suggested in this chapter. The following pages contain the formats for all the components of high-quality academic papers. These recommendations should be strictly adhered to when writing and when evaluating papers to ensure exemplary standards and performances.

B. Parts Quick Check List

The following parts are the key components of an exemplary paper:

Title Page

Outline -- Table of Contents

Introduction

Body

Summary

Conclusion

Personal Response

Reference List (APA)

Citations (APA)

Graphic Organizer(s)

Attached Article(s)

C. Parts in Detail

Five parts comprise a high-quality academic writing. The explicit details pertain especially to the one-page paper assignments, but if your can write an exemplary one-page paper, you can write an exemplary ten- or hundred-page paper. Remember, "More is not necessarily better."

1. Title page. The title page is the first thing your reader (your teacher, professor, or evaluator) sees. A good title page enhances your presentation of your writing and includes the title of your paper, the type of assignment such as " presented to…, in partial fulfillment of the requirements for ___ class, by _(your name or student number)__, and the date submitted."

2. Table of Contents. The table of contents is really a three-level outline of your paper. It briefly (in short phrases or key words) outlines the main ideas (at least three) and the supporting details (at least three each) for each main idea. It includes the introduction, body (at least three main idea paragraphs plus at least three supporting details for each main idea), summary, conclusion, personal response, reference list, graphic organizer, and attached article (if applicable). Make each level parallel in construction.

3. Paper. Write the paper following the outline you generated from your graphic organizer. Your reader should be able to outline your paper and come up with the same (or similar) outline as your table of contents. Therefore, readily identifiable by your reader should be the following: a) introduction, b) body, c) summary, d) conclusion, e) personal response, and f) reference list as well as g) graphic organizer, and h) attached article (if applicable).

    a. Introduction: The introduction paragraph lists the topic of the paper, states the thesis statement, and briefly states the key points of the paper; it tells the reader what you are going to say.

    b. Body. There are at least three body paragraphs – one for each main idea or key point. Each body paragraph explains a main idea with at least three supporting details. Each paragraph follows the paragraph guidelines of the Part III of this text. Your reader should be able to outline your content easily; if he/she cannot, you are "padding" or "rambling." The body succinctly says what you want to say. There should be at least one source citation (APA format) per body paragraph. Where did your ideas/information come from? Acknowledge your sources of information.

c. Summary. The summary paragraph recaps the three (or more) main ideas or key points. It tersely states what you said in the body of your paper. It is very parallel to the introduction. No new information should show up at this point. A heading helps your reader.

d. Conclusion. The Conclusion paragraph states something you infer or deduce from what you have read and written. The conclusion answers the questions, "So, what?" and/or "Of what significance is this information anyway?" A heading helps your reader.

e. Personal Response. After you read and wrote all this information, you formed an opinion about your data. English research papers typically are to be impersonal, but this Personal Response provides the writer an opportunity to state his position or thoughts about the content of his paper. A heading helps the reader.

4. Reference List. The Reference List is an alphabetical list of sources actually used or referred to in writing the paper. This is usually on a separate page immediately following the paper text. This should follow APA format, because most educational and social science journals use APA format for citations and for reference list. {Other citation formats are provided in Appendix C.} [Per the APA Manual (1994, 4th edition), a reference list "cites works specifically supporting a particular article or paper. ...A bibliography cites works for background or for further reading" (p. 174).] Therefore, academic papers usually request a reference list as defined here, rather than a bibliography as defined here. APA format guidelines are provided in next subsection, and other citation formats are presented in the Appendices.

5. Graphic Organizer. A graphic organizer graphically or pictorially links the main ideas and supporting details from the prewriting/brainstorming step of your writing process. Select one of the samples in Appendices or create one of your own accomplishing the same purpose.

6. Attached Article. The attached article is a photocopy of the article(s) referenced; use a computer printout for Internet articles used. This helps you and your instructor identify plagiarism issues.

Notes & Questions

C. Example Title Page (centered):

Comparing Various Reading Programs {title}
-- A Review of Literature – {assignment type}
.. {at least 5 spaces down}
. Presented to
Dr. Dianne M. Haneke {professor}
Concordia University at Austin {school}

.In Partial Fulfillment of the Requirements for
RDG 3310 Fundamentals of Writing {course # and title}

by
Johnny J. Jumpup {your name}
March 32, 2006 {date submitted}

*{This is a an example of the **highest quality** title page for a paper or a project. { } provide cues. To center entire page: FILE...PAGE SETUP... LAYOUT, center text from center of page. To center each line, highlight text and use line centered from tool bar icon on top of screen.}*

E. Table of Contents Example:

TABLE OF CONTENTS *(Example)* *{centered}*

I. Introduction {overview of contents of paper: main/key points}

II. Three Reading Programs {body; Use title or the first topic of your paper here.}

    A. Guided Reading {first main idea, key point}

        1. Small group instruction {supporting details…}

        2. In-classroom

        3. Graded text literature

        4. Successful experiences

        5. Integrated reading and writing

    B. Success for All {second main idea, key point}

        1. Joplin plan grouping {supporting details}

        2. Whole class instruction

        3. Integrated reading and writing

        4. Successful experiences

    C. Whole Language {third main idea, key point}

        1. Whole class instruction {supporting details}

        2. Flexible grouping

        3. Integrated reading and writing

        4. Integrated curriculum

III. Summary {brief… recap/list of main/key ideas; in this case, also key similarities and differences}

IV. Conclusion {brief… so what? Why significant?}

V. Personal Response {brief… I think… opinion/position statement}

Reference List {APA format; alphabetical list of references used}

Graphic Organizer {graphic used to organize/link ideas}

Articles attached {photocopy of journal articles or printout of Internet articles; use both kinds}

{This is a sample Table of Contents – 3-level Outline.
Above { } at side provide cues.
This outline can be used with research and literature review papers, most writings, and perhaps with other projects.}

F. Introduction Paragraph (example)

The Introduction introduces the topic of the paper, states the thesis statement, and briefly states the key points of the paper (telling the reader what you are about to say). For example...

Children learn to read in a variety of ways. Many reading programs purport to enhance children's reading skills. So, this paper focuses on some research literature about three prominent reading programs – Reading Recovery, Guided Reading, and Success For All. Comparisons and contrasts highlight various aspects of the programs.

G. Body Paragraphs (tips)

The Body explains the topic through at least three main ideas each having at least three supporting details. Each paragraph follows the paragraph guidelines of the Part III of this text. Your reader should be able to outline your content easily; if not, you are "padding" or "rambling." The body succinctly says what you want to say. There should be at least one source citation (APA format) per body paragraph. [Ideas do not just fall out of the sky, so where did your ideas come from? Acknowledge your sources of information.] No illustration of the paper's body is provided here. The paragraph development from Part III should enable you to generate effective body paragraphs.

H. Summary Paragraph (example)

The Summary recaps the three (or more) main ideas (keypoints); it tersely states what you said in the body of your paper. For example...

Three prominent reading programs – Reading Recovery, Guided Reading, and Success For All – exhibit similarities and differences in ways to enable children to develop reading efficiency. Reading Recovery (Clay, 1993) provides a 1:1, individualized, sequential program for enabling beginning readers. Guided Reading (Fountas Pinnell, 1996) applies Reading Recovery principals to classroom, group reading instruction. Success For All (Slavin, 1996) teaches reading and language arts skills in homogenous, cross-age/cross-grade groups throughout an entire school. All three programs offer unique aspects for reading instruction, especially for primary grades K-3.

I. Conclusion Paragraph (example)

The Conclusion paragraph shares what you might infer or deduce from what you have read and written and answers questions like, "So, what?" "Of what significance is this information?" For example, continuing with the above illustration,

Obviously, Guided Reading and Success for All offer classroom, small group instruction, whereas, Reading Recovery offers 1:1, individually prescribed tutoring. One major similarity is the use of "leveled books" to guarantee successful reading experiences. Strategies and processes taught in Reading Recovery and Guided Reading are helpful for all readers at all levels.

J. Personal Response (example)

After you read and write all this information, you formed an opinion about your data. Research papers written for English classes typically are to be impersonal, but this personal response provides the writer an opportunity to state his position or thoughts about the topic such as:

I find Reading Recovery and Guided Reading to be the more help-ful and reasonable programs to consider, especially when teaching reading to primary grade children. Though there may be strengths in the cross-grade grouping approach, Success for All appears to be more skills-based and less successful-reading-of-text-based. I want to learn more about Guided Reading for use in my classroom – even for middle school levels.

K. Reference List (APA)

The Reference List, Bibliography, or Works Cited is an alpha-betical list of sources actually used when writing the paper. Since most educational journals use APA format for citations and for reference lists, use APA. Per the APA Manual (1994, 4th edition), a reference list "cites works specifically supporting a particular article or paper. A bibliography cites works for background or for further reading" (p. 174). Teachers usually request a reference list as defined here, rather than a bibliography. Master's theses and Doctoral dissertations must adhere to all APA formatting guidelines, but you are accountable for what is simplified here as important for the assignments by most instructors.

APA varies from MLA and other formats as follows: Only last names and initials for authors. Capitalize only first word of title and first word of subtitle. Comma after city, state (2 capital letter state ab-breviation, e.g., *TX*): simple publisher name. Underline book and jour-nal titles. After the journal title comes the volume (underlined) and the issue (in parentheses) followed by page numbers (numbers only).

Be sure to check the syllabus for each course to be sure you at-tend to things you are accountable for in each course. The { } notations are for your information; do not include in the actual list. The follow-ing APA Reference List example includes entries for a book, a chapter of a book, a journal article, a newspaper article, and an Internet article. If you need format information for another types of entry for APA, consult the latest edition of the <u>Publication Manual of the American Psychological Association.</u>

L. Reference List Example

Reference List (APA example): {centered}

Allington, R. L., Walmsley, S. A. (1995). Redefining and reforming instructional support programs for at-risk students. In R. L. Allington S. A. Walmsley, <u>No quick fix: Rethinking literacy in America's elementary schools</u> (pp. 19-41). New York: Teachers College Press, and Newark, DE: International Reading Association. {book chapter}

American Psychological Association. (1994). <u>Publication Manual of the American Psychological Association (4th ed.),</u> Washington, DC: APA.

http://www.amihome.com. Reading Recovery in California (home page). {Internet}

Clay, M. M. (1993a). <u>An observation survey: Of Early literacy achievement.</u> Portsmouth, NH: Heinemann. {book}

Clay, M. M. (1993b). <u>Reading Recovery: A guidebook for teachers in training.</u> Portsmouth, NH: Heinemann. {book}

Haneke, D. M. (1996, June 12). Balanced diet of reading approach is best. <u>Austin American Statesman,</u> p. A12. {newspaper article}

Lipson, M. Y., Wixson, K. K. (1996). <u>Assessment and instruction of reading writing disability: An interactive approach (2nd ed.).</u> New York: Addison-Wesley. {book}

http:www.readingrecovery.org. Reading Recovery. {Internet article}

Spiegel, D. L. (1995). A comparison of traditional remedial programs and Reading Recovery: Guidelines for Success for All programs. <u>Reading Teacher, 49</u> (2), 86-96. {journal}

L. Citations in Text (APA)

All citations in text follow APA format. As a "rule of thumb," you should present at least one citation per body paragraph. Again, ideas do not just "fall out of the sky." Where did your ideas come from? What inspired your notions? Acknowledge your sources. Master's theses and Doctoral dissertations must adhere to all APA formatting guidelines. You are accountable for this simplified version as important for assignments depending upon your teacher or professor.

1. APA for Ideas Cited In Text

There are three ways to indicate citation for sources of ideas in the text of your paper...

a. Fountas Pinnell (1996) found

b. In 1996, Fountas and Pinnell found

c. xxx (Fountas Pinnell, 1996).

[NOTE: No first names; only last names and dates]

2. APA for direct, Word-for-Word Quotes In Text

There are three ways to indicate citation for sources of actual verbage – word-for- word quotations – in the text of your paper...

a. Fountas and Pinnell (1996) say, "Reading and writing are complementary processes" (p. 13).

b. In a 1996 study, Fountas and Pinnell report "Reading and writing are complementary processes" (p. 13).

c. "Reading and writing are complementary processes" (Fountas Pinnell, 1996, p. 13).

[NOTE: only last names and dates; capital letter starts quote; no terminal punctuation at end of quote, just " then (source, date, p. __)]

M. Graphic Organizer

The graphic organizer graphically or pictorially presents the main ideas and the supporting details for your paper. You may select one of the samples in Appendices or create one of your own accomplishing the same purpose – organizing your ideas and details to enable you to write more coherently.

N. Attached Article

The attached article is a photocopy of the article(s) referenced; use a computer printout for Internet articles used. This helps you and your instructor identify plagiarism issues needing to be addressed.

Notes & Questions

O. Table IV-27-O--Paper Evaluation Rubric

Name_____ Fa___ Sp___ Su ___

Total points: ____/_____ = _____%

Paper	Match Goals Paper (_/20)	Follows Format Issues (__/20)	Organized Flow of Ideas (___/20)	Sentence Structure (__/20)	Grammar Spelling Mechanics (__/20)	Total Score (___/100)
1-Narrative: Précis/Abstract /Summary	____/ 20	____/ 20	_____/ 20	____/ 20	_____/ 20	_____ _/100
2- Expository: Précis, Abstract	___/ 20	___/ 20	____/ 20	___/ 20	____/ 20	____ /100
3- Expository: Action Research	___/ 20	___/ 20	____/ 20	___/ 20	____/ 20	____ /100
4- Expository: Review of Literature	___/ 20	___/ 20	____/ 20	___/ 20	___/ 20	____ /100
5- Expository: Compare/ Contrast	___/ 20	___/ 20	____/ 20	___/ 20	___/ 20	____ /100
6- Expository: Critique/ Analysis Evaluation	___/ 20	___/ 20	____/ 20	___/ 20	___/ 20	____ /100
7- Expository: Editorial/ Opinion	___/ 20	___/ 20	____/ 20	___/ 20	___/ 20	____ /100
Total Scores...	____ /140	___/ 140	____/ 140	___/ 140	____/ 140	__/ 700

P. Paper Evaluation (continued)

1. Overall Perceptions:

a. Well done. Proceed to next level. _____

b. Adequate, but would benefit from more work. _____

c. Definitely needs more review and practice. _____

d. Rank order of skills from stronger to weaker:

    1) Matching goals for paper _____

    2) Organization & Flow of ideas _____

    3) Sentence Structure _____

    4) Spelling, grammar, & mechanics _____

2. Suggestions for Improvement:

a. Use Graphic Organizers to organize ideas. _____

b. Use Outline to organize flow of ideas. _____

c. Follow KISS principle: keep it simple;
tighten it up. _____

d. Consider presentation;
Is it inviting to a reader? _____

e. Presentation: Is it easy for reader
to identify the key _____
    points or message you are presenting?

Q. Paper Evaluation Questions

1. Does the writing match the assignment? Follow required formatting? Include all components?

2. Is the flow of ideas coherent and well organized? Can you outline the paper in simple form?

3. Are sentence structures appropriate and "user friendly"?

4. Do spelling, grammar, or mechanical errors hinder your reading of the paper?

5. Additional Comments:

Notes & Questions

R. Title Page Practice

Use the example Title Page in Chapter 26 to make copies and practice creating high-quality title pages.

Chapter 27

Peer Reviewing, Revising, and Editing

A. Introduction

Writing improves when others provide feedback for the author. Feedback affirms or challenges the writer's ideas. Feedback also validates or challenges development of mechanical aspects of writing. This chapter discusses procedures for peer reviews, providing feedback, making suggestions for revising, and making suggestions for editing.

B. Peer Reviews

At all levels of schooling, including university professors, peer reviews provide feedback to writers – writers of articles, papers, books, etc. This text encourages you to use peer review of paragraphs and papers of your classmates and expects you to solicit from your classmates peer reviews of your writings. Reviewers from outside your class, while they may provide valuable and valid assistance, are not aware of the instruction and guidelines you are expected to follow. So, seek feedback from your classmates who are receiving the same instruction at the same time for paragraphs and papers for this course, or share with your reviewers what you are asking of them and the standards of writing excellence you are pursuing.

C. Feedback

You are probably asking, "What kind of feedback do I ask for?" or "What kind of feedback do I provide in a peer review?" Two levels of peer review provide feedback to the writer:

1. Revision. Check the organization and flow of ideas (including grammar) on the first draft as a basis for revision [Process step 3]; Outline their paragraph or paper at this point; Do the ideas flow logically? Is there coherence?

2. Editing. Check the mechanical, spelling, and punctuation aspects of later drafts as a basis for editing [Process step 5]; are there errors hindering your understanding?

Provide feedback for EITHER revising idea organization OR editing mechanical issues. DO NOT ADDRESS BOTH IN ONE REVIEW. Throughout peer reviews, try to retain the writer's own "voice" – as if they were speaking to you.

Procedurally, first, ask the writer... What are you asking for? Where are you in the process of this writing? Would you rather I use pencil, ink, highlighter, or red pen to indicate suggestions or identify areas for you to reconsider, modify, or correct? Always read through entire writing BEFORE making any comments. Always find at least one positive comment to make (whether or not it is solicited). Consider the significance of errors; set priorities; point out only 2-3 key issues at a time. Always try to retain the writer's own "voice."

D. Revising

Focus on the organization of ideas (including grammar), the purpose for which you are writing, and your intended audience. Be sure to get at least two peer reviews. Do you have <u>at least</u> three main ideas? (You may have more.) Does each main idea have <u>at least</u> three supporting details? (Again, you may have more). Does your writing address the purpose of your writing? Does your writing address the audience you intend it? You may need to revise several times to get the main ideas and the details to form a superstructure for your writing. Rewrite and rewrite until you feel comfortable with the flow of ideas and details.

E. Editing

Focus on spelling, punctuation, and mechanics in general. You are polishing your writing in preparation for publication, posting publicly, or evaluation. This is the last step of the writing process. Not every piece of writing makes it to this step. Not every piece of writing needs to be evaluated or graded. Take pride in your final product.

Now, let's write… in your own words

Ideas for Writing Topics

Chapter 28

Paper 1: Narrative: Abstract/ Summary/Précis Paper

A. Introduction

Write an **abstract** (brief statement of essential thoughts of book, article, etc.; summary). Write a **summary** (brief statement of main points or substance; abridgment). Write a **précis** (a concise abridgment; summary; abstract). These are approximately the same assignment, so select whichever you prefer, but be aware of the various terms instructors use when calling for this type of assignment. This should be the easiest paper to write.

B. Procedure

The following steps will help you write this assignment:

1. Select a brief book or short story.

2. Generate a title page; more help is available in Chapters 18 and 24.

3. Identify the key points the author makes; there should be at least three.

4. Log the key main ideas on a graphic organizer; see Chapter 17 for more help. Use words, not sentences.

5. On your graphic organize, log the details supporting each main idea; there should be at least three, but list all significant details under the main idea they support or explain.

6. Create the three-level outline/table of contents; guidelines are in Chapters 16 and 24.

7. Write an introduction paragraph to introduce the topic's main ideas. Helps are available in Chapters 16, 24, and 26.

8. Write the Body: a paragraph for each main idea or key topic; support main ideas with details presented. Be sure to cite sources of information – at least one citation per body paragraph – in this case, per main idea. Consult Chapters 24 and 26 for assistance.

9. Solicit peer reviews for revising the flow of ideas. See Chapters 16, 24, and 27 for help.

10. Solicit peer reviews for editing mechanical errors. See Chapters 16, 24, and 27 for help.

11. Write the summary. Consult Chapter 16, 19, 24, and 26 for guidelines and helps.

12. Write the conclusion. Consult guidelines presented in Chapters 16, 24, and 26.

13. Write your personal response to the material your have read and written about. See Chapters 24 and 26 for guidelines and helps.

14. Have a final draft peer review before you submit it – just in case there's a need.

15. Generate a reference list of sources consulted for this paper. See Chapters 16, 24, and 26 for guidelines and helps.

16. Polish your graphic organizer and attach it to the paper.

17. Attach photocopies of articles or printouts of Internet articles to your paper.

18. Double-check your checklist of components, parts, and pieces for final presentation.

19. Submit your final copy for evaluation or publication.

20. Take pride in your final product!

D. Practice Writing Narrative Abstract/ Summary/Précis

Directions: Write a brief, one paragraph Abstract/Summary/Précis about your all-time favorite novel.

_____

_____

_____

_____

_____

_____

_____

_____

_____

_____

==

An exemplary writer uses such colorful and rich description the reader feels like she is right there – experiencing it first-hand.

=================================

Chapter 29

Paper 2: Expository: Abstract/ Summary/Précis Paper

A. Introduction

Write an **abstract** (brief statement of essential thoughts of book, article, etc.; summary). Write a **summary** (brief statement of main points or substance; abridgment). Write a **précis** (a concise abridgment; summary; abstract). These are approximately the same assignment, so select whichever you prefer, but be aware of the various terms instructors may use when calling for this type of assignment. This should be the easiest paper to write. This paper differs from the last Abstract paper in that this one is for expository text. The following steps will help you.

B. Procedure

1. Select a brief article on math, science, social studies, etc. (not a narrative story).

2. Generate a title page; more help is available in Chapters 18 and 24.

3. Identify the key points the author makes; there should be at least three.

4. Log the key main ideas on a graphic organizer; see Chapter 17 for more help. Use words, not sentences.

5. On your graphic organize, log the details supporting each main idea; there should be at least three, but list all significant details under the main idea they support or explain.

6. Create the three-level outline/table of contents; guidelines are in Chapters 16 and 24.

7. Write an introduction paragraph to introduce the topic's main ideas. Helps are available in Chapters 16, 24, and 26.

8. Write the Body: a paragraph for each main idea or key topic; support main ideas with details presented. Be sure to cite sources of information – at least one citation per body paragraph – in this case, per main idea. Consult Chapters 24 and 26 for assistance.

9. Solicit peer reviews for revising the flow of ideas. See Chapters 16, 24, and 27 for help.

10. Solicit peer reviews for editing mechanical errors. See Chapters 16, 24, and 27 for help.

11. Write the summary. Consult Chapter 16, 19, 24, and 26 for guidelines and helps.

12. Write the conclusion. Consult guidelines presented in Chapters 16, 24, and 26.

13. Write your personal response to the material your have read and written about. See Chapters 24 and 26 for guidelines and helps.

14. Have a final draft peer review before you submit it – just in case there's a need.

15. Generate a reference list of sources consulted for this paper. See Chapters 16, 24, and 26 for guidelines and helps.

16. Polish your graphic organizer and attach it to the paper.

17. Attach photocopies of articles or printouts of Internet articles to your paper.

18. Double-check your checklist of components, parts, and pieces for final presentation.

19. Submit your final copy for evaluation or publication.

20. Take pride in your final product!

C. Practice Writing Expository Summary/ Abstract/Précis

Directions: Write a brief, one paragraph Abstract/Summary/Précis about your all-time favorite animal.

_____

_____

_____

_____

_____

_____

_____

_____

_____

_____

"Give me the facts…
Just the facts."

(Sgt. Joe Friday, <u>Dragnet</u>, 1960s TV series)

Notes & Questions

Grammar Improves Writing

Chapter 30

Paper 3: Expository: Action Research Paper

A. Introduction

Action Research is research you, the individual writer, actively observe and record. Usually, observing and recording at least ten occurrences of the issue at hand is sufficient for gathering data for this paper, though it is an insufficient sampling for most action research assignments. Examples of action research include the following: (Asking at least ten people) What is your favorite dessert? What is your favorite ice cream? What is your favorite food? What is your favorite pet? What is your all-time favorite vacation spot? What is your favorite sport? What is your favorite basketball team? Be creative! Do not be limited by these examples though any of these ideas is fine to use as the basis for gathering your data. Some students have used email to gather data, too. This also should be an easy paper to write as well as fun to carry out the research. The following steps will help you:

B. Procedure

1. Select a topic requiring brief, simple action research -- limiting the scope for this practice paper. Action research consists of live observations of occurrences. Gather your data (in person, via writing, or via email. Set up a grid to tally your observations.

2. Conduct your research. Analyze your results. Summarize your data – clustering and totaling responses.

3. Generate a title page; more help is available in Chapters 18 and 24.

4. Identify the key points the author makes; there should be at least three.

5. Log the key main ideas on a graphic organizer; see Chapter 17 for more help. Use words, not sentences.

6. On your graphic organizer, log the details supporting each main idea; there should be at least three, but list all significant details under the main idea they support or explain.

7. Create the three-level outline/table of contents; guidelines are in Chapters 16 and 24.

8 Write an introduction paragraph to introduce the topic's main ideas. Helps are available in Chapters 16, 24, and 26.

9. Write the Body: a paragraph for each main idea or key topic; support main ideas with details presented. Be sure to cite sources of information – at least one citation per body paragraph – in this case, per main idea. Consult Chapters 24 and 26 for assistance.

10. Solicit peer reviews for revising the flow of ideas. See Chapters 16, 24, and 27 for help.

11. Solicit peer reviews for editing mechanical errors. See Chapters 16, 24, and 27 for help.

12. Write the summary. Consult Chapter 16, 19, 24, and 26 for guidelines and helps.

13. Write the conclusion. Consult guidelines presented in Chapters 16, 24, and 26.

14. Write your personal response to the material your have read and written about. See Chapters 24 and 26 for guidelines and helps.

15. Have a final draft peer review before you submit it – just in case there's a need.

16. Generate a reference list of sources consulted for this paper. See Chapters 16, 24, and 26 for guidelines and helps.

17. Polish your graphic organizer and attach it to the paper.

18. Attach photocopies of articles or printouts of Internet articles to your paper.

19. Double-check your checklist of components, parts, and pieces for final presentation.

20. Submit your final copy for evaluation or publication.

21. Take pride in your final product!

C. Action Research Practice

Directions: Write a brief (one paragraph) sample of Action Research. List at least 3 points of findings. Include Introduction, summary, conclusion, and personal response.

_____

_____

_____

_____

_____

_____

_____

_____

_____

_____

Chapter 31

Paper 4: Expository:
Review of Literature Paper

A. Introduction

      This assignment also may be labeled "a research paper" using journal articles, books, or other references. The purpose is to see what information is available on the topic. Skim at least three short articles on a topic of your choosing. Identify at least three key points of research findings from each source/article. Graphically represent your findings including overlapping points. This should be a useful paper to write for any subject. The following steps may make it easier for you to carry out this assignment:

B. Procedure

1. Select and read three brief articles on a topic of your choosing.

2. Generate a title page; more help available in Chapters 18 and 24.

3. Identify the key points the author(s) make(s); there should be at least three.

4. Log the key main ideas on a graphic organizer; see Chapter 17 for more help. Use words not sentences.

5. Log on your graphic organizer the details supporting each main idea; there should be at least three, but list all significant details under the main idea they support or explain.

6. Create the three-level outline/table of contents; guidelines in Chapters 16 and 24.

7. Write an introduction paragraph to introduce the topic's main ideas. Helps available in Chapters 16, 24, and 26.

8. Write the Body… a paragraph for each main idea or key topic; support main ideas with details presented. Be sure to cite sources of information – at least one citation per body paragraph – in this case, per main idea. Consult Chapters 24 and 26 for assistance.

9. Solicit peer reviews for revising the flow of ideas. See Chapters 16, 24, and 27 for help.

10. Solicit peer reviews for editing mechanical errors. See Chapters 16, 24, and 27 for help.

11. Write the summary. Consult Chapter 16, 19, 24, and 26 for guidelines and helps.

12. Write the conclusion. Consult guidelines presented in Chapters 16, 24, and 26.

13. Write your personal response to the material your have read and written about. See Chapters 24 and 26 for guidelines and helps.

14. Have a final draft peer review before you submit it – just in case there's a need.

15. Generate a reference list of sources consulted for this paper. See Chapters 16, 24, and 26 for guidelines and helps.

16. Polish up your graphic organizer and attach it to the paper.

17. Attach photocopies of articles or printouts of Internet articles to your paper.

18. Double-check your checklist of components, parts, and pieces for final presentation.

19. Submit your final copy for evaluation or publication.

20. Take pride in your final product!

C. Practice Writing Review of Literature

Directions: Skim at least three short articles on a topic of your choosing. Write a brief (1 paragraph) sample of Review of Literature. List at least three points of research findings. Include introduction, summary, conclusion, and personal response.

_____

_____

_____

_____

_____

_____

_____

_____

_____

_____

_____

Avoid Plagiarism!!

Read sources. Discuss with someone.

Write paper using your own words.

Practice truth and honesty.

Chapter 32

Paper 5: Expository: Compare-Contrast Paper

A. Introduction

This assignment also may be labeled "a research paper using journal articles" or a Review of Literature paper. Compare and contrast the similarities and differences of at least two (but preferably not more than three for this assignment) items, programs, topics, issues, etc. Acceptable compare/contrast papers range from comparing dogs and cats as pets to comparing various business or educational programs at a specific level. This should be a useful paper to write enabling you to write more successfully papers for other courses. The following steps may make it easier for you to do this assignment:

B. Procedure

1. Select two to three things to compare and contrast.

2. Generate a title page; more help available in Chapters 18 and 24.

3. Identify the key points the author(s) make(s); there should be at least three.

4. Log the key main ideas on a graphic organizer; see Chapter 17 for more help. Use words not sentences.

5. Log on your graphic organizer the details supporting each main idea; there should be at least three, but list all significant details under the main idea they support or explain.

6. Create the three-level outline/table of contents; guidelines in Chapters 16 and 24.

7. Write an introduction paragraph to introduce the topic's main ideas. Helps available in Chapters 16, 24, and 26.

8. Write the Body... a paragraph for each main idea or key topic; support main ideas with details presented. Be sure to cite sources of information – at least one citation per body paragraph – in this case, per main idea. Consult Chapters 24 and 26 for assistance.

9. Solicit peer reviews for revising the flow of ideas. See Chapters 16, 24, and 27 for help.

10. Solicit peer reviews for editing mechanical errors. See Chapters 16, 24, and 27 for help.

11. Write the summary. Consult Chapter 16, 19, 24, and 26 for guidelines and helps.

12. Write the conclusion. Consult guidelines presented in Chapters 16, 24, and 26.

13. Write your personal response to the material your have read and written about. See Chapters 24 and 26 for guidelines and helps.

14. Have a final draft peer review before you submit it – just in case there's a need.

15. Generate a reference list of sources consulted for this paper. See Chapters 16, 24, and 26 for guidelines and helps.

16. Polish up your graphic organizer and attach it to the paper.

17. Attach photocopies of articles or printouts of Internet articles to your paper.

18. Double-check your checklist of components, parts, and pieces for final presentation.

19. Submit your final copy for evaluation or publication.

20. Take pride in your final product!

C. Practice Writing Compare/Contrast

Directions: Write a one-page "paper" to compare and contrast having a dog or a cat for a pet. Articulate at least three points of comparing the two and at least three contrasting points for each pet. Introduction, summary, conclusion, and personal response should be included.

_____

_____

_____

_____

_____

_____

_____

_____

_____

_____

_____

Notes & Questions

Chapter 33

Paper 6: Expository: Critique/ Analysis/Evaluation Paper

A. Introduction

This assignment also may relate to or be part of several of the above papers. Analyze the strengths and weaknesses of something as a basis for the critique or evaluation. For example, critique the evening news on TV, the sports or music program at your school, college advisory service available through the school's counseling and guidance office, etc. Be creative. Select a topic of interest to you. This should be a useful paper to write enabling you to write more successfully papers for various courses. The following steps may make it easier for you to do this assignment:

B. Procedure

1. Select some thing to critique or evaluate.

2. Generate a title page; more help available in Chapters 18 and 24.

3. Identify the key points the author(s) make(s); there should be at least three.

4. Log the key main ideas on a graphic organizer; see Chapter 17 for more help. Use words not sentences.

5. Log on your graphic organizer the details supporting each main idea; there should be at least three, but list all significant details under the main idea they support or explain.

6. Create the three-level outline/table of contents; guidelines in Chapters 16 and 24.

7. Write an introduction paragraph to introduce the topic's main ideas. Helps available in Chapters 16, 24, and 26.

8. Write the Body... a paragraph for each main idea or key topic; support main ideas with details presented. Be sure to cite sources of information – at least one citation per body paragraph – in this case, per main idea. Consult Chapters 24 and 26 for assistance.

9. Solicit peer reviews for revising the flow of ideas. See Chapters 16, 24, and 27 for help.

10. Solicit peer reviews for editing mechanical errors. See Chapters 16, 24, and 27 for help.

11. Write the summary. Consult Chapter 16, 19, 24, and 26 for guidelines and helps.

12. Write the conclusion. Consult guidelines presented in Chapters 16, 24, and 26.

13. Write your personal response to the material your have read and written about. See Chapters 24 and 26 for guidelines and helps.

14. Have a final draft peer review before you submit it – just in case there's a need.

15. Generate a reference list of sources consulted for this paper. See Chapters 16, 24, and 26 for guidelines and helps.

16. Polish up your graphic organizer and attach it to the paper.

17. Attach photocopies of articles or printouts of Internet articles to your paper.

18. Double-check your checklist of components, parts, and pieces for final presentation.

19. Submit your final copy for evaluation or publication.

20. Take pride in your final product!

C. Practice Writing a Critique or Evaluation

Directions: Write a one-page "paper" to critique or evaluate your extra-curricular activities available to you such as band, art, sports, etc. Articulate at least three strengths and at least three weaknesses for each item. Be sure to include an Introduction, summary, conclusion, and personal response.

_____

_____

_____

_____

_____

_____

_____

_____

_____

_____

_____

Notes & Questions

Grammar Improves Writing

Chapter 34

Paper 7: Expository: Editorial/Personal Opinion/Personal Reflection/Position Paper

A. Introduction

An editorial/opinion/reflection/position paper assignment may be labeled by any of these titles as well as a persuasive paper. Usually, the point is to take a stand for or against an issue – often to solve a problem. This also should be a useful paper to write enabling you to write more successful papers for various courses as well as good preparation for formal debates.

C. Procedure

1. Select a topic of your choosing.

2. Generate a title page; more help available in Chapters 18 and 24.

3. Identify the key points the author(s) make(s); there should be at least three.

4. Log the key main ideas on a graphic organizer; see Chapter 17 for more help. Use words not sentences.

5. Log on your graphic organizer the details supporting each main idea; there should be at least three, but list all significant details under the main idea they support or explain.

6. Create the three-level outline/table of contents; guidelines in Chapters 16 and 24.

7. Write an introduction paragraph to introduce the topic's main ideas. Helps available in Chapters 16, 24, and 26.

8. Write the Body... a paragraph for each main idea or key topic; support main ideas with details presented. Be sure to cite sources of information – at least one citation per body paragraph – in this case, per main idea. Consult Chapters 24 and 26 for assistance.

9. Solicit peer reviews for revising the flow of ideas. See Chapters 16, 24, and 27 for help.

10. Solicit peer reviews for editing mechanical errors. See Chapters 16, 24, and 27 for help.

11. Write the summary. Consult Chapter 16, 19, 24, and 26 for guidelines and helps.

12. Write the conclusion. Consult guidelines presented in Chapters 16, 24, and 26.

13. Write your personal response to the material your have read and written about. See Chapters 24 and 26 for guidelines and helps.

14. Have a final draft peer review before you submit it – just in case there's a need.

15. Generate a reference list of sources consulted for this paper. See Chapters 16, 24, and 26 for guidelines and helps.

16. Polish up your graphic organizer and attach it to the paper.

17. Attach photocopies of articles or printouts of Internet articles to your paper.

18. Double-check your checklist of components, parts, and pieces for final presentation.

19. Submit your final copy for evaluation or publication.

20. Take pride in your final product!

C. Practice Writing Editorial/Personal Opinion/Personal Reflection/ Position Paper

Directions: Write a brief editorial (at least three paragraphs) expressing your personal opinion and personal reflection to state a position regarding... Should "under God" be removed from the Pledge of Allegiance to the American flag? Articulate at least three points. Include introduction, summary, and conclusion.

_____

_____

_____

_____

_____

_____

_____

_____

_____

_____

_____

_____

Notes & Questions

Chapter 35

Practicing Writing Paper Components

A. Introduction

The following pages provide additional practice in the various components of writing a paper. Use as needed, if at all. Note, more practice on most of these components of a paper are afforded in the preceding chapters of this book.

B. Practicing a Title Page

Use the example Title Page in Chapters 24 and 26 to make copies and practice creating high-quality title pages.

C. Practicing Graphic Organizers

Make photocopies of the Graphic Organizers provided in chapter 17 of this text. Make as many as you need to practice organizing your ideas on a Graphic Organizer.

D. Practicing a Three-Level Outline/ Table of Contents

Write a three-level outline on the topic of your choice. This becomes your Table of Contents. Be sure the body has at least three main points each supported by at least three details; remember, you may have more key points and more details. On your outline, be sure to include the introduction, summary/conclusion, and reference list/ bibliography headings.

I._____ [Intro: topic]

II._____ [Body]

   A._____ [Key Point 1]

      1._____

      2._____

      3._____

   B._____ [Key Point 2]

      1._____

      2._____

      3._____

   C._____ [Key Point 3]

      1._____

      2._____

      3._____

III._____ [Summary]

IV._____ [Conclusion]

V._____ [Personal Response]

_____ [Reference List]

_____ [Graphic Organizer]

_____ [Attached Articles]

Grammar Improves Writing

E. Practicing an Introduction Paragraph

Write an introductory paragraph for your topic outlined in # 2 above.

_____

_____

_____

_____

_____

_____

_____

_____

_____

F. Practice Writing Body Paragraphs

Write a (brief) body of at least three paragraphs, each clearly having a main idea and at least three supporting details.

_____

_____

_____

_____

_____

_____

_____

_____

_____

_____

_____

_____

_____

G. Practice Writing a Summary Paragraph

Write a brief (one to two sentences) summary of your writing above.

H. Practice Writing a Conclusion Paragraph

Write a brief conclusion (one or two sentences) about the writing you wrote above.

_____

_____

_____

_____

_____

_____

_____

I. Practice Writing a Personal Response Paragraph

Write a brief personal response (1-3 sentences) about your writing.

_____

_____

_____

_____

_____

_____

_____

M. Practice Writing a Reference List

Write a sample Reference List including at least three (imaginative but realistic) sources, one being an Internet source. Use APA format.

_____

_____

_____

_____

_____

N. Practice Writing with APA Citations in Text

1. How would you provide citation for the following quotation cited in the text of a paper?

"Give me liberty or give me death!"

2. How would you provide citation for the following general idea cited in the text of a paper?

"Democracy is a government by the people, for the people, and of the people."

O. Practice Revising

Directions: Revise the following paragraph to better organize the ideas:

Reading and writing go hand in hand. Speaking and listening are related, too. I like speaking best of all. Good readers usually write well, and good writers usually read well. Reading is a receptive language skill, whereas writing is an expressive language skill. I don't think reading and writing use the same basic skills, but I'm not sure. There are three steps in reading: pre-reading (getting ready), reading, and post-reading (reflecting on what you read). There are eight steps in writing: pre-writing (brainstorming), First draft, revising, editing, and publishing. I enjoy both reading and writing; I find them relaxing.

P. Practice Editing

Directions: Edit the following paragraph to correct spelling, grammar, and punctuation:

"all we can do is hang on to our colons punctuation is bound to change like the rest of language punctuation is made for man not man for punctuation a good sentence should be intelligible without the help of punctuation in most cases and if you get in a muddle with your dots and dashes you may need to simplify your thoughts and shorten your sentence " [Philip Howard] What questions would you like to ask mr howard what bothers you about his paragraph quoted above sure it is a long sentence but can you write one that effectively illustrates the need for punctuation of various kinds i think that might be difficult

Q. Practicing Peer Review and Feedback

Provide succinct peer review feedback to the writer of either paragraph one or two above. Provide at least one positive comment. Focus on not more than three points.

_____

_____

_____

_____

_____

_____

_____

R. Practice Writing an Abstract or Summary

Read the following paragraphs and do one of the following:

1. Write an **abstract** of the text {brief statement of essential thoughts of book, article, etc.};

2. Write a **summary** of the text {brief statement of main points or substance; abridgment};

3. Write a **précis** of the text{a concise abridgment; summary; abstract}.

As children move from grade to grade, their attitude toward writing generally worsens. Knudson's research (1991, 1992, 1993) also found younger students have more positive attitudes toward writing than older students. This long-range decline in positive writing attitudes parallels changes in other academic areas, especially reading (McKenna, Kear, Ellsworth, 1995). Many factors undoubtedly play a part in this trend. For example, children must eventually come to realize writing, good writing in particular, is effortful. In addition, many of their experiences with writing may involve tedium, lack of choice, and negative feedback. For these reasons, teachers face an uphill battle as they attempt to foster positive writing attitudes in their students. We believe this battle can be won. Effective teaching strategies and engaging opportunities to write successfully can make real inroads in student perspectives. [Kear, et. al., 2000, The Reading Teacher, 54 (1), pp. 10-23.]

_____

_____

_____

_____

_____

_____

_____

S. Practice writing Action Research

Write a brief (one paragraph) sample of Action Research. List at least three points of findings. Include introduction, summary, conclusion, and personal response.

_____

_____

_____

_____

_____

_____

_____

_____

T. Practice Writing a Review of Literature

Skim at least three short articles on a topic of your choosing. Write a brief (one paragraph) sample of Review of Literature. List at least three points of research findings. Include introduction, summary, conclusion, and personal response.

_____

_____

_____

_____

_____

_____

_____

_____

_____

U. Compare/Contrast Practice

Write a one-page "paper" to compare and contrast having a dog or a cat for a pet. Articulate at least three points of comparing the two and at least three contrasting points for each pet. Introduction, summary, conclusion, and personal response should be included.

_____

_____

_____

_____

_____

_____

V. Practicing Writing Critique/ Analysis/Evaluation

Read a brief article. Critically analyze and evaluate the validity and the value of the information printed. Articulate at least three points of evaluation. Introduction, summary, conclusion, and personal response should be included.

_____

_____

_____

_____

_____

_____

W. Practice Writing Editorial/Personal Opinion/Personal Reflection/ Position Paper

Write a brief editorial (at least three paragraphs) expressing your personal opinion and personal reflection to state a position regarding students' rights to attend the public or private school of their choice. How does this relate to the School Voucher issue? Articulate at least three points. Include introduction, summary, conclusion, and personal response.

Part V

Appendices and Other Resources

Epilogue

Addendum: Answer Keys

Appendix A: Writing Tips in Brief

Appendix B: Spelling With Phonics: Phonics in Brief

Appendix C: Spelling With Syllables, Roots, Affixes, and Contractions

Appendix D: Citation Formatting Styles: MLA, Turabian, and Chicago

Appendix E: Personal Résumé, Cover Letter,
and Professional Portfolio

Glossary

Index

Bibliography

Some Thoughts to Ponder

* * * * *

My computer and "my tongue is the pen of a ready skillful writer…" or

"I am as full of words as the speediest writer pouring out his story".

What does this mean? What are you ready to write?

[source: Psalm (45:1)]

* * * * *

"Write all the words I have spoken to you in a book."
What does this suggest? What words or ideas have you heard?
[source: Jeremiah 30:2]

* * * * * *

Epilogue

To Those Who Use this Resource,

Underlying Principle: The principle underlying this work is **"Grammar Improves Writing."** I firmly believe success in handling grammatical issues dramatically affects writing efficiency.

Perspective: I come to this project with the perspective of language, literacy, and remedial reading and writing instruction. This is a unique vantage point because most texts and resources for writing are created by English majors who usually specialize in an area of literature studies. Thus, I know working through this resource enhances every aspect of functionality with the English language – reading, writing, speaking, and listening.

Vision: My vision is to review the basics of grammar and writing specific kinds of papers – affording individuals the opportunity to "plug the gaps" in these skills so they feel more relaxed and empowered to share their thoughts in writing.

Challenge: The challenge facing me was how to organize these concepts and principles in such a way the principle and the vision can become a living reality embodying my perspective.

My sincerest desire and objective is that you experience a dramatic improvement in your writing by digesting and implementing the contents of this resource. As you review many considerations for word choice, may you find it easier to select more appropriate words to generate sensible sentences. As you review various aspects of sentences, may your be empowered to use this information to generate powerful paragraphs. As you review various aspects of paragraphs, may you write well-organized papers to persuade your readers to seriously consider what you share in writing about any subject.

I pray this academically-based book positively affects and enhances your life. May you come away believing in yourself as a competent writer and a more valuable person in our world.

I invite you to provide me feedback. Which part or chapter helped you the most? What would like to see added to this book to make it more helpful? What do you suggest be deleted? I invite any other comments you may desire to share with me. All feedback, suggestions, and comments may be sent to me at...

Dianne M. Haneke PhD

12408 Johnson Road

Manor, TX 78653 USA

Thank you for the privilege of serving you in this capacity. It has been my pleasure.

Sincerely,

Dianne M. Haneke, author and fellow sojourner

Addendum: Answer Keys

Part I-Answer Key

Chapter 1:

I-1.1.   R: Listening -- Reading

I-1.2.   Acquire: 1) listening, 2) speaking, 3) reading, and 4) writing

I-1.2.   Size: 1) listening, 2) reading, 3) speaking, and 4) writing

Writing is last and smallest vocabulary; we are less comfortable writing.

Chapter 2:

I-2.1.   1) see 2) hear 3) feel (large muscles) 4) touch (small muscles)

I-2.2.   1) word, language 2) number, logic 3) art, drawing 4) music, rhythm, beat 5) full body, dance, acting 6) cooperative, small group 7) independent, self 8) nature, out-of-doors

Chapter 3:

I-3P-1. Parts of Speech Quiz:
1) D 2) A 3) E 4) B 5) C 6) F 7) J 8) G 9) H 10) I.

I-3P-2. Parts of Speech Pre-test 2:
1) N 2) C 3) PN 4) N 5) V 6) PR 7) ADJ 8) N 9) PR 10) V 11) ADJ 12) ADJ 13) N 14) PR 15) PN 16) ADJ 17) N 18)PN 19) V 20) ADV

21) C 22) ADJ 23) N 24) V 25) ADV 26) I 27) V 28) N 29) ADV 30) HV 31) PN 32) V 33) V [34] N.

I-3-1. Nouns:
A. people, order, union, justice, tranquility, defense, welfare, blessings, liberty, posterity.
B. Nature, God, Creator, United States, Constitution, United States, America.

I-3-2. Pronouns:
1) them, her 2) us 3) They, she She, whomever 5) Whomever He, himself 7) Whose, we
8) They, we 9) them, me 10) whom Them 12) I, she, He, who Whose 14) He, she.

I-3-3. Adjectives and Articles:
1) beautiful, spacious, amber, purple, mountain, the, fruited, shining.
2) The, the, the, one, indivisible.
3) A, grand, ole, a high-flying, The, the, the, the, the, Every, the, a, Ole, your, the, grand, ole.

I-3-4. Verbs and Helping Verbs:
11) hold, are(HV), created, are(HV), endowed, are.
12) Form, establish, insure, provide, promote, secure, do(HV), ordain, establish.
1) is 2) expects 3) have 4) shed 5) Do, does 6) marches, beat 7) need 8) do cause 10) is, say 11) Does, have, go 12) makes 13) upsets.

I-3-5. Adverbs:

1) very, slightly, grossly; 2) fairly, quickly, very; 3) extremely, certainly, accurately; 4) very, suddenly, skillfully; 5) artfully, horrendously; 6) enthusiastically, wildly, accurately, closely; 7) extremely, well; 8) lavishly; 10) painstakingly, very, finely; 11) gracefully.

I-3-6. Prepositions:

A) of the United States, in order, to form, for the common defense, of liberty, to ourselves and our posterity, for the United States, of America.

B) to the flag, of the United States, of America, to the Republic, for which it stands, under God, with liberty and justice, for all.

B) For spacious skies, for amber fields, of grain, for purple mountains' majesties, above the fruited plain, on thee, with brotherhood, from sea, to shining sea.

I-3-7. Conjunctions:

1) and, and; 2) and, and, and, where, or; 3) and, however, so, and; 4) after, and, and, and, and, and, and, so; 5) although, because, nor, nor, nor, and.

I-3-8. Interjections:

1) Wow! 2) Yippee! 3) Whew! Me, too! 4) What a shame! 5) Heavens! 6) Aha! 7) No! 8) Yes! 9) I do declare! 10) Ah! 11) Mmm! 12) Yes, Sir! 13) Watch out! 14) Run! 15) All right! 16) Run, boy, run! 17) Sink it! 19) Thank Heavens! 20) Congratulations, John! 21) Yikes! 23) Oops! 24) Look out! 25) Wow!

I-3. Parts of Speech Mastery Check-up:

I (PR) pledge (V) allegiance (N) to (PRE) the (ART) flag (N) of (PRE) the (ART) United (N) States (N) of (PRE) America (N) and (CON) to (PRE) the (ART) Republic (N) for (PRE) which (PN) it (PN) stands (V) one (ADJ) nation (N) under (PRE) God (N), indivisible (ADJ), with (PRE) liberty (N) and (CON) justice (N) for (PRE) all (N).

1) Super (ADJ) job (N)! {or INT} Each; (ADJ) team (N) ingenuously (ADV) demonstrated (V) its (PN) part (N) of (PRE) speech (N) – meeting (V) different (ADJ) learning (ADJ) modalities (N) and (CON) the (ART) eight (ADJ) multiple (ADJ) intelligences (N).

2) The (ART) students (N) all (ADJ) worked (V) hard (ADV) to (PRE) prepare (V) their (PN) parts (ADJ) of (PRE) speech (N) presentations (N).

3) Team (N) five (ADJ) illustrated (V) how (ADV) adverbs (N) add (V) to (PRE) verbs (N), adjectives (N), and (CON) other (ADJ) adverbs (N).

4) Team (N) six (ADJ) cleverly (ADV) demonstrated (V) prepositions (N) showing (V) positional (ADJ) relationships (N) between (PRE) words (N).

5) Team (n) one (ADJ) presented (V) nouns (N) as (PRE) the (ART) names (N) of (PRE) persons (N), places (N), and (CON) things (N).

6) Team (N) three (ADJ) involved (V) everyone (PN) in (PRE) a (ART) game (N) to (PRE) match (V) adjectives (N) to (PRE) nouns (N).

7) Team (N) four (ADJ) engaged (V) the (ART) class (N) to (PRE) actively (ADV) demonstrate (V) verbs (N) through (PRE) some (ADJ) skits (N).

8) Team (N) two (ADJ) vividly (ADV) depicted (V) pronouns (N) taking (V) the (ART) place (N) of (PRE) nouns (N).

Dianne M. Haneke, Ph.D.

Chapter 4:

I-4-1. Homonym Pre-test:
1) C 2) A 3) B 4) B 5) A 6) A 7) B 8) my 9) A 10) C 11) B 12) C 13) A 14) B 15) A 16) B 17) B 18) A 19) A 20) B.

I-4-3. Commonly Confused Words Pre-test-1:
1) A 2) B 3) B 4) A 5) A 6) B 7) C 8) A 9) B 10) B 11) D 12) C 13) A 14) B 15) B 16) D 17) C 18) A 19) D 20) C.

I-4-4. Commonly Confused Words Pre-test-2:
1) B 2) A 3) A 4) B 5) B 6) A 7) A 8) B 9) B 10) A 11) B 12) A 13) B 14) A 15) B 16) A 17) A 18) B 19) B 20) A.

I-4-5. Commonly Confused Words Pre-test-3:
1)B 2) A 3) A 4) B 5) B 6) A 7) B 8) A 9) A 10) B 11) A 12) B 13) B 14) A 15) A 16) B 17) C 18 B 19) A 20) B.

Chapter 5:

I-5-1. Pre-test on Plurals:
1) A 2) B 3) B 4) B 5) B 6) A 7) C 8) C 9) C 10) C 11) B 12) A.

I-5-2. Pre-test on Possessives:
1) C 2) B 3) C 4) C 5) C 6) C 7) A 8) A 9) D 10) B 11) D 12) A.

I-5-5. Plurals Posttest:
1) C 2) C 3) A 4) C 5) C 6) A 7) B 8) A 9) B 10) D 11) A 12) C.

I-5-6. Possessives Posttest:
1) D 2) B 3) A 4) B 5) A 6) D 7) A 8) D 9) B 10) A 11) B 12) B.

Chapter 6:

I-6-1. Antonym Pre-test:

1) A 2) B 3) C 4) D 5) B 6) B 7) E 8) A 9) B 10) C 11) C 12) A 13) C.

I-6-2. Synonym Pre-test:

1) A 2) C 3) E 4) C 5) A 6) B 7) C 8) B 9) C 10) B 11) A 12) C 13) D.

I-6-3. Analogies Pre-test:

1) B 2) A 3) D 4) B 5) A 6) C 7) B 8) A or D 9) C 10) B 11) A 12) A 13) B 14) A or B 15) C 16) A 17) D 18) B 19) B or C 20) C 21) A 22) B.

I-6-7. Antonyms – Posttest-1:

1) A 2) A 3) D 4) B 5) A 6) D 7) C 8) B 9) A 10) B 11) B 12) A.

I-6-8. Synonyms – Posttest-2:

1) A 2) B 3) C 4) B 5) C 6) C 7) A 8) B 9) C 10) A 11) C 12) A.

I-6-9. Analogies – Posttest-3:

1) B 2) A 3) A 4) B 5) C 6) A 7) B 8) A B or C 9) C 10) B 11) B 12) B 13) C.

Part II-Answer Key

Chapter 7:

II-7-1. Pretest 4 Kinds of Sentences:
1) IN 2) D 3) E 4) IN 5) D 6) IN 7) D 8) IM 9) E 10) IN 11) D 12) IN 13) D 14) D 15) D 16) D 17) D or E 18) D 19) D or E 20) D or E 21) E 22) IN 23) D 24) IN 25) D.

2) Practice: Answers will vary.

Chapter 8:

II-8-1. Simple, Complete, Compound Sentences Pre-test:

A. Whole sentences…

1) circle: boy ; box: ran; vertical line: boy | ran; one line: <u>The tall, lanky farm boy</u>

two lines: <u>ran quickly across the field chasing the horse.</u>

2) circle: Rebecca, Mary, and Joan; box: studied; vertical line: Joan | studied

one line: <u>Rebecca, Mary, and Joan;</u> two lines: <u>studied together for their chemistry final exam.</u>

3) circle: policeman; box: guided; vertical line: policeman | carefully; one line: <u>The tired, weary policeman;</u> two lines: <u>carefully guided motorists around the scene of the horrible accident.</u>

4) circle: Dean Smith; box: called; vertical line: smith | sternly; one line: <u>Stately Dean Smith</u>

two lines: <u>sternly called the four sophomore men into his office to reprimand them for their behavior.</u>

5) circle: Mom and dad; box: came; vertical line: dad | came; one line: <u>Mom and dad</u>

two lines: <u>came gladly to the Parents' Weekend and Homecoming activities, because they are proud alumnae.</u>

6) circle: Thomas, Britt, and Bill; box: tried out; vertical line: Bill | tried; one line: <u>Last night, Thomas, Britt, and Bill;</u> two lines: <u>tried out for the varsity basketball team</u>.

7) circle: professors; box: talk; vertical line: professors | often; one line: <u>Researching professors;</u> two lines: <u>often talk over the heads of their undergraduate students</u>.

8) circle: principal; box: makes; vertical line: principal | usually; one line: <u>A caring principal;</u> two lines: <u>usually makes all the difference in the world</u>.

B. Compound subjects... (circle)

9) Loretta, George, Tom, and Susan

10) Robert and Sharon

11) Tennis and swimming

12) James and Mary

13) Rob and Laura

14) Dennis and Charlene

C. Compound predicates... (box)

15) ate and drank

16) ran and greeted

17) play, walk, and swim

18) bought and attended

19) missed and lost

20) swims, plays, or jogs

Chapter 9:

II-9-1. Fragments Pretest:
1) C 2) F 3) F 4) C 5) F 6) C 7) C 8) F or C 9) F 10) C 11) F.

II-9-2. Run-ons Pretest:
12) RO 13) C 14) C 15) RO 16) RO17) C 18) C 19) RO 20) RO 21) C 22) C.

II-9-3. Punctuation Pretest:
1) I-incorrect; capitalize *Which*; remove comma after *donuts*.
2) C-correct.
3) I-incorrect; need comma after *mix* and before ".
4) C-correct.
5) I-incorrect; capitalize *How*; change final period to *?*.
6) C-correct.
7) I-incorrect; capitalize *Macaroni Grill*, *Red Lobster*, and *El Chico*; add commas after *Grill* and *Lobster*.
8) C-correct.
9) C-correct.
10) I-incorrect; capitalize *Where* and *San*; add *?* after *born*; add period at end of second sentence.
11) I-incorrect; change final period to *?*.

Chapter 10:

II-10-1. Subject-Verb Pretest:
1) DN 2) AN 3) AN 4) DN 5) DN 6) AN 7) AN (disagree tense) 8) DN (agree tense) 9) AN (agree tense) 10) DN (disagree tense) 11) AN (disagree tense) 12) DN (disagree tense) 13) AN (agree tense) 14) DN (agree tense) 15 AN 16) DN 17) AN 18) DN 19) DN 20) AN.

Chapter 11:

II-11-1. Pronoun-Antecedents:

1) girls; they; they>>girls.

2) team; its; its>>team.

3) class; their; their>>class (their papers).

4) friend and I; We; we>>friend and I.

5) John; him; him>>John.

6) Julie; She; She>>Julie.

7) Bob and Corey; their; their>>Bob and Corey.

8) Neither; his; his>>neither.

9) Each; her; her>>each.

10) Everyone; his; his>>everyone.

11) Nancy; her; her>>Nancy (her = possessive pronoun for car).

12) Planes; their; their>>planes.

13) You; your; your>>you.

14) Passengers; their; their>>passengers.

15) Crew; their; their>>crew (because each has his/her own luggage; they do not share the luggage; they share the flight.)

16) Jury; it; it>>jury (because a jury gives one verdict as a whole unit, not several verdicts; they agree on one verdict.)

17) Crewmen; their; their>>crewmen.

18) Council; its; its>>Council.

19) Members; their; their>>members.

20) Firemen; their; their>>firemen.

21) John and Mark; their; their>>John and Mark.

22) Debbie, Erik, and Alyssa; their; their>> Debbie, Erik, and Alyssa.

23) Family; its; its>>family.

24) Marie and Dominick; their; their>> Marie and Dominick.

25) John and Dianne; their; their>>motor home.

Chapter 12:

II-12-1. Verb Tense Pretest:
1) DN-AT ; 2) AN-AT; 3) AN-AT; 4) DN-AT; 5) DN-AT; 6) AN-AT; 7) AN-DT; 8) DN-AT; 9) AN-AT; 10) DN-DT; 11) DN-AT; 12) AN-AT

II-12-2. Verb Tense Pretest:
1)AN-DT; 2) DN-DT; 3) AN-AT; 4) DN-AT; 5) AN-AT; 6) AN-AT; 7) DN-AT; 8) DN-AT; 9) AN-AT; 10) AN-DT; 11) AN-AT.

Chapter 13:

II-13-1. Parallel Construction Pretest:
1) NP; ^to play sports. 2) NP; ^a tuner 3) NP; ^a swimmer. 4) P 5) P 6) NP; ^to scuba dive 7) NP; ^the tuba, ^the saxophone 8) NP; ^a piano 9) NP; ^made me anxious. 10) P 11) NP; ^an elk, ^an antelope 12) P.

II-13-2. Parallel Construction Pretest:
1) NP; ^one yellow tuna, ^one blue marlin 2) P 3) NP; ^With delight 4) NP; ^to stand, ^to walk 5) P 6) NP; ^likes basketball OR ^plays basketball, and enjoys football (typo) 7) P; 8) typo: computers hardware) 9) NP; ^traveling, ^enjoys painting 10) P; ^likes fishing 11) better) 12) P 13) P 14) P.

Chapter 14:

II-14-1. Active/Passive Voice Pretest:
1) P 2) A 3) P 4) A 5) P 6) A 7) A 8) P 9) A 10) P 11) A 12) P 13) A 14) P 15) P 16) A

II-14-2. Active/Passive Voice Pretest:
17) A 18) P 19) P 20) A 21) A 22) P 23) A 24) P 25) A 26) P.

Chapter 15:

II-15-3. Misplaced Modifiers Pretest:
1) MM; pulling the bow-string>>arrow. 2) C 3) MM; Running at top speed>>wig. 4) C 5) C 6) MM; While driving down the highway>>cell phone. 7) C 8) MM; plodding up the mountain>>earthquake. 9) C 10) C 11) MM; hurtling through space>> camera. 12) C 13) MM; while playing the piano >>doorbell. 14) C 15) MM; "pouring cats and dogs">> siren. 16) C 17) MM; approaching the accident intersection>>center lane. 18) MM; while flying>>birdbath. 19) C 20) C.

II-15-4. Awkward/Choppy/Stringy/ Wordy Sentence Pretest:
1) AWK 2) OK 3) CH 4) CH 5) W or S 6) W (some extra unnecessary words) 7) W (some extra unnecessary words) 8) OK 9) OK 10) W (some extra unnecessary words).

II-15-5. Awkward/Choppy/Stringy/ Wordy Sentence Pretest:
1) W (some extra, unnecessary words) 2) CH 3) CH 4) 5) CH 6) W (some extra unnecessary words) 7) W (some extra unnecessary words) 8) W (some extra unnecessary words) 9) W (some extra unnecessary words) 10) AWK 11) AWK.

PLEASE NOTE: For all writings in Part III paragraphs and Part IV papers, students' answers and responses will vary, so no key is provided.

Part III-Answer Key

Chapter 16:

III-16-B. Writing Process Check-up:
A. 1=brainstorming, 2=writing drafts, 3=revising, 4=editing, 5=publishing.

B. Matching:
1-publishing=B 2-editing=C 3-pre-writing=D 4-revising=A 5-writing=E

Part IV-Answer Key

Part IV Introduction...

IV-1. Text Types Refresher Activity:
1. N-narrative 2. E-expository 3. P-persuasive 4. A-academic.

Some More Thoughts
to Ponder

* * * * *

"Write the vision, and make it plain upon tablets, so he may run who reads it."
What does this mean?
What impact might your writing have?
[resource: Habakkuk 2:2]

* * * * * * * *

"Write the things you have seen, the things that are, and the things that are coming;"
What does this mean?

What have you seen, do you see, and do you understood to be coming?

[resource: Revelation 1:19]

* * * * * * * *

Appendix A

Writing Tips in Brief

The following is a recap of each of the four parts of this book: writing tips in brief:

A. Part I - Basic Word Elements -— English Writing and Reading

1. Four Aspects of Language: reading, writing, listening, speaking
2. Two Models of Learning Styles:
   a. VAKT: Visual, Auditory, Kinesthetic, Tactile
   b. Gardner's 8 Multiple Intelligences: verbal/linguistic, math/logical, spatial/artistic, musical, bodily/kinesthetic, inter-personal, intra-personal, and naturalistic
3. Spelling patterns follow rules of phonics and graphophonic principles.
4. Parts of Speech describe the way a word is used in a sentence. Check the dictionary.
   a. Nouns: names of persons, places, things, or ideas.
   b. Pronouns: take the place of nouns {= for, on behalf of nouns}
   c. Adjectives: describe or modify nouns
   d. Articles: *a, an, the*
   e. Verbs: show action or state of being; tell what noun is doing
   f. Helping/linking verbs: enable verbs to express past, present, and future tenses, such as *was* walking, *is* walking, and *will be* walking.
   g. Adverbs: add to the verb or modify an adjective or another adverb; look for *ly*

h. Conjunctions: link words or parts of sentences {= with or for junction}

i. Prepositions: show position of noun to other words in sentence {= position}

j. Interjections: provide emphasis and filler {look for exclamation!}

5. Commonly Confused Words: words similar in pronunciation, sound, or meaning.

6. Plurals: nouns meaning more than one;

   a. Usually add *s* or *es*... ***boy/boys***   ***leaf/leaves***

   b. Some noun forms remain the same... ***deer/deer***

   c. Some noun forms change totally... ***mouse/mice***

7. Possessives: nouns changed to show possession or ownership

   a. Usually add ***'s*** to words ending in other than an ***s***. *man's, men's*

   b. Usually add ' to words ending in the letter ***s***. *class', classes'*

8. Antonyms: words meaning the opposite... *hot:cold*

9. Synonyms: words meaning the same or similar... *cold:cool::icy: chilly*

10. Analogies: show relationships of words to each other

   a. Based on synonyms such as *hot:warm::cold:cool.*

   b. Based on antonyms such as *hot:cold::warm:cool.*

   c. Based on other relationships such as *bird:flies::cat:walks.*

B. Part II – Basic Sentence Structures – English Grammar and Usage

1. Four kinds of sentences: statement, question/interrogative, command, exclamation

2. Two Parts of Sentences: Subjects and Predicates:

   a. Simple subject = who/what sentence is about (noun or pronoun)

b. Simple predicate = what subject is or is doing (verb)

c. Complete subject = all words describing/clarifying the simple subject

d. Complete predicate = all words describing/clarifying the simple predicate

e. Compound subject = more than one noun as simple subject

f. Compound predicate = more than one verb as simple predicate

3. Fragments: parts of sentence; prepositional phrase or a clause lacking either a clear subject or a clear predicate

4. Run-ons: two or more sentences run together; can be resolved through appropriate:

a. Punctuation or separation into two or more separate sentences. Typically occurs when writer wants to link two ideas closely together.

5. Punctuation: includes…

a. Capitalization to start a new sentence

b. Periods, questions marks, and exclamation marks to end a sentence

c. Commas, colons, and semi-colons in the middle of sentence to indicate separation

d. Quotation marks to indicate conversation or direct quotes.

6. Subject-verb Agreement in number:

a. Single subject takes single verb; Plural subject takes plural verb

b. If subject does not end in s (singular), verb usually ends in s.

c. If subject ends in s (plural), verb usually does not end in s.

d. Subjects connected by *and* are plural.

e. Singular subjects connected by conjunctions such as *either/ or* stay singular.

f. A singular and plural subject connected by *either/or* -- verb agrees with closest subject.

g. *There* is never the subject of a sentence; then the subject follows the verb.

h. *Anybody, anyone, each, another, everyone.* are singular and take a singular verb.

i. Relative pronouns like *who, which, and that* – look to see the noun the relative pronoun is standing for and make the verb match it.

j. Collective nouns such as *family, committee, team, jury* almost always act singularly

k. Numbers representing a single unit are singular: *forty percent, eight years.*

7. Sentence Agreement: Pronouns and Antecedent Referents

8. Pronoun must refer to preceding noun; when it does not, meaning is unclear.

9. Use a singular pronoun with a singular antecedent (noun it references).

10. Use a plural pronoun with a plural antecedent (noun it references).

11. Sentence Agreement: Tenses must agree ... = form of verb placing the action in time:

a. Past tense = action in past; Present tense = present action; Future tense = future action

b. Six basic tenses plus the continuous or *–ing* form of all six.

12. Sentence Agreement: Parallel Construction:

a. Sentences or parts of sentences connected by an idea should be expressed in similar form. Check for parallel nouns, adjectives, prepositional phrases, and clauses.

13. Sentence Agreement: Active/Passive Voice:

a. Active voice: the subject acts; more powerful and easily understood by readers.

b. Passive voice: the subject receives the action

14. Misplaced Modifiers:

a. Put modifying phrases next to the subjects they clarify. Say what you mean!

b. When comparing actions, include both verbs and the correct subject pronoun.

c. When comparing nouns, be sure both nouns are in sentence and nouns are comparable.

15. Select the correct word for the situation; know what your words mean. Avoid redundancy.

D. Part III – Basic Paragraph and Text Structures

1. Eight-Step Process Writing

a. Brainstorm/pre-write -- generate Graphic Organizer to cluster ideas.

b. Generate three-level outline to organize data into logical flow of ideas.

c. Write first draft

d. Review (personal and peer) for Revising (organization, flow of ideas)

e. Rewrite considering revision input.

f. Review (Personal and peer) for Editing (mechanics, grammar, punctuation, etc)

g. Write final daft considering editing input.

h. Publish for others to see the final copy.

2. Seven Graphic Organizers... (use words not sentences)

a. Bubble chart: organize ideas in clusters (loosely organized)

b. Sequential Time Line: organize ideas in order, sequence

c. Venn Diagram: organize ideas for compare/contrast paper (loosely organized)

d. Concept Map: organize ideas; helpful stepping stone to outline and writing

e. Cause/Effect Diagram: organize ideas for cause/effect papers

f. Problem/Solution Diagram: organize ideas for problem/solution papers

g. Strengths/Weaknesses Chart: organize ideas for critique or analysis

3. Three-Part Handy Model...for each book, chapter, paper, and paragraph...

　　a. Main idea/thesis (thumb)

　　b. Supporting Details (at least three; three middle fingers)

　　c. Summary/conclusion/personal response (each; all three; small finger)

4. Two Major Kinds of Text:

　　a. Narrative (story; story grammar)

　　b. Expository (informational text; organized seven ways)

　　　　1) Summary/Abstract/Précis

　　　　2) Descriptive (narrative and expository)

　　　　3) Sequential/How-to/Chronological

　　　　4) Compare/Contrast

　　　　5) Cause/Effect

　　　　6) Problem/Solution

　　　　7) Persuasive/Position... take a stand or position using any of the above text formats.

E. Part IV - Basic Genres of Writing and Reading

1. Audiences, Styles, Purposes and Processes – see text for more

　　a. Consider audience for whom you are writing.

　　b. Styles vary by kind of text structure, purpose of writing, type of paper assigned, and narrative versus expository.

　　c. Processes -- Process Writing has eight steps:

　　　　1) Brainstorm/pre-write -- generate Graphic Organizer to cluster ideas.

　　　　2) Generate three-level outline to organize data into logical flow of ideas.

　　　　3) Write first draft

4) Review (personal and peer) for Revising (organization, flow of ideas)

5) Rewrite considering revision input.

6) Review (personal and peer) for Editing (mechanics, grammar, punctuation, etc)

7) Write final daft considering editing input.

8) Publish for others to see the final copy.

b. Procedures:

1) Follow format requested by instructor or professor.

2) Include all parts requested.

3) Use all hints and suggestions made by instructor or professor.

4) Review scoring sheet(s) to see how writing is to be scored; what is evaluator looking for?

5) Take pride in your final product – a good job well done.

c. Getting Organized…use Graphic Organizers (see Chapter 17 for models):

1) Bubble chart: to dump ideas in clusters (loosely organized)

2) Sequential Time Line

3) Venn Diagram: dump ideas for compare/contrast paper (loosely organized)

4) Organizational chart: organize ideas; stepping stone to outline and writing

5) Cause/Effect and Problem/Solution Flow Charts

6) Evaluation/Critique Strengths/Weaknesses Table

d. Parts of any writing: Handy Model; Each book, chapter, paper, and paragraph needs…

1) Main idea/thesis (thumb)

2) Supporting Details (at least three; three middle fingers)

3) Summary/conclusion/personal response (each; all three; small finger)

e. Formatting: APA Formatting for citation. see above text Section IV.

f. Revising and Editing…Peer reviewing and Feedback

1) Focus on no more than three aspects/skills to work on at a time

2) Retain writer's "voice" at all times; revising and editing not to override writer's voice

g. Seven kinds of papers…

1) Papers 1 and 2: Abstract/Summary/Précis: brief recap of key points

a) Discuss at least three major points of article, book, or source.

2) Paper 3: Action Research

a) Extract at least three patterns from your data gathering.

b) Discuss any unique findings – special contributions to knowledge base.

3) Paper 4: Review of Literature: consult at least three sources

a) Discuss at least three key points from each source.

b) Discuss at least three key points held in common

c) Discuss any unique findings – special contributions to knowledge base.

4) Paper 5: Compare/Contrast: How are two (or more) things alike? Different?

a) Discuss at least three details of shared likeness.

b) Discuss at least three details of unique differences for each.

5) Paper 6: Critique/Analysis/Evaluation of Article and/or Research: Strengths and Weaknesses

   a). Discuss at least three strengths and at least three weaknesses.

   b) Evaluate relative strength of the article or study.

6) Paper 7: Editorial/Personal Opinion/Personal Reflection/Position Paper: Personal conclusions

   a) Discuss at least three key points or issues regarding your stand/position.

   b) Provide supporting details, corroborating research, etc.

   c) Recap personal conclusion.

Additional Notes & Tips

Appendix B

Spelling With Phonics: Phonics in Brief

A. Introduction

Phonics comes from the Greek root, *phōnē*, meaning a sound, and *phonics* means the study of sound(s). *Graphophonics* relates symbols [writing -- *graphē*, *graphikos* (Greek), *graphicus* (Latin)] to sounds. Phonics and graphophonics aid sounding out words and writing words as symbols for sounds. This Appendix combines with the Syllabication Appendix to strengthen your spelling to enhance your writing. The following is a brief summary of phonics including definitions; see the reference list at the end of this Appendix for more resources.

B. Definitions

1. **Phonemes**: minimal sound units of speech; e.g., /t/ in top, stop, pot
2. **Graphemes**: written representations (symbols) of a phoneme; e.g., *b* for /b/, *oy* for /oi/

C. Consonants

1. **Consonants (listed)**: letters other than *a-e-i-o-u*-w-y; include *w* and *y* to start a word or syllable.
2. **Double Consonants**
   a. **Consonant Digraphs**: two consonants representing one sound;
      1) *ch sh th wh* and *gn- kn- pn- wr-* to start words: *church, shop, this, thin, when, gnat, knot, pneumonia, write*
      a. −ck −nk and −ng to end words: *rack, sink,* and *sing*

2) Sounds of **ch:** /ch/ as in *church, child, cheese;* /k/ as in *chorus, chemistry;* /sh/ as in *chic, chef;* /kw/ as in *choir*

3) Ph = /F/: ph = /f/ as in *phone, elephant, telegraph*

b. Initial Consonant Blends: two or more consonants sounded; each consonant is heard.

1) *–l* Teams: **bl**a*ck* **cl**ay **fl**y **gl**ee **pl**ay **sl**i*p* **spl**a*sh*

2) *–r* Teams: **br**i*ck* **cr**y **dr**y **fr**y **gr**ay **pr**ay **tr**y **wr**i*te* **scr**a*p* **spr**ay **str**ay **thr**o*at*

3) *--*s Teams: **sc**a*b* **sk**u*nk* **sm**a*ll* **sn**a*p* **sp**o*t* **st**o*p* **sw**i*m*

4) miscellaneous: **tw**i*n*   (and there are a few more.)

c. Final Consonant Blends: two or more consonants; each consonant is heard.

E.g., *–ld –mp –nd –sk –st* as in *m*i**ld** *l*a**mp** *st*a**nd** *m*a**sk** *m*a**st**

3. Other Consonant Considerations

a. Hard/Soft C:

1) **Hard:** When *c* is followed by **a o** or **u,** c = /k/: e.g., *cat cot cut*

2) **Soft:** When *c* is followed by **i e** or **y,** c = /s/: e.g., *city cent cymbal*

3) **Hard/Soft G:**

4) **Hard:** When *g* is followed by **a o** or **u,** *g* = /guh/: e.g., *gate got gut*

5) **Soft:** When *g* is followed by **i e** or **y,** *g* = /j/: e.g., *ginger gentle gym*

b. Sounds of *S*:

1) /s/ as in *sidewalk, song*

2) /z/ as in *as, is, has, was*

3) /sh/ as in *sugar, sure*

4) /zh/ *pleasure, treasure*

c. Sounds of Qu: /k/ as in *unique, technique;* /kw/ as in *queen, quit, quiet*

d. *W* and *Y* as consonants and as vowels:

 1) W and *Y* are **consonants** when they start words; e.g., *wagon, will, yard,* *yes*

 2) W and *Y* are **vowels** when they end words; e.g., *fly, try; knew, know.*

 3) W and Y are **vowels** when they team with vowels; e.g., *cow, day*

e. Silent Consonants:

 1) Words with double medial consonants, first is sounded, second not: *luggage*

 2) Diagraph *–ck* is pronounced */k/: thick, trick.*

 ***3)** –gh* usually not sounded when preceded by *I: nigh, sigh*

 4) In words beginning with *kn-,* the *k* is usually silent: *knight, knot, knew*

 5) In words starting with *wr-,* the *w* is usually silent: *write, wrong, written*

 6) In words ending with *–mb,* the *b* is usually silent: *lamb, plumb, thumb*

 7) In words ending with *–ten,* usually the t is silent: *kitten, written,*

D. Vowels

1. **Vowels** (definition) letters "carrying" the sound in words – *a, e, i, o, u,* and sometimes *w* and *y.*

2. **Long Vowel Rule 1 {VCE}:** If a syllable or one-part word has two vowels, usually the first is long and the second is silent; the final silent *e* makes the preceding vowel long.

 [VCE Rule = Vowel + Consonant + final E]; e.g., *gate, lake, cane, tame, cake, coke*

3. **Long Vowel Rule 2 {CVVC}:** "When two vowels go walking, usually the first one does the talking." **[CVVC = Consonant + Vowel + Vowel + Consonant]** applies to only four vowel sets: **ee**

(98%), **oa** (97%), **ea** (66%), and **ai/ay** (64%) (Heilman, 1998, p. 91).

    a. **[closed syllable long //]** e.g., *peep, seen; boat, loaf; bead, heat, knead; brain, rain*

    b. **[open syllable long //]** e.g., flee, *teepee; sea, tea; day, play*

    c. Exceptions to these vowel sets:

        1) **ee** = /ĕ/: *been*

        2) **oa** = /ŏ/: *broad*

        3) **ai** = ă: *again, against, said;* **ai** = ī : aisle (Heilman, 1998, p. 98).

        4) **ea** = /ā/: *great, steak*; **ea** = /ĕ/: *bread, dead, head*

4. **Long Vowel Rule 3 {CV or CCV}**: If a syllable or a word has one vowel, and it comes at the end of the syllable or word, the vowel is usually long in the "open syllable."

    a. **[CCV = Consonant + Consonant + Vowel] = [open syllable]**: e.g., *fly, try, tripod*

5. **Long Vowel Rule 4 -- Y as a vowel / ī/** : If **Y** is the only vowel at the end of a one-syllable word, **Y** has the sound of long **I**: *by, my, try, fly, fry*

6. **Long Vowel Rule 5 – Y as a vowel /ē /**: If **Y** is the only vowel at the end of a word of more than one syllable, **Y** has a sound like long **E**: *baby, funny, sunny, hilly, Tony, tabby*

7. **Short Vowel Rule {VC or CVC}**: If a syllable or a word has only one vowel and the vowel comes at the beginning or between two consonants, the vowel is usually short.

    a. **[VC] = [closed syllable]**: e.g., *is, am, it, if, at, an, in*

    b. **[CVC] = [closed syllable]**: *rag, beg, rig, dog, rug, rabbit*

8. Controlled Vowels

    a. R-Controlled Vowels: Vowel sounds change slightly when paired with an *r*...

        1)**r** = /ar/: bar, *car, far, hard, jar, lard, mar, par, smart, tar*

        2)**er/ir/ur** = /er/: *her, per; dirt, fir, girl, shirt, sir; burr, church, fur, hurt, purr*

3)or = /or/: *core, door, for, horn, lord, more, nor, poor, sore, tore, worn, yore*

b. -L, -LL, -W, and –U-Controlled Vowels:

1) The vowel *a* sounds like *ô* /aw/ when followed by *l, ll, w,* and *u.*

2) *Balk, chalk, halt, malt, psalms, salt, talk, walk,*

3) *All, ball, call, fall, hall, mall,*

4) *Awl, bawl, caw, jaw, law, paw, raw, saw, yaw*

5) *Fault, Gaul, haul, maul, Paul, Saul, vault*

c. Vowels *e, i, o,* and *u* are also controlled by *–l or –ll*… as in *bell, bill, loll, pull*

d. Vowels *e* and *o* are also controlled by w: as in *few, pew; flower, power*

9. Double Vowels

a. Irregular Double Vowels – Vowel Digraphs {CVVC}: Double vowels not following the Long Vowel Rule # 1:{CVVC: 1st vowel long, 2nd silent} but represent a **single vowel sound** such as **ea** (see # 17 above) and the following:

b. u = /aw/ in *auto, autograph*

c. aw = /aw/ in *paw, lawn*

d. ei = /ī/ in *eight, freight, weight*

e. Oo = /ōō/: *boot, cool, loon, moon, moot, pool, room, soon, school, tooth*

f. Oo = /ŏ/: *book, brook, crook, foot, good, hook, look, nook, took, wood*

10. **Diphthongs:** Two vowels blend together to form a compound speech sound. The tongue glides from one vowel sound to another moving the jaw. The following are diphthongs:

a. oi = /ō-ē/ as in *oil, boil, coil, foil, poi, toil*

b. oy = /ō-ē/ as in *boy, joy, Roy, soy, toy, voyage*

c. ou = /o-w/ as in *count, foul, hour, out, pout, Scout*

d. ow = /o-w/ as in *brown, cow, how, howl, jowl, power*

e. **ew** = /o-o/ as in *brew, few, hewn, Jewish, mew, new, pew*

11. **Vowel Teams with 2 or More Sounds:**

    a. ea: 1) */long ā/ great*   2) /short *ĕ*/ *head*   3) /long *ē*/ *knead*

    b. oo: 1) /long *ō*/ *school, food*   2) /short *ŏ*/ *hood, good*

    c. ou: 1) /short *ŏ*/ *should*   2) /*ow*/ *shout*   3) /*aw*/ *thought*   4) /long *ō*/ *though*

    d. ow: 1) /long *ō*/ *snow*   2) /*ow*/ *cow*

    e. gh: 1) /*f*/ *enough*   2) /silent/ *though, thought*

12. **Schwa Sound** occurs in the less stressed syllable of multi-syllabic words, softens the vowel sound, and is represented with the upside-down-*e* symbol. This becomes important when sounding out words in the dictionary. Examples include… the -*ti*- in *beautiful,* the –*en* in *happen,* and the –*er* in *wonder.*

Onset and Rime

    Onset and Rime help people to visualize and spell parts of larger, multi-syllabic words. Historically, Linguistic analysis led to Word Families — more recently known as onset and rime. Below are some examples of onset-rime or word families. See Fry's <u>Reading Teacher's Book of Lists</u> or Heilman's <u>Phonics in Perspective</u> for more complete listings.

-ag: bag, gag, lag, nag, rag, sag, tag, wag, zigzag
-all: ball, call, fall, hall, mall, tall, wall
-an: ban, can, Dan, fan, Jan, man, Nan, pan, ran, Stan, tan, van
-at: bat, cat, fat, gnat, hat, mat, rat, sat, vat
-ell: bell cell dell fell sell tell well
-et: bet, get, jet, let, met, net, pet, set, wet
-ew=/oo/: dew, few, hew, mew, new, pew-ew=//: sew
-ide: bide, glide, hide, ride, side, tide, wide
-ike: bike, hike, like, Mike, pike
-in: bin din fin gin kin pin sin tin win
-ight: fight height light might night right sight tight
-oo: boo, coo, moo, too
-ot: cot, dot, got, hot, jot, lot, not, rot, tot
-ough=ō: bough, dough-ough=/aw/: cough, rough, tough

-ought: bought fought sought thought
-ud: bud, cud, dud, mud
-ue: cue, due, flue, glue, hue, sue
-ug: bug, dug, hug, jug, lug, mug, pug, rug, tug
-ule: mule, rule
-y: by, my, why

F. Recap

Yes, the English language tends to have some irregular forms, but using these phonics and phonics-related guidelines (as well as the syllabication and morphology of the next Appendix) enables you to predict linguistic patterns and to spell more effectively in all your writings.

G. Phonics References

Fry, E. B., Kress, J. E., Fountoukidis, D. L. (2000). <u>The reading teacher's book of lists (4th ed.)</u>. Englewood Cliffs, NJ: Prentice-Hall.

Heilman, A. W. (1998). <u>Phonics in proper perspective (8th ed.)</u>. Upper saddle River, NJ: Merrill/Prentice Hall.

Hull, M. A., Fox, B. J. (1998). <u>Phonics for the teacher of reading: Programmed for self-instruction (7th ed.)</u>. Upper Saddle River, NJ: Merrill/Prentice Hall.

H. Additional Notes – Spelling With Phonics

Appendix C

Spelling With Syllables, Roots, Affixes, and Contractions

I. Syllables, Roots, and Affixes

A. Introduction

Structural analysis of words develops better spelling by identifying root words, compound words, prefixes, suffixes, syllables, and contractions. This Appendix combined with the Phonics Appendix strengthens your spelling to enhance your writing. The brief summary of morphology (root words, prefixes, suffixes, and inflectional endings), compound words, syllabication, and contractions incorporates definitions. A reference list at the end offers more resources.

B. Morphology in Brief

Morphology means the study of the meaningful parts of words or word structure. Webster's New World College Dictionary defines *morphology* as "the branch of linguistics dealing with word structure and with functional changes in the forms of words such as inflection and compounding;" (Agnes Guralnik, 2000, p. 938). This overview of morphology covers morphemes, root words, affixes including prefixes and suffixes, and inflectional endings.

Morphemes are the smallest units of meaning in a word in any language. It may be a root word, a prefix, or a suffix. Examples of morphemes as meaning units include the following:

Homograph: homo = same; graph = writing; homographs have same spelling/letters

Homophone: homo = same; phone = sound; homophones sound alike

Homonym: homo = same; nym = name; homonyms have same name

Microscope: micro = small, scop = see; microscope helps to see small things

Microphone: micro = small, phon = sound; microphone magnifies small sound

Telescope: tele = far off; scop = see; telescope helps see from a distance

Telephone: tele = far off; phon = sound; telephone sends sound far off

Television: tele = far off; vis = see; television helps see pictures far off

C. Root Words

Root Words are the fundamental basic units of a word in any language; they are the basic word parts for adding prefixes and/or suffixes. The morpheme illustrations above show some root words, but many English root words come from Latin or Greek roots.

1. Greek and Latin Roots

The following illustrate examples of Greek (G) and Latin (L) Root Words:

aqua (L) = water:	*aquarium, aquatic*
biblio (G) = book:	*bibliography, Bible*
cycl (G) = circle/ring:	*bicycle, cycle, cyclone, encyclopedia, recycle, tricycle*
duc (L) = lead:	*aquaduct, conduct, duct, educate, induction*
flect, flex (L) = bend:	*deflection, flex, flexible, reflection, reflexes*
geo (G) = earth:	*geography, geological, geometric, geophysics*
graph (G) = write:	*autobiography, autograph, photography*
junct (L) = join:	*conjunction, junction, juncture*
loc (L) = place:	*allocation, dislocated, local, locate, location*
meter (G) = measure:	*barometer, centimeter, diameter, metric, thermometer*
ped (G) = child:	*encyclopedia, pedagogical, pediatrics, pediatrician*
ped (L) = foot:	*biped, pedal, pedestal, pedestrian*
pod (G) = foot:	*podiatric, podiatrist, podium, tripod*
rad (L) = ray/spoke:	*radiation, radio, radiology, radioactive, radius*
struct (L) =build:	*construction, destruct, constructor, instructor, structure*
urb (L) = city:	*suburb, suburban, urban, urbanism*
var (L) = different:	*invariable, variation, variety, various, variegated*

2. See Fry's <u>Reading Teacher's Book of Lists</u> for a more complete list of root words.

3. Root words we can build upon by adding various prefixes and suffixes include the following:

faith:	faith**ful**, **un**faith**ful**, **un**faith**fulness**
give:	giv**ing**
love:	lov**ing**, **un**lov**ing**, love**ly**
pay:	pay**ing**, pay**less**
thank:	thank**ing**, thank**ful**, **un**thankful, thank**less**

D. Prefixes

Prefixes are **morphemes** (meaning-bearing syllables) added to the front/beginning of root words. Using the above root words, here are some examples of prefixes in use...

*inter*faith   *for*give   *un*love(d)   *pre*pay   *un*thank(ful)

1. **Basic, beginning level prefixes** include the following: (Fry, 2000, p.85)

anti- = against:	*antiwar, antifreeze*
dis- = not, opposite:	*disagree, dishonest, disappear*
ex- = former:	*ex-teacher, ex-president*
im-, in- = not:	*immature, impossible, inactive, independent*
inter- = among between:	*international, Internet, intermission*
intra- = within:	*intramural, intrastate*
micro- = small, short:	*microphone, microscope, microwave*
mis- = wrong, not:	*misbehave, misconduct, mistake*
multi- = many, much:	*multitude, multiply*
non- = not:	*nonstop, nonfiction, nonsense*
over- = too much:	*overactive, overdo, overdue,*
post- = after:	*postdate, postpone, postwar*
pre- = before:	*prefix, preamble, preface*
pro- = favor:	*pro-American, proactive, pro-education, pro-trade*
pro- = forward:	*progress, produce, project, prophet*
re- = again:	*redo, rewrite, repeat*
re- = back:	*rebate, recall, retell,*
sub- = under, below:	*subtract, submarine, subfreezing*
super- = above, beyond:	*superhuman, superman, supernatural, supervisor*
tele- = distant, far:	*telephone, telegraph, telescope, television*

trans- = across:	*transfer, transportation, translation, transoceanic*
un- = not:	*unable, unhappy, unsure, uncomfortable*
under- = below, less than:	*underage, underground, underneath*

2. Fry (2000) provides several other helpful lists of prefixes including the following **Intermediate to Advanced Prefixes:**

    a. *mid- = middle:*   *midday, midnight, midway*

    b. Number-Expressing Prefixes such as…

        1)bi-, bin- = two: *bicycle, bifocals, bimonthly*

        2)mega- = large, million: megabyte, megaton, megahertz, megawatt

    c. Size-Describing Prefixes such as…

        1)macro- = large/long: *macrocosm, macroeconomics, macroscopic*

        2)micro- = small/short: *microcosm, microeconomics, microscopic*

    d. When-Describing Prefixes such as…

        1)post- = after: *postdate, postdoctoral, posterior, postpone*

        2)pre- = before: *preamble, precautions, prefixes, prejudiced*

    e. Where-Describing Prefixes such as…

        1)sub- = under: *subject, submarine, submersion, subscript*

        2)super- = over: *superimpose, supernatural, superscript, supersede*

    f. Amount- or Extent-Describing Prefixes such as…

        1)equi- = equal: *equally, equator, equidistant, equivalent*

        2)omni- = all: *omnibus, omnipotent, omnipresent, omniscient*

g. Togetherness-/Separateness-Expressing Prefixes such as…

    1)ab- = *away from:*   *abdicate, abduct, aberrant, absent*

    2)con- = *with:*   *concert, concurred, conduct, consent*

    3)together prefixes: *co-, syl-, sym-, syn-… syllable, symbol, synonym*

    4)with prefixes: *col-, com-, con-…collect, community, contract*

h. Negation-Expressing Prefixes such as…

    1)not prefixes: *a-, an-, for-, il-, im-, in-, ir-, ne-, neg-, non-*

        a)atheist, anemia, forget, illegal, immature, inactive, irate, never, negative, nonfat

    2)opposite prefixes: *counter- counteract, de- depart, un- unable*

i. Judgment-making Prefixes such as…

    1)against prefixes: *anti- antibody, contra- contradiction*

    2)for prefixes: *pro- pro-American, proactive*

    3)good prefixes: *bene- benefit, eu- eulogy*

    4)bad prefixes: *dys- dysfunctional, mal- maladjusted, mis- misconduct*

See Fry's <u>Reading Teacher's Book of Lists</u> for a more complete list of prefixes with meanings.

E. Suffixes – Inflectional Endings

Suffixes and Inflectional endings are two types of meaning-bearing units added to the end of a word to change its meaning.

1. **Suffixes** are **morphem**es (meaning-bearing units consisting of a letter, a syllable, or a group of syllables) added to the back/end of a root or base word to change its meaning.

2. **Inflectional Endings** are **morphemes** (meaning-bearing units consisting of a letter, a syllable, or a group of syllables) added to the back or end of a root or base word to change its meaning.

Inflectional endings "indicate the grammatical form of words…" (Fry, 2000, p. 95).

a. Noun Inflectional Suffixes.

1) The suffix –s indicates plural for most noun root words such as… *apples, apricots, bananas, grapes, lemons, limes, oranges, pears, plums.*

2) The suffix –es indicates plural for nouns ending with a –ch, -sh, -ss, -x, or -z … *churches, peaches; brushes, bushes; kisses, misses; fixes, mixes; jazzes, quizzes.*

3) The suffix –ies indicates plural for nouns ending in y such as… *baby—babies, candy—candies, fly—flies, pantry—pantries*

b. Adjective Inflectional Suffixes.

1) Many nouns and/or verbs change to adjectives by adding a suffix such as…

a) –y: *bag—baggy, boss—bossy, tang—tangy*

b) –like: *child--childlike, lady—ladylike, life—lifelike*

c) –ful: *faith—faithful, fear—fearful, wonder—wonderful*

d) –ish: *child—childish, fool—foolish, Spain—Spanish*

e) –ic: *geography—geographic, history—historic, scene—scenic*

f) –ese: *China—Chinese, Japan—Japanese*

g) –ward: *east—eastward, north—northward, to—toward*

h) –en: *froze—frozen, spoke—spoken, write—written*

2) Compare adjectives with one another using suffixes such as…

a) –er: *fatter, skinnier, shorter, taller, rounder, longer*

b) –est: *fattest, skinniest, shortest, tallest, roundest, longest*

c. Verb Inflectional Suffixes.

   1) Verb-Inflectional Endings include the following:

   a) *–ed* shows past tense: *cared, dried, loved, shared, walked*

   b) *–ing* shows present participle: *caring, drying, loving, sharing, walking*

   c) *–en* shows past participle: *driven, eaten, frozen, forgiven*

   d) *–s* shows 3ʳᵈ person singular(he/she/it): *cares, drives, eats, forgives, loves*

d. Adverb Inflectional Suffixes.

   1) Adverb Inflectional Suffixes include the following:

   a) *–ly* indicates an adverb: *fairly, goodly, honestly, lovingly*

   b) *–ily* indicates an adverb for words ending in y: *happy—happily*

   2) Many adjectives can be changed into adverbs by adding *–ly* or *–ily* such as…

   a) Clean—cleanly, dear—dearly, sweet—sweetly, swift—swiftly

3. Suffixes – General

   Suffixes are **morphemes** (meaning-bearing units consisting of a letter, a syllable, or a group of syllables) added to the back/end of a root or base word to change its meaning.   Using the illustrative root words from above, here are some examples of suffixes in use…

faithful forgiveness   *loveable*   *payable*   *thankfulness*

a. Basic, beginning level suffixes include the following: (Fry, 2000, p. 93)

-able, -ible = is, can be:	*comfortable, learnable, edible, combustible*
-ar, -er, -or = one who:	*actor, doctor, liar, teacher, learner, waiter*
-en = to make:	*fasten, fatten, shorten, strengthen, weaken*
-er = more:	*faster, lower, nearer, shorter, taller*
-ess = one who (female):	*actress, hostess , seamstress, waitress*
-est = most:	*fastest, lowest, nearest, shortest, tallest*
-ette = small:	*barrette, diskette, pipette*
-ful = full of:	*careful, cheerful, faithful, fearful, joyful, thankful*
-ish = relating to:	*bookish, childish, selfish*
-less = without:	*ageless, careless, fearless, thankless, thoughtless*
-like = resembling:	*childlike, homelike, lifelike*
-ly = resembling:	*brotherly, fatherly, motherly, sisterly, scholarly*
-ment = action or process:	*developmental, endowment, experiment, governmental*
-ness = state or quality of:	*emptiness, fullness, goodness, happiness, kindness*
-ship = state or quality of:	*citizenship, friendship, hardship, internship, worship*

Fry (2000) provides several other helpful lists of suffixes including the following:

b. Intermediate to Advanced Suffixes such as...

    1)–an,-ian, -ial = relating to: American, Californian, Hawaiian, Texan, veteran

    2)–ism = doctrine of: Americanism, capitalism, patriotism, socialism

c. Inflectional Suffixes [See separate section above].

d. Noun Suffixes. Fry (2000) lists nearly 100 noun suffixes – letters or syllables changing the meaning of the root when added to the end of the word such as... (p. 96-97).

    1) *–sion, -tion, -ation = state or quality of: action, inspiration, relation, tension*

    2) *–ology = study or science of: biology, psychology, sociology, zoology*

e. Adjective Suffixes. Fry (2000) lists 44 adjective suffixes – most meaning *relating to, inclined to, state or quality of, or full of* -- such as... (p. 98-99).

    1) *–ful = full of:*   *faithful, joyful, peaceful, restful, thankful*

    2) *–ous = full of:*   *joyous, virtuous, wondrous*

f. Verb Suffixes. Fry (2000) lists sixteen verb suffixes showing action, process, person, or tense such as...

    1)–d, -ed = past tense: *believed, hiked, placed, soaked*

    2) –ate, -en, -fy, -ize = to make: activate, shorten, beautify, computerize

g. Adverb Suffixes. Fry lists three adverb suffixes such as...

    1) *–ly = forms adverb from adjective:*   *faithfully, joyfully, musically*

    2) *–ways = manner:*   *always, crossways, sideways*

    3) *–wise = manner, direction:*   *clockwise, lengthwise*

For more complete lists of various suffixes, see Fry (2000).

4. Rules for Adding Suffixes

   a. When a word of one syllable ends with a single consonant letter preceded by a single vowel letter, **double the consonant** letter before adding a suffix beginning with a vowel letter such as... *bat—batter, run—running, sun—sunny—sunning, swim--swimming;* exception: the consonant letter *x /ks/* as in *box—boxes, fix--fixing.*

   b. When a multi-syllable word's last syllable is stressed and ends with a consonant preceded by a single vowel letter, **double the consonant** letter before adding suffixes beginning with a vowel such as... *admit—admitte—admitting, bet—betting, regret—regretted.*

   c. If a word ends with a *-y*, **change the *y* to *i* and add *es*** such as...*baby—babies, candy—candies, fly—flies.*

   d. When a word ends with a *-y*, **keep the *y* before adding a suffix beginning with an *i*** such as... *baby—babying—babyish, cry—crying, fly—flyer—flying, try—trying.*

   e. When a word ends with a *-y* preceded by a consonant, **change the *y* to *i* before adding suffixes other than *–ing*** such as... *fly—flies, try—tried—tries.*

   f. When a word ends with a *-y* immediately preceded by a **vowel *(-y* digraphs and diphthongs), usually keep the *y*** before adding a suffix such as... *boy—boyish, buy—buying, play—playful—playing.*

   g. When a word ends with a *silent-e*, usually **drop the *final* e** before adding a suffix beginning with a vowel such as... *bake—baking, fence—fencing, late—later, love—loving.*

   h. When a words ends with an *-e* immediately preceded by any other vowel, usually **drop the *final* e** before adding a suffix beginning with a consonant such as... *awe—awful—awesome, sue—suing, true—truly.*

   i. When a word ends with an *-f* or *-fe*, usually change the *–f* or *–fe* to a *v* before adding the suffix such as... *calf—calves—calving, half—halves—halving, knife—knives.*

F. Compound Words

Compound words are larger words made up of two or more smaller words.

1. Examples include the following: *airplane = air + plane, baseball = base+ ball, basketball = basket + ball, doghouse = dog + house, football = foot + ball, horseback = horse + back, policeman = police + man, sandlot = sand + lot, Thanksgiving = thanks + giving, waterfall = water + fall.*

2. Often, the meaning of compound words can be determined by thinking about the meaning of the smaller words forming it such as… *birdhouse = house for birds, pigpen = pen for pigs, towrope = rope for towing, and whirlpool = pool that whirls.*

3. Sometimes, compound words have a hyphen *(-)* between them such as… *Chinese-Americans, half-hour, man-of-war, merry-go-round, shell-like, sixty-one, sixty-first, and state-of-the-art technology.*

4. Often, a hyphen *(-)* joins two words describing a noun if the descriptors precede the noun, but not if they follow the noun such as… *bright-red shirt* but *shirt that is bright red; well-known fact* but *fact that is well known;* and *foreign-car dealer.*

Recognizing smaller words in larger words supports better spelling and better writing.

G. Syllabication in Brief

1. **Syllables.** Syllables are **morphemes:** words or parts of words pronounced with a single, uninterrupted sounding of the voice. These units of pronunciation consist of one vowel sound along with one or more consonants. Syllabication aids word analysis and spelling with both phonics and structural analysis principles.

H. Syllabication Guidelines

1. **Number of vowel sounds heard = number of syllables.** Usually, there are as many syllables in a word as there are vowel sounds heard (not just vowels seen). The following words illustrate vowels sounds seen versus vowel sounds heard:

a. beautiful	5 vowels seen – 3 vowel sounds heard
b. casual	3 vowels seen – 3 vowel sounds heard
c. phonics	2 vowels seen – 2 vowel sounds heard
d. pleasure	4 vowels seen – 2 vowel sounds heard
e. syllables	2 vowels seen – 2 vowel sounds heard

2. **Divide between double consonants.** Usually, syllables divide between double and/or two consonants in words such as

a. bal·let	*bas·ket·ball*	*com·pare*	*coun·sel*
b. don·key	*gar·den*	*hap·pen*	*ten·der*

3. **Divide in front of a single consonant.** Usually, a single consonant between vowels goes with the second vowel in words such as… *be·fore, ce·ment, di·rect, fi·nal, po·lice* unless the first vowel is accented and short such as in *spo-ken, wag-on.*

4. **Do not divide consonant digraphs or blends.** Usually, never divide consonant digraphs (*ch, sh, wh, th, ph, -ng,* etc) and consonant blends (*bl, cl, fl, gl, pl, sl, spl; sp; br, cr, fr, gr, pr, spr, tr, wr; st,* etc.) in words such as… *teach·er; preach·er; past·or; ath·lete.*

5. **Divide between digraph or blend and a third consonant.** Usually, divide between the blend or digraph and the third consonant when there are three consonants between vowels in words such as… *tum-bler; strug-gling; tramp-ling; wran-gler; wrest-ler.*

6. **Consonant+le endings form final syllable.** Usually, the word endings *–ble, -cle, -dle, -gle, -kle, -ple, -tle, and –zle* are the final syllable in words such as *an-gle, Bi-ble, bu-gle, pad-dle, gen-tle.*

7. **Prefixes and suffixes are syllables.** Usually, prefixes and suffixes form separate syllables in words such as… *be-lieve-able, grate-ful, thank-ful-ness, un-thank-ful, un-likel-ly.*

8. **Suffix -y.** Usually, the suffix *–y* picks up the preceding consonant to form a separate syllable in words such as… *ba-by, migh-ty, whim-py.*

9. **Suffix –ed.** Usually, the suffix *– ed* forms a separate syllable only when it follows a root ending in *–d* or *–t* in words such as… *ce-ment-ed, dent-ed, land-ed, plant-ed.*

10. **Suffix –s.** Usually, the suffix –*s* never forms a syllable except sometimes when it follows an *e* in words such as... *class-es, cours-es, danc-es.*

11. **Compound words.** Always divide compound words such as these... *blue-bird, dog-house.*

Using your knowledge of these syllable guidelines can strengthen your spelling ability and enhance your writing.

II. Contractions in Brief

A. Contractions:

Contractions are the shortenings of a word or phrase by the omission of one or more sounds or letters. An apostrophe (') indicates letters are omitted. The following are some examples of common contractions:

B. Verb contractions:

Verb contractions include... are not > aren't; cannot > can't; could not > couldn't; did not > didn't; do not > don't; does not > doesn't; had not > hadn't; has not > hasn't; have not > haven't; here is > here's; is not > isn't; that is > that's; there is > there's, there shall/will > there'll; was not > wasn't; were not > weren't; what is > what's; where is > where's; will not > won't; would not > wouldn't. [20]

C. Pronoun plus verb contractions.

Pronoun plus verb contractions include... (by pronoun) [28]
1. *he is > he's; he had/would > he'd; he shall/will > he'll;*
2. *I am > I'm; I have > I've; I shall/will > I'll; I had/would > I'd;*
3. *it had/would > it'd; it is > it's; it shall/will > it'll;*
4. *she is > she's, she had/would > she'd, she shall/will > she'll,*

5. *they are > they're; they had/would > they'd; they have > they've; they shall/will > they'll;*

6. *let us > let's; we are > we're; we had/would > we'd; we have > we've; we shall/will > we'll;*

7. *who is > who's; who had/would > who'd; who shall/will > who'll;*

8. *you are > you're; you have > you've; you had/would > you'd; you shall/will > you'll;*

Your knowledge of contractions will help your informal writing, but contractions are not generally acceptable in formal writing.

III. References for Structural Analysis

Fry, E. B., Kress, J. E., Fountoukidis, D. L. (2000). The reading teacher's book of lists (4th ed.). Englewood Cliffs, NJ: Prentice-Hall.

Heilman, A. W. (1998). Phonics in proper perspective (8th ed.). Upper saddle River, NJ: Merrill/Prentice Hall.

Hull, M. A., Fox, B. J. (1998). Phonics for the teacher of reading: Programmed for self-instruction (7th ed.). Upper Saddle River, NJ: Merrill/Prentice Hall.

Notes on Spelling with Syllables and Contractions

Appendix D

Citation Formats

A. Introduction

"There are nearly 1000 publishing styles..." (*Citation-7*, Software, 1995). Large groups of journal and academic press editors prefer some publishing styles, and some styles are specified by particular journals to document sources of information. In Part IV, the APA (American Psychological Association) format is explained in a brief synthesis of the key points when citing ideas and direct quotations in text and in a reference list. This Appendix provides the following additional citation formats so you have them available if/when your instructors request them instead of APA Style: MLA, Turabian, and the University of Chicago styles.

B. Preferences

Each academic discipline tends to prefer a specific citation format, though some instructors will accept whatever format the student submits. Usually, **APA Style** is the choice for psychology, education, social sciences (Delaney, 2002) and technical writing (Schiffhorst Pharr, 1997). **MLA Style** (Modern Language Association) is the choice for literature, arts, and humanities. **Turabian Style** "is designed for college students to use with all subjects" and **Chicago Style** is "used with all subjects in the 'real world' by books, magazines, newspapers, and other non-scholarly publications" (Delaney, 2002, p. 1). Medicine, health, and biological sciences prefer the AMA (American Medical Association) format is not included here. The four formats included in this text offer some citation choices for students if/when their instructor does not specify a particular format.

C. MLA Style– Modern Language Association: Short Version

1. **MLA** (Modern Language Association) documents citations for literature, arts, and humanities, and MLA is the format usually taught by high school and college English instructors.

2. Citations in Text (MLA)

The following citations follow the MLA format. As a "rule of thumb," present at least one citation per body paragraph. What inspired your notions and ideas? Acknowledge your sources. Master's theses and Doctoral dissertations must adhere to all formatting guidelines, but you are accountable for this simplified version depending upon what your instructor requires.

2-a. <u>Ideas</u> Cited in Text (MLA)

Three ways cite sources of ideas – paraphrased and summarized materials – in the text of your paper. By using the same examples used for APA, you can compare the MLA with APA and note the differences. Gerald J. Schiffhorst and Donald Pharr (269) provide the format.

   a. Irene C. Fountas and Gay Su Pinnell (13) relate reading and writing...

   b. According to Irene C. Fountas and Gay Su Pinnell (13), reading and writing...

   c. Reading and writing complement each other... (Irene C. Fountas and Gay Su Pinnell, 13).

   [NOTE: MLA uses full names, a page number, and no dates.]

2-b. <u>Direct</u>, Word-for-Word <u>Quotes</u> in Text (MLA)

Three ways cite direct quotations in text...

   a. Irene C. Fountas and Gay Su Pinnell say, "Reading and writing are complementary processes" (13).

   b. In a 1996 study, Irene C. Fountas and Gay Su Pinnell report, "Reading and writing are complementary processes" (13).

c. "Reading and writing are complementary processes" (Irene C. Fountas and Gay Su Pinnell, 13).

3. Endnotes (MLA)

To provide your reader with additional information that cannot appropriately be included in your paper's body, MLA offers Endnotes -- typically typed on a separate page at the end of the chapter or paper, listed in the sequence presented in text, and labeled "Notes." Write consecutive note numbers in superscript in the text right after the sentence it references.[1] Bibliographical material is placed in the Works Cited, not in the Endnotes.[2]

3-a. Endnotes –Example (MLA)

[1] Gerald J. Schiffhorst and Donald Pharr (272) provided much of this information.

[2] Citation software automatically formats all citations in text, in Endnotes (when applicable), and in the Works Cited or Reference List. It follows whatever citation protocol you select, and it can use the same bibliographical database to shift formats however needed.

4. Works Cited (MLA)

MLA's Works Cited is like APA's Reference List. It alphabetically lists resources used/cited in the paper -- double-spaced, indented-second and following lines, and listed by title when no author is provided (Delaney, 2).

4-a. Works Cited (Example- MLA)

The following illustrate MLA citation format for Works Cited:

Allington, Richard I., and Sean Walmsley. "Redefining and Reforming Instructional Support Programs for At-Risk Students." <u>No Quick Fix: Rethinking Literacy in</u> <u>America's</u> <u>Elementary Schools.</u> New York: Teachers College Press, 1995. 19-41. {book chapter}

<u>Citation7.</u> CD-ROM. Nota Bene/Oberon. 1995.{Electronic Media: CD-ROM}

Delaney, Robert. "Citation Style for Research Papers." <u>B. Davis Schwartz Memorial Library.</u> 2001. Long Island University (LIU)/ C.W. Post Campus. June 22, 2002. {Internet article}

http://www.liunet.edu/cwis/cwp/library/workshop/citmla.htm. {website}

Haneke, Dianne M. "Balanced Diet of Reading Approach is Best." <u>Austin American Statesman</u>12 Jun. 1996: A12. {newspaper article}

Schiffhorst, Gerald J., and Donald Pharr. <u>The Short Handbook for Writers</u>. 2nd ed. New York: McGraw-Hill, 1997. {book: two or more authors}

Spiegel, Dixie L. "A Comparison of Traditional Remedial Programs and Reading Recovery: Guidelines for Success for All Programs." <u>Reading Teacher</u> 49.2 (1995): 86-96. {journal}

5. Additional Notes on MLA

See MLA's website for additional information and for information not covered here in this short version of MLA.

D. Turabian Style– Short Version

Turabian Style documents citations for any subject and is a format generally introduced at the college level. This abbreviated version of Turabian style is based on the 6th edition of Kate Turabian's <u>A Manual for Writers of Term Papers, Theses, and Dissertations</u> (1996) as presented in two Internet websites: D.S. 1997, 4 (Concordia University at Irvine, CA) and Delaney 2002, 4 (Long Island University – C.W. Post Campus).

1. Citations in Text (Turabian Style)

    Turabian permits two forms of citation – the traditional method of footnotes with a bibliography and the more recent method of parenthetical references with a Reference List at the end. The following citations illustrate the Turabian parenthetical format. As a "rule of thumb," present at least one citation per body paragraph. What inspired your ideas and notions? Acknowledge your sources. Master's theses and Doctoral dissertations must adhere to all formatting guidelines.

2. Ideas Cited in Text –(Turabian Style)

    Three ways cite sources of ideas – paraphrased and summarized materials – in the text of your paper. Compare Turabian with APA; note the differences re: page number and some dates. These guidelines pattern after D.S. (1997) from the Concordia University-Irvine (CA) Website.

    1. Fountas and Pinnell 1996 (13) relate reading and writing.

    2. According to Fountas and Pinnell 1996 (13), reading and writing are highly correlated literate activities.

    3. Reading and writing complement each other and strengthening one usually strengthens the other (Fountas and Pinnell 1996, 13).

3. Direct, Word-for-Word Quotes in Text (Turabian Style)

    Turabian uses three ways to cite direct quotations in text as illustrated in the following:

    a. Fountas and Pinnell say, "Reading and writing are complementary processes" (1996, 13).

b. In a 1996 study, Fountas and Pinnell report, "Reading and writing are complementary processes" (13).

c. "Reading and writing are complementary processes" (Fountas and Pinnell 1996, 13).

4. Reference List (Turabian Style)

Turabian's Reference List is like MLA's Works Cited and APA's Reference List – a single-spaced list of resources used or cited in the paper. Each item is indented second and following lines, listed by title or organization when no author is provided. It also may be called "References," "Works Cited," or "Literature Cited" (D.S., 1).

4-a. Reference List Example (Turabian Style)

The following illustrate Turabian's formatting for APA's Reference List and MLA's Works Cited:

Allington, Richard I., and Sean Walmsley. 1995. "Redefining and Reforming Instructional Support Programs for At-Risk Students." No Quick Fix: Rethinking Literacy in America's Elementary Schools. New York: Teachers College Press. {book chapter}

Citation7. 1995. CD-ROM. Nota Bene/Oberon. {Electronic Media: CD-ROM}

Delaney, Robert. 2001. "Citation Style for Research Papers." B. Davis Schwartz Memorial Library. Long Island University (LIU)/C.W. Post Campus. {Internet article}

http://www.liunet.edu/cwis/cwp/library/workshop/citmla.htm; accessed 22 June 2002.

D.S. 1997. "Documentation Guide – Turabian." Concordia University at Irvine CA. {Internet}

http://juno.concordia.ca/faqs/turlynx.html ; accessed 22 June 2002.

Haneke, Dianne M. 1996. Balanced Diet of Reading Approach is Best. <u>Austin</u> <u>American Statesman,</u> 12 Jun. 1996: A12. {newspaper article}

Schiffhorst, Gerald J., and Donald Pharr. 1997. <u>The Short Handbook for Writers</u>. 2nd ed. New York: McGraw-Hill. {book: two or more authors}

Spiegel, Dixie L. 1995. A Comparison of Traditional Remedial Programs Reading Recovery: Guidelines for Success for All Programs. <u>Reading Teacher,</u> 49 (Oct): 86-96. {journal}

Turabian, Kate. 1996. <u>A Manual for Writers of Term Papers, Theses, and Dissertations.</u> 6th ed. Chicago: University of Chicago Press.

5. Additional Information (Turabian Style)

For further details, consult Kate Turabian's manual cited above or conduct an Internet search for "Turabian" where you find several university library resources for citation formatting. [NOTE: Obvious differences between MLA and APA or Turabian are the date placements and the issue indications for journals. APA uses last names and initials; MLA and Turabian use full names.]

E. Chicago Style– Short Version

Chicago Style documents citations in any subject area as well as books, magazines, newspapers, and other non-scholarly publications. This short version is based on information posted on the Internet by Long Island University – C.W. Post Campus' B. Davis Schwartz Memorial Library and by the University of Wisconsin – Madison Writing Center.

1. Citations in Text (Chicago Style)

The following citations display the Chicago Style (or Turabian Style) – also sometimes called "**humanities style**" or "**documentary note style.**"[1] As a "rule of thumb," present at least one citation per body paragraph. What inspired your notions and ideas? Acknowledge your sources. Chicago usually documents sources as Notes at the bottom of a page or the end of a paper – sometimes called a "note system" – but also offers guidelines for parenthetical documentation and reference lists.[2] Master's theses and Doctoral dissertations must adhere to all guidelines, but you are accountable for this simplified version depending upon what your instructor requires.

2. Ideas Cited in Text (Chicago Style)

Three ways cite sources of ideas – paraphrased and summarized materials – in the text of your paper. Note Chicago's differences from APA, and note Chicago's similarities with Turabian and MLA. The Internet sites provide the format. First references to sources provide entire bibliographic data in the Notes (here illustrated as at the end of the section or paper – following *In Text* examples). Subsequent references use a shorter form – providing only last name, comma, page number, and a period. Write the consecutive note numbers in superscript in the text right after the sentence they reference.[3]

2-a. Long form. First paraphrased idea citations in text may look like any of the following:

a. Irene C. Fountas and Gay Su Pinnell (13) relate reading and writing…[4]

b. According to Irene C. Fountas and Gay Su Pinnell (13), reading and writing…[4]

c. Reading and writing complement each other. (Irene C. Fountas and Gay Su Pinnell, 13).[4]

[NOTE: Chicago, like MLA and Turabian, uses full names, a page number, and no dates.]

2-b. Short form. Subsequent paraphrased idea citations in text may look like any of the following:

a. Fountas and Pinnell (13) relate reading and writing…[4]

b. According to Fountas and Pinnell (13), reading and writing…[4]

b. Reading and writing complement each other. (Fountas and Pinnell, 13).[4]

[NOTE: Chicago Style, like MLA and Turabian, uses last names, page number, and no dates.]

3. Direct, Word-for-Word Quotes in Text (Chicago Style)

Similarly, three ways cite direct quotations in the text of your paper. Note Chicago's differences from APA, and note Chicago's similarities with MLA and Turabian. Write the consecutive (sequential) note numbers in superscript in the text right after the sentence it references.[5] The Internet sites illustrate the format.

3-a. Long form. First direct quotation citations in text may look like any of the following:

a. Irene C. Fountas and Gay Su Pinnell say, "Reading and writing are complementary processes" (13).[4]

b. In a 1996 study, Irene C. Fountas and Gay Su Pinnell report, "Reading and writing are complementary processes" (13).[4]

c. "Reading and writing are complementary processes" (Irene C. Fountas and Gay Su Pinnell, 13).[4]

3-b. Short form. Subsequent direct quotation citations in text may look like any of the following:

a. Fountas and Pinnell (13) relate reading and writing…[4]

b. According to Fountas and Pinnell (13), reading and writing…[4]

c. Reading and writing complement each other. (Fountas and Pinnell, 13).[4]

[NOTE: Chicago Style, like MLA and Turabian, uses last names, page number, and no dates.]

4. Endnotes (Chicago Style)

To provide your reader with full bibliographic data in sequence of presentation in paper, Chicago offers Notes. Notes are numbered and typed on a separate page at the end of the chapter or paper and labeled "Notes." Place full bibliographical data both in the Notes (first citation) and Works Cited or References, and use the shorter form – last name, comma, page number, and period – in subsequent citations of same source in Notes.[6,7] Indent the second and following lines. If no author is provided, start with title, then date. Use italics for titles, but if italics are unavailable, underline the title.[8]

4-a. Endnotes Example (Chicago Style)

The following illustrate the Chicago Style Endnotes:

a. Documentation: Chicago Style. 2001. In *University of Wisconsin–Madison Writing Center Writer's Handbook* [online]. Madison, WI: University of Wisconsin-Madison, 2001. [cited 22 June 2002]. Available from World Wide Web: http://www.wisc.edu/writing/Handbook/DocChiNotes.html

b. Ibid.

c. Chicago Style: General Information. 2001. In *University of Wisconsin–Madison Writing Center Writer's Handbook* [online]. Madison, WI: University of Wisconsin-Madison, 2001. [cited 22 June 2002]. Available from World Wide Web: http://www.wisc.edu/writing/Handbook/DocChiNotes.html

d. Fountas, Irene C., and Gay Su Pinnell. 1996. *Guided Reading: Good First Teaching for All Children.* Portsmouth, NH: Heinemann Publishing.

e. Chicago Style: General Information. 2001. In *University of Wisconsin–Madison Writing Center Writer's Handbook* [online].

f. Chicago Style: Sample Notes (First References). In

University of Wisconsin–Madison Writing Center Writer's Handbook [online]. Madison, WI: University of Wisconsin-Madison, 2001. [cited 22 June 2002]. Available from World Wide Web: http://www.wisc.edu/writing/Handbook/DocChiNotes.html

g. Chicago Style: Sample Notes (Second or Subsequent References).). In *University of Wisconsin–Madison Writing Center Writer's Handbook* [online]. Madison, WI: University of Wisconsin-Madison, 2001. [cited 22 June 2002]. Available from World Wide Web: http://www.wisc.edu/writing/Handbook/DocChiNotes.html

h. Delaney, Robert. 2001. Chicago Citation Style: Chicago Manual of Styles, 14ᵗʰ ed. *In B. Davis Schwartz Memorial Library* [online]. Long Island, NY: Long Island University, 2001[cited 22 June 2002]. Available from World Wide Web:

5. Works Cited (Chicago Style)

Chicago Style's Works Cited (also called **Selected Bibliography** or **References**) is like APA's Reference List – an alphabetical list of resources used and cited in the paper (Wisconsin-Madison Writing Center Handbook, 1). Double space, indent second and following lines, and list by the title when no author is provided (Delaney, 2).

5-a. Works Cited (Examples)

The following illustrate Chicago Style's Works Cited similar to APA's and MLA's Reference List:

a. Allington, Richard I., and Sean Walmsley. Redefining and Reforming Instructional Support Programs for At-Risk Students. In *No Quick Fix: Rethinking Literacy in America's Elementary Schools.* New York: Teachers College Press, 1995. 19-41. {book chapter}

b. Chicago Editorial Staff. 1993. *The Chicago Manual of Style: The essential Guide for Writers,Editors, and Publishers.* 14ᵗʰ ed. Chicago, IL: University of Chicago.

c. Chicago Style: General Information. 2001. In *University of Wisconsin–Madison Writing Center Writer's Handbook* [online]. Madison, WI: University of Wisconsin-Madison, 2001. [cited 22 June 2002]. Available from World Wide Web: {Internet article} http://www.wisc.edu/writing/Handbook/DocChiNotes.html

d. Chicago Style: Sample Notes (First References). In *University of Wisconsin–Madison Writing Center Writer's Handbook* [online]. Madison, WI: University of Wisconsin-Madison,2001. [cited 22 June 2002]. Available from World Wide Web: {Internet article} http://www.wisc.edu/writing/Handbook/DocChiNotes.html

e. Chicago Style: Sample Notes (Second or Subsequent References). In *University of Wisconsin–Madison Writing Center Writer's Handbook* [online]. Madison, WI: University of Wisconsin-Madison, 2001. [cited 22 June 2002]. Available from World Wide Web:

f. http://www.wisc.edu/writing/Handbook/DocChiNotes.html {Internet article}

g. Citation7. CD-ROM. Nota Bene/Oberon. 1995. {Electronic Media: CD-ROM}

h. Delaney, Robert. "Citation Style for Research Papers." B. Davis Schwartz Memorial Library. 2001. Long Island University (LIU)/C.W. Post Campus. June 22, 2002. {Internet article}

i. http://www.liunet.edu/cwis/cwp/library/workshop/citmla.htm.

j. Documentation: Chicago Style. 2001. In *University of Wisconsin–Madison Writing Center Writer's Handbook* [online]. Madison, WI: University of Wisconsin-Madison, 2001. [cited 22 June 2002]. Available from World Wide Web: {Internet Article}

k. http://www.wisc.edu/writing/Handbook/DocChiNotes.html

l. Fountas, Irene C., and Gay Su Pinnell. 1996. *Guided Read-*

ing: Good First Teaching for All Children. Portsmouth, NH: Heinemann Publishing.{book: two or more authors}

m. Haneke, Dianne M. "Balanced Diet of Reading Approach is Best." Austin American Statesman 12 Jun. 1996: A12. {newspaper article}

n. Spiegel, Dixie L. "A Comparison of Traditional Remedial Programs and Reading Recovery: Guidelines for Success for All Programs." Reading Teacher 49.2 (1995): 86-96.{journal}

o. University of Wisconsin–Madison Writing Center Writer's Handbook. 2001. Madison, WI: University of Wisconsin, 2001. [cited 22 June 2002]. Available From World Wide Web: http://www.wisc.edu/writing/Handbook/DocChi-Notes.html {Internet article}

F. Additional Citation Internet Sites

The following sites may be helpful (http://library.concordia.ca/services/citations.html):

1. APA Style

   A Guide for Writing Research Papers Based on APA… (Capital Community College)

   APA Citation Style Examples (Northwest Missouri State University)

   APA Style Guide PDF format (Concordia University Libraries)

   Electronic References (APA)

   Using American Psychological Association (APA)… (Purdue University On-Line Writing Labs)

2. Chicago Style

   Documentation: Chicago Style (University of Wisconsin-Madison Writing Centers)

3. MLA Style

   A Guide for Writing Research Papers Based on MLA… (Capital Community College)

   MLA Citation Style Examples (Northwest Missouri State University)

   MLA Style Guide PDF format (Concordia University Libraries)

   NoodleBib The MLA Bibliography Composer. Create an MLA Style bibliography--online forms.

   Using Modern Language Association (MLA) Format (Purdue University On-Line Writing Labs)

4. Turabian Style

   Turabian Citation Styles Examples (Northwest Missouri State University)

   Turabian (6th ed.) Samples for a Bibliography (Ithaca College Library)

Turabian Styles Guide: (University of Southern Mississippi Libraries)

Turabian Style Guide PDF format (Concordia University Libraries)

Turabian Styles: Sample Footnotes Bibliographic Entries (6th ed.) (Bridgewater State College)

F. General Comments.

Additionally, for all four styles, see Long Island University-CW Post Campus-B. Davis Schwartz Memorial Library at http://www.luinet.edu/cwis/cwp/library/workshop.html.

This Appendix D highlights four major citation formats utilized across the curriculum in most educational settings. However, it is important to be aware that sixty-plus citation formats exist, and your may be asked to use one other than these four. Why so many? Well, each academic area of study – mathematics, sciences, social sciences, education, medicine, etc. requires its students learn and use its somewhat unique citation and reference list or bibliography format. Thus, at higher levels of educational pursuit, you may concurrently write several papers -- each requiring it own citation format. The format people recall the most is MLA, because it is the format style used in English classes; but we encounter many other options while writing papers throughout our schooling.

Appendix E

Personal Résumé, Cover Letter, Professional Portfolio

A. Job Application Process

At some point in your life, applying for a job may be viewed as a three or four-part process. It is helpful to keep in mind the purpose and function of each part as you go through the process. The parts and their roles are as follows:

1. Application

The application provides the potential employer with personal information about you and your work experience. Work experiences are usually listed chronologically. Since applications vary in structure and data requested, no example is presented here, but be prepared to supply previous positions, businesses, managers, dates, and job descriptions.

2. Personal Résumé

The résumé promotes your skills and work experiences focused around a few key strengths. Because managers and interviewers review your résumé in 60 seconds or less, the résumé should be short, simple, and to the point. Prioritize three skills or strengths, and briefly list your experience with each of those points. Set the skill priorities in terms of what best qualifies you for the position. Do not repeat everything from the application. Reserve some information for the interview. See example provided below. Adapt as needed. When you mail in a résumé, always send it with a cover letter. (See example below.)

3. Interview

The interview promotes your character and the way you present yourself. There is no need to repeat everything stated on the application or in the résumé. Be yourself but "put your best foot forward." Dress appropriately. Be early. Be a good listener. Conserve your words and energy. Having investigated the business, ask intelligent questions about the company, its products, and its vision for future expansion. Thoughtfully share how you fit into its vision and what you can contribute to the success of its mission. No example shown.

4. Professional Portfolio

The portfolio demonstrates the quality of the work you do. It is like an artist's portfolio – a sampling of the best of each kind of work accomplished. See portfolio guidelines below.

B. Personal Résumé

The following outline offers a basic format for creating a resume for applying for work positions:

RESUMÉ
for
YOUR NAME (all caps)

College Address: Permanent Address:
Your Address {upper/lower case}   Address
Your City, State {upper/lower case}   City, State
Your Phone   Phone

OBJECTIVE: To secure a position as a _____,

EDUCATION:
BA/BS: (major),_____
College/University at _____ (20___).

CERTIFICATION (if applies):
Certified in _____
for the State of_____.

EXPERIENCE: {Use what applies}
Student Teaching in grades ___ at _____ school in
_____, TX.
Sales Clerk in _____ Department at _____,
_____.

RELATED EXPERIENCE: {Use what applies}
Recreation leader, Sunday School teacher, grades: _____, summer camp counselor, sports coach, etc.

HONORS and AWARDS: {Use what applies}
Dean's list, honor society, honors, awards, special recognitions, etc. – school and non-school

INTERESTS and HOBBIES: {Use what applies but be specific}
Sports, music, art, travel, languages, etc.

REFERENCES: {two professional/work-related references plus one character reference}
Name, position, address, phone number

Name, position, address, phone number

Name, position, address, phone number
[OR... References furnished upon request]

B-1. Résumé Sample

The following is the resume of an imaginary person:

RESUMÉ
for
TUKIE DEE VANDENSNORT
1515 Southern Belle Drive
Plainole, TX 78000-2000
(777) 777-7777

OBJECTIVE: a teaching position in grades 4-8, especially in language arts or social sciences.

EDUCATION:
BA: Reading and Social Studies Composite, Timbuktu University (2000)

CERTIFICATION:
Texas Provisional for grades 1-8 (2000).

EXPERIENCE:
Student Teaching: grade 5, Zion Hill Elementary School in Plainole, TX.

RELATED EXPERIENCE:
Student Assistant in Social Science Department; Sunday School teacher (grades 3-8), First Church, Plainole; Girl Scout summer camp counselor; VBS (gr 6-8); recreation leader (all ages); coach Special Olympics soccer and bowling.

HONORS and AWARDS:
Dean's list (8 semesters), Honor Society, Summa Cum Laude graduate.

INTERESTS and HOBBIES:
tennis, swimming, guitar, singing, travel, and languages.

REFERENCES:

Dr. Joe Bloe, Dean of Education University Supervisor, Timbuktu University, 300 North I-300, Plainole, TX, 78000-2000, (777) 888-9999.

Mr. Bo Didley, cooperating teacher, Zion Hill Elementary, 777 Education Way, Plainole, TX 78000-2000, (777) 666-7777.

Rev. Joshua Caleb, pastor, First Church, Plainole, TX 78000, (777) 333-4444.

C. Sample Cover Letter

The following is a cover letter to accompany the job application for an imaginary person:

Tukie Dee Vandensnort
1515 Southern Belle Drive
Plainole, TX 78000-2000
(777) 777-7777

July 10, 2002

Mrs. Allfora Education
XYZ Middle School
1900 Success Drive
Plainole, TX 78000

Dear Mrs. Education,

In response to your posting in the <u>Daily Local</u>, I am applying for the position of middle school social studies teacher.

Enclosed, please find a copy of the application and my résumé.

I would appreciate the opportunity to discuss this available position with you at your earliest convenience. I can be reached at the number provided above or on my cell phone (777) 333-3333 any day after 1:00 p.m.

Thank you for your thoughtful consideration and help in this matter.

Sincerely,
Tukie D. Vandensnort
Tukie D. Vandensnort

Encl: re'sume'
Cc: files

D. Professional Portfolio

Remember, your personal professional portfolio demonstrates the quality of work you have accomplished, whereas the application provides history, the résumé highlights skills, and the interview showcases your personality. Therefore, the portfolio does not duplicate the others, but it reveals how you pursue excellence in your work. The following guidelines help you start and continue to develop your personal professional portfolio. It is a growing document, so, over time, your more recent achievements replace your earlier ones. Place all the artifacts in top-loading plastic slip covers in a 3-ring binder with a copy of your title page in the slip of the front cover and similarly use tabs on dividers for major division of your portfolio. If you have two areas in which you might apply for a position, create a personal professional portfolio for each professional area of employment. The following are recommended contents of your portfolio:

1. Title Page. {inside and cover}
2. Table of Contents. {shows how you organized your portfolio}
3. Introduction. {Brief paragraph explaining purpose and scope of portfolio}
4. Résumé. {a copy}
5. Sample of each major area of work or study. Photos help. Elementary teachers include the following:
   a. Sample of Language Arts/Reading/Writing Instruction [include best lesson plan]
   b. Sample of Mathematics Instruction [include best lesson plan]
   c. Sample of Science Instruction [include best lesson plan]
   d. Sample of Social Studies Instruction [include best lesson plan]
   e. Sample of Computers Integrated into Instruction [include best lesson plan]
   f. Sample of Multicultural Instruction and Resources re: Black Americans, Hispanic Americans, Native Americans, and Asian Americans

g. Block Plan {shows Planning Instruction for a Year}

h. Unit Plan {shows Planning a Thematic Unit for One to Four Weeks}

i. Samples of Bulletin Boards Created Used {photographs}

j. Sample Lesson Plan providing for Multiple Intelligences various learning styles

k. Sample Lesson Plan showing use of Bloom's Higher levels of thinking

6. Sample of Computer Literacy, Knowledge, and Programs

7. Samples of Special Projects {e.g., Science Fair, UIL competition, etc.}

8. Samples of Special Talents Abilities {in art, music, sports, languages, drama, etc.}

D-1. Professional Portfolio Guidelines and Tips

The following guidelines and tips support your pursuit of excellence in presenting samples of the best of work you have accomplished in your field.

1. Use a hard 3-ring binder with a front slip pocket {so you can change the front title page as you grow in your career.}

2. Use plastic slipcovers {for all pages including displaying all materials.}

3. Generate an inside Title Page {lists your career and your name such as Teaching Portfolio for Dianne M. Haneke, Ph .D.}

4. Generate a Table of Contents {to show how you organized it your way.}

5. Generate Computer Graphics {to enhance your Portfolio as much as seems reasonable.}

6. Use dividers and tabs {to enable your reader to find specific items quickly.}

7. Generate an introduction to each section {to explain what the section is about; for example, "The following Block Plan demonstrates planning social studies instruction for a sixth grade class

for an entire year as student study the world. It is coded to the TEKS."}

8. Include graphic organizers {with examples of how it is used in content areas. Consider, KWL Charts, semantic webs, Venn diagrams, concept maps, etc.}

9. Include things revealing the quality of your expertise. {Select items demonstrating your excellence as a worker (teacher) – your personal ability to apply the knowledge you acquired in your training.}

10. Type, double-spaced, minimum 1-inch margins. Beware of mechanical errors in grammar, usage, spelling, punctuation, capitalization, etc.

11. Take pride in your Portfolio as an on-going, evolving documentation of your work ethic and performance excellence.

E. Additional Notes

Glossary

Most terms are defined as they are introduced throughout this book, so this Glossary just highlights key terms. Parentheses list the chapter where term or phrase first appears.

Abstract paragraph paper: brief statement of essential thoughts of book, article, etc.; summary. (18, 28, 29)

Action Research: research you, the writer, actively observe and record what you see. (30)

Active voice: subject is active, subject does the action, subject is the doer. (14)

Adjectives: describe or add to nouns; usually answer *How* questions. (3)

Affixes: parts of words added to root words to clarify or enhance the meaning. (Appendix C)

Adverbs: describe or add to the verb, to an adjective, or to another adverb; usually answer *How*, *How much*, *How many*, and *Why* questions; often end in *ly*. (3)

Analogies: show relationships between words and their various meanings. (6)

Antonyms: mean the opposite or nearly the opposite. (6)

APA (American Psychological Association): citation formatting style choice for psychology, education, social sciences, and technical writing. (Appendix D)

Apostrophes: used to replace letters in contractions and to indicate possession. (5 & Appendix C)

Articles: specific adjectives (a, an, and the); describe or add to nouns. (3)

Aspects of Language: reading, writing, listening, and speaking. (1)

Attached article: a photocopy of the article(s) referenced or a computer printout for Internet articles used. (26)

Audience: those whom you anticipate will read your writing. (24)

Awkward sentences: usually do not present readily identifiable errors, are simply written poorly, confusing, illogical, unclear, or obscure. (15)

Bibliography: alphabetical list of sources actually used or referred to in writing the paper (26); specifically -- cites works for background of a paper or for further reading (26); generally – used interchangeably with, so see also Reference List or Works Cited. (26) and Appendix D.

Body: main ideas with supporting details (says it); each main idea has own paragraph. (16)

Bubble charts: cluster main ideas and their supporting details. (17)

Cause-Effect flow charts, paragraphs, papers: organize causes and effects for cause-effect papers. (17, 22)

Chicago Style: citation format used with all subjects in the "real-world" by books, magazines, newspapers, and other non-scholarly publications. (Appendix D)

Choppy sentences: several short sentences following one another with abrupt starting and stopping that does not strengthen the writing. (9, 15)

Citation formatting styles: the formatting styles used to document sources of information, ideas, and direct quotations in text and in a bibliography or reference list. (26) (Appendix D)

Comma splice run-on: run-on that has a comma but no connective. (9)

Common nouns: name general persons, places or things. (3)

Compare-Contrast graphic organizer, paragraph, paper: also labeled "a research paper using journal articles" or a Review of Literature paper; compare and contrast the similarities and differences of at least two items, programs, topics, issues. (17, 21, 32)

Comparative adjectives: add -er to express comparison when comparing two items such as taller in Joe is taller than Jim. (3)

Complete predicate: simple or compound predicate (verb) and all the describing modifiers. (8)

Complete subject: simple or compound subject (noun or pronoun) and all the describing modifiers. (8)

Compound adjectives: comprised of more than one word and are hyphenated; e.g., *state-of-the-art, 12-year-old*, etc. (3)

Compound predicate: two or more actions (verbs) by the same subject. (8)

Compound subject: two or more subjects doing the same action – using the same verb. (8)

Concept maps: organize ideas in a manner helping develop the 3-level outline. (17)

Conclusion: states a conclusion you drew from what you read and wrote (says what you conclude from this activity). (16, 26)

Conjugation: complete listing of a verb's forms by person, number, voice, tense, and mood. (3)

Conjunctions: connect/join two or more nouns, pronouns, verbs, adverbs, prepositional phrases, or independent clauses in a sentence. (3)

Conjunctive adverbs: join sentence elements; include *accordingly, also, anyhow, besides, consequently, furthermore, however, indeed, moreover, nevertheless, otherwise, still, then,* and *therefore.* (3, 9)

Contractions: shortened forms of two words merged into one word. (Appendix C)

Coordinating conjunctions: join sentence elements of equal form, weight, or function such as two nouns or two subject + verb units; include *and, but, for, not, or, so,* and *yet.* (3)

Critique/analysis/evaluation: critically analyze and evaluate the validity and value of the information presented. (33)

Dangling modifiers (dangling participles): "dangle" when there is no clearly logical word for the "dangler" to modify. (15)

Declarative sentence: makes a statement, gives information, or tells what happens. (7)

Definite article: *The* is a definite article; refers to a specific noun. (3)

Descriptive/Elaboration Narrative: interestingly describes persons, places, things, or situations. (19)

Editing: checks spelling, punctuation, and mechanics in general. (16, 27)

Editorial/Personal Opinion/Personal Reflection/Position Paper: sometimes called a persuasive paper, takes a stand for or against an issue, often to solve a problem. (34)

Ellipses (...): signal words are intentionally left out. (9)

Exclamatory sentence: sentence shows strong emotion or feeling. (7)

Expressive language: speaking and writing (1)

Finite verb: together with a subject, can form a complete sentence: *She writes. He is writing.* (3)

Fragments: incomplete sentences – lacking either a subject or a predicate or both. (9)

Gerunds: verbs used as nouns such as *writing* in *Writing is fun.* (3)

Graphic Organizer: graphically or pictorially organizes the main ideas and the supporting details for your paper. (17)

Haneke's Handy Model: uses the hand to remember the five basic parts of paragraph and paper structure -- organizing the main idea and supporting details of any paragraph, chapter, or paper. (16)

Helping, assisting, or auxiliary verbs: such as *can, may, could, should, would, might,* and *must*; usually followed by the base or infinitive form of the verb (3)

Helping/linking verbs: enable verbs to express past, present, and future tenses such as *was, is,* and *will.* (3)

Homographs: look alike – are spelled alike -- but have different meanings and origins. (4)

Homonyms: words having the same name; include homophones, homographs, and seem-a-likes. (4)

Homophones: sound alike but have different spellings and meanings. (4)

Imperative sentence: gives a command – telling someone to do something. (7)

Indefinite articles: *A* and *an* **are indefinite articles;** refers to a general noun. (3)

Infinitive: base form of verbs; verbs used as nouns, adjectives or adverbs such as *sing* in the following: (n) <u>*Singing*</u> is my favorite pastime. (adj) *The* <u>*Singing*</u> *Nuns made a CD.*(3)

Interjections: exclaim excitement; are followed by an exclamation point (!).(3, 9)

Interrogative sentence: asks a question; ends with question mark (?).. (7, 9)

Intransitive verbs: have no object such as *singing* in *She is singing.* (3)

Introduction: introduces the topic of the paper, states the thesis statement, and briefly states the key points of the paper (tells what you are about to say). (16, 17, 24)

Irregular verbs: change in various ways to create the past tense and past participle forms. (3)

Learning Modalities Theory: learning theory based on the basic senses – auditory, visual, kinesthetic, and tactile. (2)

Learning Styles: Ways people assimilate knowledge.

Linking verbs: occur in two structures. In one, the verb is followed by an adjective describing the subject such as *is* in *It is beautiful.* In the other structure, the noun following the verb links back to the subject such as *He is my husband. She is my girlfriend.* (3)

Misplaced modifiers: words not applying or relating clearly or accurately to the specific word or words you want them to modify or describe. (15)

MLA (Modern Language Association): citation formatting style choice for literature, arts, and humanities. (Appendix D)

Mnemonics: handy clues to remember information. (all)

Modifiers: a word or groups of words adding something specific to the meaning of the word it describes, modifies, relates to, or applies to; adjectives and adverbs. (15)

Multiple Intelligences Theory: learning theory based on at least eight "ways of knowing" or modes for learning (2)

Nonfinite – verbal: verb acting as another part of speech. (3)

Nouns: name a person, place, or thing; usually answer Who, What, and Where questions. (3)

Objective case pronouns: used as direct objects of the verb or objects of prepositions, usually receiving an action or an object. (3)

Oral language: received (receptive) through auditory/hearing/listening; expressed (expressive) through speaking. (1)

Paper: follows the outline; it contains seven main parts: introduction, body, summary, conclusion, personal response, reference list, graphic organizer, and article. (24)

Paragraph: distinct section of a paper presenting one of the key points of the paper. (16)

Parallel construction: expressing parallel ideas of a series in a like manner. (13)

Participles: verbs used as adjectives such as *winning* in *Ricky hit the winning run.* (3)

Parts of Speech: Ways in which words are used in sentences to convey meaning; nouns, pronouns, verbs, adverbs, adjectives, prepositions, conjunctions, etc. (3)

Passive voice: subject is passive, receives the action, is the receiver such as *A new record was set by the athlete.* (3, 14)

Peer review editing: Ask a classmate or friend to read your second draft looking at the mechanics, spelling, punctuation, etc. (16, 27)

Peer review revision: Ask a classmate or a friend read your rough first draft looking primarily at the flow of ideas. (16, 27)

Peer reviews: classmates or professionals give feedback on writings. (16, 27)

Person: six persons (in English) – first-, second-, third person singular and first-, second-, third person plural. (3)

Personal editing: check paper for grammar, spelling, punctuation, and mechanics. (16, 27)

Personal response: presents your thoughts and opinions about what you read and wrote. (24)

Personal revision: check organization of ideas, writing purpose, intended audience. (16, 27)

Phonics: science or study of sound; acoustics; method of teaching beginners to read or pronounce words by learning to associate certains letters or groups of letters with sounds they represent. (Appendix B)

Plagiarism: "1) the act of plagiarizing; 2) an idea, plot, etc. plagiarized." "to take (ideas, writings, etc.) from (another) and pass them off as one's own." from the Latin word *plagiarius* meaning "kidnapper, literary thief." (25)

Plurals: indicate more than one of that noun; e.g., one horse, two horses; one deer, two deer. (5)

Possessive case pronouns: show possession either as a modifier or used alone. (3)

Possessives: indicate that the noun or pronoun owns or possesses something(s); for example, John's horse; Casey's three fish; Mark's dolphins. (5)

Précis: a concise abridgment; summary; abstract. (18, 28)

Predicate: what the subject is doing. (8)

Prepositions: indicate positional relationship between two nouns; usually answers *Where?* (3)

Pre-writing: jot down ideas; cluster main ideas and details on a graphic organizer. (16)

Problem-Solution flow charts paragraphs: help writers organize problems and possible solutions. (17, 23)

Pronoun antecedent: word/group of words that pronoun stands for, refers to, or replaces; noun referred to precedes pronoun. (11)

Pronoun referent: noun (word, phrase or clause) the pronoun references; noun referred to may precede or follow the pronoun. (11)

Pronouns: substitute for nouns—for (pro) nouns; answer Who or What questions. (3, 11)

Proper nouns: name specific persons, places, and things and as such are capitalized. (3)

Purposes: explicit assignment as stated by the instructor or professor such as summarize, action research, review literature, compare/contrast, critique, or position. (24)

Receptive language: listening and reading. (1)

Reference list: alphabetical list of sources actually used or referred to in writing the paper (24); term used by APA Style and Turabian Style. (Appendix D). [See also Bibliography and Works Cited.]

Reflexive case pronouns: reflect back to the subject. (3, 11)

Regular verbs: past tense and past participle forms are created by adding *–ed* to the base form as in *walk, walked, walked.* (3)

Review of literature: also may be labeled "a research paper" using journal articles, books, or other references; purpose is to see what information is available on the topic. (31)

Revising: checks the organization of ideas, the purpose for your writing, and your intended audience. (16, 27)

Roots: basic word components, usually from Latin or Greek, to which affixes (prefixes and suffixes) are added. (Appendix C)

Run-ons: two or more sentences not correctly connected. (9)

Seem-a-like homonyms: seem alike but differ in meaning. (4)

Sequential time lines: flow charts of how-to, history or scientific development over time. (20)

Silent language: received (receptive) through visual/seeing/reading; expressed (expressive) through writing. (1)

Simple predicate: simplest word telling what subject is/did; usually a verb or verb clause. (8)

Simple subject: Who or what the sentence is about; a noun, a pronoun, or *you* (understood); usually one word unless the subject is a multi-word proper noun. (8)

Split infinitive: places one or more words between *to* and the verb. (3)

Squinting modifiers: either/or modifying words that stand in the middle of the sentence and can apply to either what precedes or what follows it in the sentence. (15)

Strengths and Weaknesses tables: assist writer to list strengths and weaknesses for a critique. (17)

Stringy sentences: tie together many ideas that should be expressed in separate sentences; ignores logical stopping places. (15)

Styles: narrative and expository styles of five text structures: descriptive, compare/contrast, sequential/how-to, cause/effect, and problem/solution. (24)

Subject: who/what the sentence is about. (8)

Subjective/nominative case pronouns: used as subjects, i.e., usually doing the action. (3)

Subordinating conjunctions: join and show relationship between two elements of unequal importance. (3)

Summary: recaps the main ideas/key points (says what you said) (18); brief statement of main points or substance; abridgment. (18, 28)

Superlative adjectives: add *–est* to express the extreme of a range when comparing three or more items such as *tallest* in *Joe is taller than Jim but John is the tallest of the three.* **(3)**

Syllable: "word or part of a word pronounced with a single sound." (Appendix C)

Synonyms: words that mean the same or something similar. (6)

Table of Contents: a three-level outline of your paper -- briefly outlining the main ideas and the supporting details for each main idea. (16, 24)

Tense: indicates time of action for three time divisions: present, past, future. English has six tenses: present, past, future, present perfect, past perfect, and future perfect. (3)

Text Structures: Ways in which words are put together to convey certain meanings and achieve particular goals. (Part III)

Three-Level Outlines: outlines presenting information in hierarchical levels of main ideas (key points) and supporting details. (17)

Title page: provides your title, the assignment, name of course and instructor, your name, and the date submitted. (24)

Transitive verbs: have an object such as *singing* in *She is singing the song.* (3)

Turabian Style: citation formatting style designed by Kate Turabian for college students to use in all subjects. (Appendix D)

Venn diagrams: help writer list likenesses and differences to compare and contrast two or more people, places, or things. (17)

Verb Tenses: verb forms indicating past, present, and future as well as acting or acted upon; usually presented in verb conjugation lists.

Verbs: indicate action or state of being; usually answer, "What is happening?" questions. (3)

Vocabulary: body of words one reads, writes, speaks, or listens to with understanding of meanings. Each individual has a reading vocabulary, listening vocabulary, speaking vocabulary, and writing vocabulary. All vocabularies are expanded through life experiences as well as by considering antonyms, synonyms, and analogies of any given word. (1, 6)

Voice: verb form that tells whether the subject does the action (active) or receives the action (passive). (14)

Wordy sentences: use more words than necessary – more words than the meaning and style of writing assignment require; clouds the meaning and weakens the impact of the statement. (15)

Works Cited: alphabetical list of sources actually used or referred to in writing the paper (26); term used by MLA Style and Chicago Style formats. (App D) [See also Bibliography and Reference List.]

Additional Words for Glossary

Index

Grammar Improves Writing

Grammar Improves Writing

Grammar Improves Writing

Grammar Improves Writing

Bibliography

Agnes, M. , Guralnik, D. B. (2000). <u>Webster's new world college dictionary (4th ed.).</u> Cleveland, OH: Webster's New World.

American Psychological Association. (1994). <u>Publication manual of the American Psychological Association (4th ed.).</u> Washington, D.C.: American Psychological Association.

Behrman, C. H. (1990). <u>Hooked on writing: Ready-to-use-writing process activities for grades 4-8.</u> West Nyack, NY: The Center for Applied Research in Education.

Behrman, C. H. (1997). <u>Writing activities for every month of the school year: Ready-to-use-writing process activities for grades 4-8.</u> West Nyack, NY: The Center for Applied Research in Education.

Behrman, C. H. (2000). <u>Writing skills problem solver: 101 Ready-to-use-writing process activities for correcting the most common errors.</u> West Nyack, NY: The Center for Applied Research in Education.

Bromley, K., Irwin-De Vitis, L., Modlo, M. (1995). <u>Graphic organizers: Visual strategies for active learning (grades K-8).</u> NY: Scholastic Professional Books.

Bryant, T. (1998). <u>Writing skills flipper: A basic flip-guide to writing and speaking.</u> South Bend, IN: Christopher Lee Publications.

Buscemi, S. V., Nicolai, A., Strugala, R. (1998). <u>The basics: A rhetoric and handbook (2nd ed.).</u> Boston, MA: McGraw-Hill.

Clemmons, J., Laase, L. (1995). <u>Language arts mini-lessons: Step-by-step skill-builders for your classroom (grades 4-8).</u> NY: Scholastic Professional Books.

Corder, J. W., Ruszkiewicz, J. J. (1989). Handbook of current English (8th ed.). Glenview, IL: HarperCollins.

Dahl, K. L., Farnan, N. (1998). Children's writing: Perspectives from research. Chicago, IL: National reading Conference.

Emory, D. (1995). Improve your essays. NY: McGraw-Hill.

Fearn, L., Farnan, N. (1998). Writing effectively: Helping children master the conventions of writing. Boston, MA: Allyn Bacon.

Fry, E. B., Kress, J. E., Fountoukidis, D. L. (2000). The reading teacher's book of lists (4th ed.). Englewood Cliffs, NJ: Prentice-Hall.

Gibb, G. S., Dyches, T. T. (2000). Guide to writing quality: Individualized education programs: What's best for students with disabilities? Boston, MA: Allyn Bacon.

Graves, D. H. (1983). Writing: Teachers and children at work. Portsmouth, NH: Heinemann.

Heilman, A. W. (1998). Phonics in proper perspective (8th ed.). Upper saddle River, NJ: Merrill/Prentice Hall.

Hull, M. A., Fox, B. J. (1998). Phonics for the teacher of reading: Programmed for self-instruction (7th ed.). Upper Saddle River, NJ: Merrill/Prentice Hall.

Kemper, D., Nathan, R., Sabrenak, P. (1996). Writers express: A handbook for young writers, thinkers, and learners. Wilmington, MA: Great Source Education Group, Houghton Mifflin.

Kirk, K. (2001). Writing to standards: Teacher's resources of writing activities for prek-6. Thousand Oaks, CA: Corwin Press.

Learning Express. (1999). Learning express skill builders practice: 501 grammar and writing questions. NY: Learning Express.

Ledbetter, M. E. (1998). <u>Writing portfolio activities kit: Ready-to-use management techniques and writing activities for grades 7-12.</u> West Nyack, NY: The Center for Applied Research in Education.

Lerner, M. (1994). <u>The Princeton Review: Writing smart: Your guide to great writing.</u> NY: Random House.

Matthews, S. M., Sladky, P. (1995). <u>Improve your paragraphs.</u> NY: Macmillan/McGraw-Hill.

Mattson, M., Leshing, S., Levi, E. (1993). <u>Help yourself: A guide to writing and rewriting</u> (3rd ed.). New York: Macmillan. [out of print]

Maxwell, R. J.(1996). <u>Writing across the curriculum in middle and high schools.</u> Boston, MA: Allyn Bacon.

Motchkavitz, L. M., McKerns, D. (1998). <u>Grammar! Grammar! Extra! Extra! (Grades 4-8).</u> Torrance, CA: Good Apple (Frank Schaffer).

Muschla, G. R. (1991). <u>The writing teacher's book of lists: With ready-to-use activities and worksheets.</u> Paramus, NJ: Prentice Hall.

Muschla, G. R. (1993). <u>Writing workshop survival kit.</u> West Nyack, NY: The Center for Applied Research in Education.

O'Conner, P.T. (1996). <u>Woe is I: The grammarphoebe's guide to better English in plain English.</u> NY: Putnam.

Price, B. T. (1982). <u>Basic composition activities kit.</u> West Nyack, NY: The Center for Applied Research in Education.

Pulaski, M.A.S. (1982). <u>Step-by-step guide to correct English.</u> NY: Macmillan.

Salak, A. M. (1995). <u>Improve your sentences.</u> NY: McGraw-Hill.

Saltzman, J. (1996). <u>If you can talk, you can write: A proven program to get you writing keep you writing.</u> NY: Warner Books.

Schiffhorst, G. J., Pharr, D. (1997). The short handbook for writers (2nd ed.). NY: McGraw-Hill.

Shertzer, M. (2001). The elements of grammar: Essential guide to refining and improving grammar. NY: Barnes Noble.

Staff of the Princeton Review. (2001). The Princeton Review: Grammar smart: A guide to perfect usage (2nd ed.). NY: Random House.

Strouf, J. L. H. (1990). Hooked on language arts: Ready-to-use activities and worksheets for grades 4-8. West Nyack, NY: The Center for Applied Research in Education.

Strunk, W., White, E. B. (1999). The elements of style (4th ed.). NY: Macmillan.

Sunflower, C. (1994). Really writing: Ready-to-use writing process activities for the elementary grades. West Nyack, NY: The Center for Applied Research in Education.

Troxel,, K. (1994). Grammar songs: Learning with music. Newport Beach, CA: Audio Memory.

Weaver, C. (1996). Teaching grammar in context. Portsmouth, NH: Heinemann.

Wollman-Bonilla, J. (1991). Response journals: Inviting students to think and write about literature. New York: Scholastic Professional Books.

Also…

1) Dictionary of your choice (not more than 5 years old). Recommend…

Agnes, M., Guralnik, D.B. (2000) <u>Webster's New World College Dictionary (4th ed.)</u>. Foster City, CA: IDG Books Worldwide.

2) Thesaurus of your choice (not more than 5 years old).

A. Notes on Bibliography

TATE PUBLISHING & *Enterprises*

Tate Publishing is committed to excellence in the publishing industry. Our staff of highly trained professionals, including editors, graphic designers, and marketing personnel, work together to produce the very finest books available. The company reflects the philosophy established by the founders, based on Psalms 68:11,

"THE LORD GAVE THE WORD AND GREAT WAS THE COMPANY OF THOSE WHO PUBLISHED IT."

If you would like further information, please call
1.888.361.9473
or visit our website
www.tatepublishing.com

TATE PUBLISHING & *Enterprises*, LLC
127 E. Trade Center Terrace
Mustang, Oklahoma 73064 USA